Living in Dang

Broadening Perspectives on Social Policy
Series editor: Bent Greve

The object of this series, in this age of re-thinking on social welfare, is to bring fresh points of view and to attract fresh audiences to the mainstream of social policy debate.

The choice of themes is designed to feature issues of major interest and concern, such as are already stretching the boundaries of social policy.

This is the twelfth collection of papers in the series. Previous volumes include:

Living in Dangerous Times

Fear, Insecurity, Risk and Social Policy

Edited by

David Denney

A John Wiley & Sons, Ltd., Publication

This edition first published 2009
Originally published as Volume 42, Issue 6 of *Social Policy & Administration*
Chapters © 2009 The Authors
Book compilation © 2009 Blackwell Publishing Ltd

Blackwell Publishing was acquired by John Wiley & Sons in February 2007. Blackwell's publishing program has been merged with Wiley's global Scientific, Technical, and Medical business to form Wiley-Blackwell.

Registered Office
John Wiley & Sons Ltd, The Atrium, Southern Gate, Chichester, West Sussex, PO19 8SQ, United Kingdom

Editorial Offices
350 Main Street, Malden, MA 02148-5020, USA
9600 Garsington Road, Oxford, OX4 2DQ, UK
The Atrium, Southern Gate, Chichester, West Sussex, PO19 8SQ, UK

For details of our global editorial offices, for customer services, and for information about how to apply for permission to reuse the copyright material in this book please see our website at www.wiley.com/wiley-blackwell.

The right of David Denney to be identified as the author of the editorial material in this work has been asserted in accordance with the Copyright, Designs and Patents Act 1988.

Library of Congress Cataloging-in-Publication Data
Living in dangerous times: fear, insecurity, risk, and social policy / edited by David Denney.
    p. cm.
"Originally published as volume 42, issue 6 of Social policy & administration."
Includes bibliographical references and index.
ISBN 978-1-4051-9176-0 (pbk. : alk. paper)
1. Risk–Social aspects. 2. Social policy. I. Denney, David. II. Social policy & administration.
HM1101.L58 2009
320.6–dc22

                         2009005780

A catalogue record for this book is available from the British Library.

Set in 10.5pt Baskerville
by Graphicraft Limited, Hong Kong
Printed and bound in Malaysia by KHL Printing Co Sdn Bhd

01   2009

CONTENTS

NOTES ON CONTRIBUTORS

David Abbott is Senior Research Fellow at the Norah Fry Research Centre, University of Bristol.

Rowland Atkinson is Associate Professor and Director of the Housing and Community Research Unit at the University of Tasmania, Australia.

Gerard Delanty is Professor of Sociology and Social and Political Thought at the University of Sussex.

David Denney is Professor of Social and Public Policy at Royal Holloway, University of London.

Mary Ann Elston is Reader Emerita in Medical Sociology at Royal Holloway, University of London, and Visiting Reader at Surrey University.

Frank Furedi is Professor of Sociology at the University of Kent.

Jonathan Gabe is Professor of Sociology at Royal Holloway, University of London.

Bent Greve is Professor in the Department of Society and Globalization, Roskilde University, Denmark.

Anwen Jones is Research Fellow at the Centre for Housing Policy, University of York.

Hazel Kemshall is Professor of Community and Criminal Justice at De Montfort University.

Brian Littlechild is Professor of Social Work and Associate Head of the School of Social, Community and Health Studies at the University of Hertfordshire.

Deborah Quilgars is Senior Research Fellow at the Centre for Housing Policy, University of York.

Chris Rumford is Senior Lecturer in Political Sociology, Royal Holloway, University of London.

Jason Wood is Senior Lecturer in Youth and Community Development at De Montfort University.

1

Editorial Introduction: Living in Dangerous Times – Fear, Insecurity, Risk and Social Policy

David Denney

Insecurity, fear and risk have come to dominate individual and collective consciousness in the twenty-first century. Although global insecurity has been created by terrorism, pollution, global epidemics and famine, risks have also come to be defined with respect to more mundane aspects of everyday life. Seemingly innocuous objects including carpets, footwear, televisions, vacuum cleaners, personal stereos, mobile phones and even tea cosies are often associated with potential risk (Spicker 2001; Denney 2005).

Some events, however, have come to symbolise global insecurity. The claim that the global crisis in the banking system and September 11th 'changed the world forever' can be challenged. A sense of global fear existed before the collapse of the World Trade Center in 2001. A global economic depression had occurred previously, during the inter-war period. Government and the media present many aspects of public life including the supply of basic services as being under threat. Since 9/11 risk stories have been created around possible dangers to transportation systems, fuel, food and water supply, banking and financial systems, defence infrastructure and government itself. The impact of global warming on climate change adds to the fear of imminent mass destruction.

This volume examines how far such aggressively defensive thinking can be seen in aspects of social policy development. The nature of protection and security provided by the state has changed since the Second World War. Following Beveridge in the UK, state-funded systems were created to cushion the impact of ill health and poverty during the postwar period. The creation of the welfare state in other developed countries characterized a state sponsored approach to individual risk management. The state, individuals and their employers paid for social insurance against adversity.

In 2005 in his Dimbleby lecture, the then Metropolitan Police Commissioner Sir Ian Blair, alluding to Beveridge, described personal insecurity as the sixth great evil, along with idleness, ignorance, squalor, disease, and want (BBC 2005). Anthony Giddens, who helped guide the New Labour project, has argued for policies which develop independence and individual potential.

However, no specific suggestions are made as to how those who cannot grasp opportunities presented in the risk society can be best assisted by either the state or the private sector working together or separately. Many people feel ambivalent about risk and uncertainty and are often unable to differentiate between the progress that they experience in living standards and other pressures they feel in social life. Those at most risk from social change may see greater flexibility in society as a threat rather than an opportunity (Taylor-Gooby 2000).

Attention to risk control in social policy appears to reflect operational practices in the civil aviation industry. At airports all passengers are routinely screened to ensure that they do not pose a risk to the safety of the general public. The onus is on the passenger to prove innocence. Psychological profiling exercises, some covert, are being developed to identify risky passengers. Hand luggage is X-rayed and at some international airports every fifth passenger will have hand baggage manually examined. Once aboard videos relating to life rafts, life jackets, emergency chutes and exits are shown as passengers contemplate the consumption of their duty-free highly flammable alcohol.

Social welfare claimants and service users are treated as being potentially undeserving burdens on already overstretched social care budgets until they can prove the contrary. Needs assessments and the delivery of packages of care are designed to ensure that public funds are regulated, and that individuals draw upon their own financial and human resources before becoming dependent on the state. The use of risk assessment stretches beyond the provision of welfare. In the criminal justice system possible candidates for community sentences are assessed though a national offender risk assessment system. As is the case at the airport, service-providing agencies need regulated escape routes in a world in which the word 'accident' is becoming unacceptable. Risk regulation mechanisms provide the framework for the equivalent of seat belts, life jackets and X-ray machines in the formulation of policy.

The contributors to this volume are drawn from a wide variety of academic disciplines reflecting the multidisciplinary approach. Two central themes run through the contributions. Firstly, policies are built around the idea of public resilience, whilst simultaneously promoting notions of public vulnerability. Furedi analyses the tendency for policy-makers to 'recycle' the paradigm of vulnerability. Littlechild develops the theme of vulnerability and resilience in his analysis of the impact of risk assessment in child protection work. Gabe and Elston review zero tolerance of violence perpetrated on health care workers and interpret this in the wider context of risk anxiety and insecurity. Atkinson analyses fear and insecurity in hidden spaces inhabited by 'problem' people. Quilgars, Jones and Abbott present new research designed to investigate whether social and cultural differences along the dimensions of disability, sexuality, faith and ethnicity influence attitudes to financial risk and insecurity. Kemshall and Wood explore critical factors in the trend towards public protection and the framing of risk and risky offenders.

Secondly, the perceived erosion of social securities gives rise to policies which promote social exclusivity and the strengthening of boundaries, often at the expense of human rights. Denney examines the complex policy interplay between fear, human rights and New Labour's approach to risk. The 'precautionary principle' has come to dominate specific areas of both domestic social and foreign policy. Delanty argues that fear of others and anxieties about the future have resulted in a crisis of European solidarity and a wider crisis of collective purpose. The European project, he claims, must give more attention to social justice and inclusive forms of social solidarity in order to combat such developments. Rumford argues that fear has become central to social scientific understandings of insecurities and focuses on the means by which the world is rendered strange. Rumford goes on to analyse how uncertainty, unpredictability and insecurity can open up new forms of governance. Denney argues that both foreign and social policy have been driven by a precautionary logic which has in some cases compromised human rights and due process. Greve in his conclusion to this volume asks how possible it is for the welfare state to make a 'rational' response to 'new risks'.

All these chapters address critical contemporary questions for policy-makers and policy analysts. To what extent has a burgeoning epidemic of fear exacerbated by 9/11 and subsequent global acts of terrorism created a new impetus for reactive risk-centred social policy development? How far has due process in law and human rights become secondary to the endless regulated search for security and safety? To what extent does the policy backdrop of danger serve to increase social division?

References

BBC (2005), Dimbleby Lecture, Sir Ian Blair, 16th November Available on BBC News Channel: http://news.bbc.co.uk

Denney, D. (2005), *Risk and Society*, London: Sage.

Giddens, A. (2000), *The Third Way and its Critics*, Cambridge: Polity Press.

Jordan, B. (1998), *The New Politics of Welfare*, London: Sage.

Spicker, P. (2001), *Social Insecurity and Social Protection*, in Edwards, R. and Glover, J. (eds) *Risk and Citizenship*, London: Routledge.

Taylor-Gooby, P. (2000), *Risk, Trust and Welfare*, London: Macmillan.

2
Fear, Human Rights and New Labour Policy Post-9/11

David Denney

The events of 9/11 in New York and the attacks on London on 7/7 have been used to justify aggressively defensive thinking in many aspects of New Labour policy development on the domestic and international fronts. Threats to national and international security have justified the introduction of coercive policy measures which are unprecedented since the Second World War. It will be argued that often complex and contradictory discourses of fear have constituted a dominant theme in New Labour policy-making since 1997. A growing tension has developed between the endless search for security, due process and human rights. In this chapter three interlocking themes will be examined: first, the nature of risk and fear in the late modern world; second, the complex and at times contradictory New Labour dependency on risk control; and third, the impact of fear-driven policy on due process and human rights. The idea of fear will be related to domestic and foreign policy aims and consequences in what has become an all-encompassing precautionary logic.

Modernity and the Emergence of the Risk Society

In the traditional class society equality was a central dynamic in policy formulation, whereas in the post-traditional world safety becomes a major imperative. In analysing what he calls the 'risk society' Beck describes a process of 'reflexive modernization' in terms of changing patterns of social experiences in which values provided by social institutions are being fundamentally challenged. Whereas in the traditional society political control is institutionalized through technical competence, government directives, law and administrative procedures, political control in the post-traditional society is more fragmented and disjointed (Beck 1992, 1994). In the risk society more individualized decisions are made about employment, education and self-identity. Concomitantly, beliefs about social class, gender and the family are being overturned (Mythen 2004). It is now widely accepted that Beck has underestimated poverty and discrimination in the Western world and overemphasized a shift from mass concerns about survival to those related to insecurity (Denney 2005; see Quilgars *et al.*, this volume). Notwithstanding this,

Table 1

Fear, risk and New Labour social policy

	Causes of fear	Policy aims	Policy consequences	Examples of policy
External threats	Alien terrorist groups aiming at symbolic targets to cause maximum loss of life. High-risk population groups in specific geographical locations.	Protect vulnerable citizens. The precautionary principle – take pre-emptive action to minimize risk. Identify dangerous individuals and groups.	Privileges risk of future crime over due process, justice and human rights. Creates increased anger in targeted groups. Separates communities. Increases feelings of fear.	Terrorism Act 2000. Anti Terrorism Crime and Security Act 2001. Prevention of Terror Act 2005. Terrorism Act 2006. Imposition of control orders.
Internal threats	Dysfunctional families. Unsupervised and impressionable youths. Irresponsible parents. High-risk population groups in specific locations.	Protect vulnerable citizens. The precautionary principle – take pre-emptive action to minimize risk. Identify dangerous individuals and groups. Promote individual responsibility for risk.	Separates communities. Increases feelings of fear. Privileges risk of future crime over due process, justice and human rights. Leaves some groups without sufficient state-sponsored insurance, e.g. older people.	Anti Social Behaviour Act 2003. Crime and Disorder Reduction Partnerships. Crime and Disorder Act 1998. Criminal Justice Act 2003. Sure Start 1998.

the risk society thesis has been and continues to be significantly influential and relevant to current social science research.

Giddens, who was influential in the creation of the New Labour project, writing from a similar position, describes risk as being central to the development of post-traditional societies. The notion of 'high' or 'late' modernity describes a social transformation which is characterized by uncertainties about the nature of truth and claims to truth. This has been accompanied by a growing scepticism about the ability of experts to predict risk and danger (Giddens 1990, 1991). Although the work of Giddens and Beck shares a number of common concerns, Giddens's work is far more programmatic and has consequently influenced the development of New Labour's programme since 1997 (Giddens 1998).

What has emerged in New Labour policy is what Garland calls a 'responsibilization strategy', which has been reflected most notably in criminal justice and other policies (Garland 2001). One of Giddens's basic arguments when conceptualizing the 'third way' was the construction of a new social contract based on the idea of

'No rights without responsibilities.' Those who profit from social goods should use them responsibly and give something back to the wider social community in return. (Giddens 2000: 53)

Individualized Fear in the Risk Society

Individuals living in the risk society, according to some theorists, are living in a more knowledge-dependent society, which is mediated through global reconstruction and uncertainty (Beck 1998). The communication of risk is informed by the idea that fear itself is a risk, and must be part of policy-making (Furedi 2007). In a world society of individuals, perceptions of fear are often metaphorically constructed, guided by intuition and grounded in diffuse and complex anxieties (Beck 2000; Denney 2005; Sparks 1992).

Avoidance of the stranger infuses all aspects of life. Hubbard has shown how multiplex cinemas are often located out of town in places understood by consumers to be low-risk and where interaction between strangers is kept to a minimum. For Hubbard fear is a

Productive force shaping not just the city scape but the entire fabric of post industrial society. (Hubbard 2003: 73)

Fear also needs to be distinguished from anxiety. Anxiety is a fear that is objectless or where the object of fear is less apparent than manifest. Anxiety arises in situations where the object of fear is opaque or even invisible, while fear is based on an external threat to the self (see Delanty, this volume). The rise of an increasing societal concern with anxiety has resulted in the development of what is sometimes referred to as a 'risk community', which emanates from government, the media, industry, trade unions, the public and their representatives (Beck 2000).

Contemporary fear is highly individualized and is institutionally synthesized, often by the media and government. 'Raw' fear is less directed towards a particular danger, e.g. the fear of God or a specific event, but constitutes a more nebulous, all-pervasive anxiety state which is 'free-floating'. Such generalized forms of fear enable arbitrary links to be made between future and past fears whether real or imagined (Furedi 2007; see Furedi, this volume).

Understandings of fear represent an interplay of perception, cultural reality and personal psychodynamic aspects of fear and real danger. The complexity of the macro and the micro circuitry of understandings of fear forms the basis for perceptions of risk (Lupton and Tulloch 2000).

Legions of intermeshing and possible future scenarios create fear on a daily basis (Douglas 1992). Global warming, falling and rising house prices, biological and computer viruses, the use of long-range missiles by rogue states, the potential collapse of banking systems through internet corruption, all help to form an endless list of possible catastrophic scenarios. Particular risks to mass safety and vulnerable groups in society, most notably children and the elderly, can emanate from a plethora of internal and external sources. International terrorists, paedophiles, or groups of young people living in geographical areas designated by government as high-risk are often targeted as constituting a danger to the public. Following the attacks on the London transport system on 7 July 2005, the idea of the home-grown terrorist was presented as constituting the enemy without and within.

Full-spectrum Dominance

The events of 9/11 encouraged some Western politicians of a more hawkish disposition to argue that the result of being too diplomatic in the face of dangerous states could be the failure to take appropriate action to avoid catastrophes such as the destruction of the twin towers. During the second term of the Clinton administration, an influential group of like-minded Republican politicians formed the 'Project for the New American Century', propagating the idea that the world was a dangerous place and that the future of Western civilization was in danger. If the USA was 'forward-looking enough', it had the power to make the world a better place. The emergence of 'full-spectrum dominance' ensured that a nation's relationship with the USA was of crucial importance (Kampfner 2004: 24).

Blair and Bush argued that one particular future nightmare scenario could be avoided by taking pre-emptive action against Saddam Hussein who, they argued, had amassed weapons of mass destruction. This precautionary position was accepted by some governments (Italy, the UK, the Netherlands, Denmark and Spain, in Europe), in a situation in which an implausible risk had become horrifying reality on 9/11. Other European nations, including France, Germany and Belgium, did not support intervention in Iraq without a UN mandate.

Dealing with the Enemy Post-9/11

Internal reaction to the attacks in New York on 9/11 was swift in the USA and the UK. The passing of the US Patriot Act in 2000 reflected the urgency

7

with which the USA regarded the risk of terrorism. The legislation was introduced on 2 October and became law on 26 October. Debate was restricted by the speed at which the legislation progressed. President George W. Bush argued that

> In order to win the war, we must make sure that the law enforcement men and women have got the tools necessary within the constitution to defeat the enemy . . . we are at war and we are going to win. (cited in Thomas 2002: 95)

The state of war against an ill-defined enemy justified extraordinary government actions in the USA. The Act enabled the Secretary of State to designate any group, foreign or domestic, as terrorist. Powers of detention and surveillance were given to the executive and law enforcement agencies over which the courts were prevented from offering any significant judicial oversight. The Act also targeted a new crime, 'domestic terrorism', which included activities deemed by the executive and law enforcement agencies to potentially intimidate the civil population. Section 142 of the legislation permitted the indefinite detention of immigrants and other non-nationals.

Smiljanic has drawn attention to the contravention of the Geneva Convention on the basis that some terrorist suspects were indefinitely detained without legal representation (Smiljanic 2002). Attempts to provide legal representation to detainees proved unsuccessful. Under the Geneva Convention the USA should have released Taliban soldiers unless they were being charged with war crimes (*Guardian* 2003). The prevailing culture of fear allowed the US authorities to argue that they were holding prisoners who could provide useful intelligence, while releasing others.

In the UK the reaction to 9/11 was no less radical, appearing to put the nation on a precautionary war footing. An unknown number of prisoners were held at Belmarsh Prison under the provisions of the 2001 Anti Terrorism Crime and Security Act, which was enacted hastily despite opposition from the House of Lords following 9/11. Under this Act, 'foreign' nationals who are reasonably suspected of terrorism could be immediately returned to their own country of origin and indefinitely detained without charge. In order to pass this legislation David Blunkett, the then Home Secretary, was forced to suspend Britain from the European Convention of Human Rights. The Human Rights Act, which came into force in October 2000, incorporates the European Convention on Human Rights. The requirement that conviction by a court must precede punishment is enshrined in the European Convention of Human Rights (Article 5).

The Terrorism Act of 2000 created new offences and extended the power of the police to investigate, arrest and detain suspects, as is the case in the USA with the US Patriot Act. In December 2004 British detainees took their case to the House of Lords where it was ruled that indefinite detention without trial for foreign subjects suspected of terrorism contravened the European Convention of Human Rights in that it discriminated on the basis of nationality and migration status. They further ruled that current legislation was disproportionate and discretionary. On 26 January 2005, four

UK citizens accused by the USA of being terrorists were released from Guantanamo Bay after being detained for three years. Following questioning by the police in the UK these individuals were released without charge.

The then Home Secretary Charles Clarke, under the Prevention of Terror Act 2005, announced his intention to extend his executive power by imposing 'control orders' which could include curfew, tagging and being placed under house arrest, reporting to the police station and restricted movement. The orders could be imposed on British or foreign nationals and replaced indefinite detention (*Guardian* 2005). The Terrorism Act 2006 came into force in April and during its passage through the House of Commons Tony Blair suffered his first parliamentary defeat. During the passage of this bill through Parliament New Labour attempted to extend the time limit for detention without charge from 14 to 90 days. There was cross-party opposition to this not only in principle but also because it was seen as potentially hardening disaffection among ethnic minorities, especially young Muslims. There was particular concern that when this measure had been introduced in Northern Ireland it had led to martyrdom (Downes and Morgan 2007). A compromise solution was reached enabling the police to hold suspects for up to 28 days, which doubled the previous 14 days. This is far longer than any other comparable democracy (*Guardian* 2007a). The 2006 Act also created the new offence of 'glorification' of terror. The concept makes it illegal for individuals to celebrate terrorism in a way which others think that they should emulate. Critics of this act claim that the glorification offence could have seen people who supported Nelson Mandela's struggle against apartheid being found guilty of such an offence in the 1980s (BBC 2006).

In May 2007 John Reid, the then Home Secretary, answered emergency questions regarding three missing terror suspects. Again New Labour announced that they were considering derogation from the European Convention of Human Rights. Reid described the current control framework as not even the second-best option for tackling terrorism (*Guardian* 2007b, 2007c).

Setting Fearful Agendas

While the response to 9/11 and 7/7 has reflected the precautionary principle, its influence in domestic policy was none the less present but more complex and contradictory. The precautionary principle has been invoked to identify hazards before they occur and take, in some cases, disproportionate precautions to ensure that harm to the public is kept to a minimum. The all-pervasive fear which New Labour had helped to create post-9/11 needed to be managed carefully.

In 2005 Blair announced the implementation of the Hampton Review, which had been commissioned by the then Chancellor Gordon Brown. The Review had recommended fewer regulatory bodies and more robust risk assessment methodologies. In consequence of this Blair set up the Better Regulation Task Force in 2005 to create a better balance between risk and regulation (Blair 2005, 2006; Better Regulation Commission 2006).

New Labour effectively constructed 'risk environments' based upon the selective generation of possible scenarios which created fear (Raco 2002). Just as the invasion of Iraq had been presented by President Bush as a pre-emptive act of self-defence, similar discourses can be seen with respect to economic policies. Blair, like Giddens, argued that the major risks to the well-being of the majority in the UK were present in the powerful emergent economies, most notably India and China (Blair 2005; Giddens 1991). In 1999 Stephen Byers, the then Secretary of State for Trade and Industry, argued catastrophic consequences would result if society failed to respond to the realities of the new world order (Byers 1999, cited in Raco 2002).

This form of rhetoric did not take account of the future demands on social and economic infrastructure which accompany economic growth. Transport systems cannot safely respond to extra volumes without sufficient investment in integrated transport infrastructure. Possible environmental damage caused by the extraction of raw materials for the development of manufacturing was not mentioned by New Labour in its urgent call to meet future economic threats.

New Labour warned of the dangers posed by external threat and the need for constant vigilance, while also advocating policies which required citizens to take significantly more responsibility for their own risks. Risks to the vulnerable created by anti-social youths and dysfunctional families were used by New Labour to argue for an extension of social control in dangerous communities. Risk was also presented as constituting the basis for a new form of active, self-sufficient citizenship. Any expectation of a return to 'no fault' state risk protection was effectively removed (Kemshall 2002). This balance between individual responsibility for personal risk and government regulation to control risk became an important theme within policy development. Policy imperatives, both international and domestic, became premised on the need to mount permanent campaigns against ill-defined enemies, whether they be global terrorists or groups of young people living in communities identified as being high-risk.

While government anxiety has been created with respect to urban decline and the break-up of the traditional family, Blair believed that attempts made by governments in response to risk could stifle economic and social creativity, which in itself constituted a new risk. Excessive and over-zealous implementation of regulation by government bodies in local and central government resulted in costly bureaucracy and an unacceptable number of regulations (Blair 2005).

The need to combine private and public funding in the delivery of social care was also presented as an economic necessity with dire consequences if urgent action was not taken to develop partnerships between the private and public sectors. The Conservatives under John Major had introduced quasi-markets and 'needs-led' assessments into the social care sector with the NHS and Community Care Act in 1990. This constituted a significant departure from Beveridge. This mixed market delivery of social care was transformed by New Labour into a risk-led service (Kemshall 2002).

The consequences of this policy had a differentiated impact on groups in society (see Quilgars *et al.*, this volume). In the Green Paper *Partnership in Pensions* New Labour made it clear that individual citizens were expected to secure their own financial security in old age (Ring 2003). This is despite the fact that older people are vulnerable to the risk of suffering a major bereavement, disability, social exclusion, lack of work, unsuitable accommodation, and inadequate income (Heywood *et al.* 2002). By targeting groups in a seemingly arbitrary manner, some risks are minimized while others are exaggerated.

Targeting Risky Groups

The policy approach taken by New Labour appears to reflect what Beck calls the 'cosmopolitan significance of fear' and has in some instances led to a breakdown in the rule of law (Beck 2000). Particular groups, whether they be al-Qaeda or paedophiles, appear to be beyond due process. Following the sexual assault and murder of a small child Sarah Payne in West Sussex, a media campaign to name and shame paedophiles was launched by several tabloid newspapers. In July and August 2000 names, residential details and in some cases pictures of sex offenders were published; one of these subsequently required police protection. In the same year on the Paulsgrove estate in Portsmouth hundreds of residents rioted for five days in protest against a named paedophile allegedly living in the area. The editor of the *News of the World* claimed that the newspaper had a public duty to monitor the activities of paedophiles.

In this instance government failed to protect its citizens from summary punishment imposed by a collectivity, while also failing to uphold the rule of law. This example also illustrates how fear can be moved from one theme to another in unpredictable ways. Southern Baptist Minister Jerry Vines described Muhammad as a demon-possessed paedophile, while Allah leads Muslims to terrorism. Such arbitrary linkages reflect free-floating discourses of fear (Furedi 2007). Thematic changes and often contradictory discourses of fear can be seen in the treatment and depiction of young people, who are to be both feared and protected from risk.

Fear of Young People

New Labour claimed that risks associated with social exclusion and youth crime could be tackled through early identification of crime, understanding what works in addressing criminal behaviour, better coordination of the state agencies working with young offenders, and the balancing of personal rights and responsibilities (Blair 2006; 6; Peck 2004a).

These principles appear to have been applied selectively to specific localities designated by New Labour as being high-risk, inhabited by vulnerable, dysfunctional people (Furedi 2007). Fear, social malaise, loss of community, urban decline and the break-up of the traditional family were all risk factors which needed to be tackled (Blair 2006).

Although, as has been noted above, children and young people are seen by New Labour as being particularly vulnerable, they are at the same time targeted as a group who create fear. A recurring theme reflected in policy is the need to take action in the face of new levels of moral degeneracy among the young.

The principle of doli incapax (literally meaning 'incapable of crime') meant that children under the age of 10 could not be considered criminally responsible. The abolition of this principle in 1998, which came in the wake of the murder of 2-year-old James Bulger by two other children, led to the perception that a new level of social deviancy had been reached which was a threat to society (Muncie 1999, quoting from *The Times*, 24 November 1993). The abolition of doli incapax drew criticism from the European Commissioner for Human Rights, nor was the measure consistent with most other European countries where the age of criminal responsibility is between 12 and 15 years (Tonry and Doob 2004). The then Home Secretary Jack Straw used the abolition of doli incapax as a key feature of the get-tough responsibilization agenda which related to crime.

> The presumption that children aged 10–13 do not know the difference between serious wrong doing and simple naughtiness flies in the face of common sense and is long over due for reform. (Straw 1998, quoted in Morgan and Newburn 2007)

Other legislation including the imposition of the Anti Social Behaviour Act 2003 and consequent Anti Social Behaviour Orders (curfew orders on children under the age of 16) reflected policies with the stated aim of purifying the streets of fear (Downes and Morgan 2007).

Fear and Community Safety

The 1998 Crime and Disorder Act, New Labour's first flagship crime measure, placed a responsibility on local authorities and police to promote Crime and Disorder Reduction Partnerships. The key actors in this process are citizens activating communities, and youth offending teams comprising social services, probation and the police. Local voluntary agencies now work together to create a multi-agency approach which serves to redistribute crime control. The transformation from crime prevention to community safety was recommended in the Morgan Report in 1991 and New Labour set about implementing community safety when they came to power in 1997. The principal difference between crime prevention and community safety according to Van Swaaningen (2002) is that the former aims to reduce crime levels while the latter is designed to increase public feelings of safety. The risk-conscious discourse of community safety targets individuals and specific groups in geographical areas, and incorporates a multi-agency approach while seeking the active participation of citizens (Matthews and Pitts 2001).

One consequence of these policies has been to separate social groupings within communities. A more aggressive New Labour approach to security since 9/11 has been particularly focused on some Muslim communities throughout Britain. These areas are often materially deprived, overcrowded areas. More affluent families living near high-risk communities emulate the precautionary principle by living in gated communities, installing protection to their homes, and ferrying their children to places rather than entrusting them to public transport (Wiles and Pease 2001; see also Atkinson, this volume). The endless quest for safety can serve to increase feelings of fear and insecurity by constantly providing reminders of the potential dangers people face (Zedner 2003).

While the rich are increasingly protected from danger through commercially 'governed social spaces', the poor defend themselves in dangerous public places policed by an increasingly militarized police force. The unlawful shooting of Jean Charles de Menezes, a suspected terrorist, by officers of the Metropolitan Police at Stockwell tube station on 22 July 2005 illustrates the potential danger to the public of a shoot-to-kill policing strategy.

The Brown Administration in the UK is also concerned to govern ungovernable spaces, whether real or virtual. Hazel Blears, Secretary of State for Communities and Local Government at the time of writing, announced measures to tackle extremism among young Muslims through government-sponsored websites. Some £70 million was to be allocated to tackle ungoverned spaces including the internet, bookshops, snooker halls and clubs. Of this sum £25 million was to be spent on training imams and teaching citizenship in mosque schools (BBC 2007). In 2008 the Home Secretary Jacqui Smith announced that 300 new police and civilian staff would be employed to target radicalism in communities before it had happened (BBC 2008).

New forms of cooperative action have been introduced with the stated aim of reducing fear. Simultaneously, such forms of action create a wider spectrum of surveillance and social control (Foucault 1972). In the name of community safety 'high-risk' neighbourhoods and populations have been targeted for increased surveillance. The development of private policing and the deployment of CCTV systems are manifestations of the 'risk society'. In Beck's words risk has become a 'systematic' way of dealing with the 'hazards and insecurities' introduced by late modernity (Beck 1992: 21). Citizens now expect governments to control fear through the targeting of communities and the efficient management of risk populations. At the same time individuals assume that they are responsible for finding solutions to their own problems (Edwards and Glover 2001).

New Labour, Reflexive Modernity and Human Rights

While public spaces are becoming increasingly controlled, privatized and divided (see Atkinson, this volume), the global war against terror and the struggle to identify dangerous individuals and groups at home moves on relentlessly. The Criminal Justice and Court Services Act 2000 introduced the requirement for relevant agencies to work together to make arrangements for assessing and managing risks posed by violent offenders and those who could do harm to the public. This three-tiered protection system (Multi Agency Public Protection Authorities – MAPPA) includes the police, probation and prison services (Kemshall *et al.* 2005). Maria Eagle, a justice minister at the time of writing, describes MAPPA as one of the most advanced systems in the world for monitoring and managing dangerous offenders (*Guardian* 2007c). The over-emphasis on risk in the control of crime has been well documented over a long period (Kemshall 1997; Beaumont 1999).

Risk control has been accompanied by a tougher approach to criminal justice which has penetrated many well-established aspects of due process. The elimination of the double jeopardy rule in 2005 resulted in the possibility of individuals facing a new trial after being acquitted if new and compelling evidence emerged.

It is possible to see the precautionary principle reflected in the idea that it is better to keep a prisoner locked up than to risk the life or property of another human being. However, the relationship between New Labour, fear and human rights is a complex one. It would be difficult to make the case that New Labour has been simply authoritarian and has brazenly ignored justice and rights.

There has been a commitment to enhance the rights of some groups. The Race Relations Amendment Act 2000 recognized the reality of institutional racism following the Inquiry into the murder of Stephen Lawrence. The rights of young children and families living in areas of deprivation were recognized in the £17 billion investment in the Sure Start programme claimed by Blair since he came to office (Blair 2006). The rights of gay and lesbian people were recognized in 2004 with the passing of the Civil Partnership Act. In the 2005 Disability Discrimination Act New Labour recognized the weakness of the 1995 Disability Discrimination Act and acted to consolidate rights in this area. In October 2007 the Commission for Racial Equality, Disability Rights and Equal Opportunities was replaced by the Equality and Human Rights Commission. The stated aim of this body was to extend the government's effort to deal with discrimination to include sexual orientation age and religious belief (see website: www.epolitix.com, Trevor Phillips, Equality and Human Rights Commission, 1 October 2007). The appointment of Harriet Harman as Equality Secretary in the Brown government was another indicator of New Labour's commitment to human rights.

Although the effectiveness of these measures can be debated (see Glass 2003 on Sure Start), the constant emphasis on rising imprisonment rates and the removal of civil liberties can distract attention from measures taken by New Labour with the intended aim of enhancing inclusiveness and human rights. Even within the criminal justice system where, as has been argued, basic rights within due process appear to have been compromised, there has been a resurgence of rehabilitative and innovative restorative justice programmes (Morgan and Newburn 2007). Compliance with the Human Rights Act is normally a requirement of any new legislation and New Labour has endeavoured in the main to ensure that there can be no challenges in this area.

It is also possible to overestimate the ability of any government to use fear to promote policy since it constitutes only one aspect of the social world (Garland 2001). It is dangerous, as critics of Beck have suggested, to regard New Labour's preoccupation with risk and fear as the result of some form of all-encompassing logic. Risk has been uppermost in the minds of citizens and policy-makers throughout history (O'Malley 2000). Regulation and surveillance are never applied uniformly and the application of social control through fearful discourse should not be regarded as a mechanistic process. It has been argued that the messages sent out by New Labour reflected the changes in the nature of modernity in which, as Beck argues,

The place of the value system of the 'unequal' society is taken by the value system of the 'unsafe' society. Whereas the utopia of equality contains a wealth of substantial and positive goals of social change, the utopia of the risk society remains peculiarly negative and defensive. Basically one is no longer concerned with attaining something 'good' but preventing the worst. (Beck 1992: 49)

Human Rights, it is often argued, should form the foundation of a balance between crime control and due process (Ashworth 1995). The reflexive nature and impact of human rights policies also need to be recognized. In 2007 the Asylum and Immigration Tribunal decided not to deport Learco Chindamo on his release from prison for the murder of head teacher Philip Lawrence in 1995. Chindamo was 15 when he committed the offence outside a school gate in Maida Vale, West London. Chindamo's lawyers argued that it would be disproportionate to deport him since he had no connections with Italy and that such action would deny him the right to family life under the Human Rights Act. Frances Lawrence (Philip Lawrence's widow), herself a supporter of the Human Rights Act, argued that the decision not to deport Chindamo failed to encompass the rights of her and her family (*Guardian* 2007d). Home Office policy at the time of writing is that foreign prisoners who have committed serious offences should be deported at the end of their sentences. This example illustrates how the decision to grant rights in one case can reflexively act back on itself, compromising and complicating the rights of another.

Consequences of Fear-based Policy

There are a number of consequences which flow from New Labour's approach to risk and fear. First, a key principle of any criminal justice system is that people are only punished for the crimes that they have committed and not for future crimes. The notion of justice in popular discourse has now become synonymous with discipline, and individuals are being punished for crimes that they might commit at some future point (Hudson 2001). Policies designed to control the risk of fear have in some cases resulted in due process being given less emphasis than the politics of safety.

Second, if some person or some category of persons is categorized as a risk to public safety, there seems to be very little to suggest that they are owed justice and that due process should operate. The vocabulary of justice is almost entirely absent from debates about sexual offending, safety in public places, suspected terrorists, and mass surveillance (Hudson 2000, 2001). Increased surveillance is determined by membership of a high-risk group, rather than the seriousness of any offence committed (Feeley and Smith 1992).

Third, an over-emphasis on fear can fracture and stigmatize communities and mark out particular individuals as targets, conceptualizing them as a danger or threat. Surveillance and the notion of community safety incorporate the idea that we must distinguish between those who belong and those who do not (Hubbard 2003). This rationale applies not only to the war on terror but also to other high-risk populations including the homeless, beggars on trains, rowdy teenagers, asylum-seekers, prostitutes, and the mentally ill.

Fourth, the precautionary principles often fail to provide consistency, accuracy, predictability or accountability (Marchant 2001). This would seem to characterize the measures outlined above.

Lastly, the creation of policies which emphasize independent responsibility have created greater risk for some groups (e.g. older people) in society, who are now expected by government to be self-reliant.

Conclusion

Some tentative themes have emerged from the above discussion. It has been argued that internal and external security appear to have merged under the all-pervasive fear of global risk. The fear created by unsubstantiated linkages between rogue states, combining forces against the West, resonates with the public identification of paedophiles by national newspapers.

The effectiveness and practicability of implementing some of the policies described above seem questionable (e.g. control orders, anti-social behaviour orders). In some cases the measures adopted could create more anger and fear. Compromising due process and the rule of law could confirm terrorist accusations of Western authoritarianism and serve to increase recruitment, thereby reflexively increasing risk to personal safety. Fear management appears to have replaced coherent principles in the development of policy while the preoccupation with fear and anxiety has provided a rationale for the suspension of liberty and adoption of measures that Western democracies have only usually seen in times of war (Hudson 2001). Risks related to dangerous communities and the need to identify aliens have been exaggerated while being instrumental in creating a more exclusivist society in which problems have been reduced to simplistic certainties (Young 1999).

One of President Obama's first acts as President of the United States was to sign Executive Orders to close Guantanamo Bay over a phased period. Obama also banned harsh interrogation techniques and ordered the CIA to close secret overseas prisons. Notwithstanding the complexities involved in unravelling the anti-terror programmes described above, this act marked a significant change in policy (Landers 2009).

Leaders in previous eras have appeared less fearful in the face of adversity. In 1933 Roosevelt attempted to challenge panic with hope and optimism in the face of economic catastrophe. Roosevelt was responding to a real crisis which affected the daily lives of Americans, while Blair's pessimism was often fuelled by hypothetical future fears. The events of 9/11 appear to have created a 'moral disorientation' and 'bewilderment' in the Western cultural imagination (Furedi 2006; see also Rumford, this volume). This will remain a major feature of the New Labour legacy.

References

Ashworth, A. (1995), Principles, practice and criminal justice. In P. Birks (ed.), *Pressing Problems in the Law. 1: Criminal Justice and Human Rights*, Oxford: Oxford University Press.
BBC (2006), Terrorism Laws, *BBC News*. Available at: http://news.bbc.co.uk
BBC (2007), Internet used to target extremism, *BBC News* (31 October).

BBC (2008), Smith pledges more terror police, *BBC News* (16 April). Available at: www.bbc.co.uk.

Beaumont, B. (1999), Assessing risk in work with offenders. In P. Parsloe (ed.), *Risk Assessment in Social Care and Social Work*, London: Jessica Kingsley.

Beck, U. (1992), *Risk Society: Towards a New Modernity*, London: Sage.

Beck, U. (1994), The re-invention of politics: towards a theory of reflexive modernisation. In U. Beck, A. Giddens and S. Lash (eds), *Reflexive Modernisation: Politics, Tradition and Aesthetics in the Modern Social Order*, Cambridge: Polity Press.

Beck, U. (1998), *Democracy without Enemies*, Cambridge: Polity Press.

Beck, U. (2000), The cosmopolitan position: sociology of the second age of modernity, *British Journal of Sociology*, 51, 1: 79–107.

Better Regulation Commission (2006), *Risk Responsibility – whose work is it anyway?* (October). Available at: www.brc.gov.uk.

Blair, T. (2005), Tony Blair's speech on compensation culture, *Guardian Unlimited*. Available at: www.politics.guardian.co.uk/speeches/story.

Blair, T. (2006), Our nation's future (5 September). Available at: www.pm.gov.uk.

Denney, D. (2005), *Risk and Society*, London: Sage.

Douglas, M. (1992), *Risk and Blame: Essays in Cultural Theory*, London: Routledge.

Downes, D. and Morgan, R. (2007), No turning back: the politics of law and order into the millennium. In M. Maguire, R. Morgan and R. Reiner (eds), *The Oxford Handbook of Criminology* (4th edn), Oxford: Oxford University Press.

Edwards, R. and Glover, J. (eds) (2001), *Risk and Citizenship*, London: Routledge.

Feeley, M. and Smith, J. (1992), The new penology: notes on the emerging of correction and its implications, *Criminology*, 30: 449–74.

Foucault, M. (1972), *The Archaeology of Knowledge*, London: Routledge.

Furedi, F. (2006), Five years after 9/11: the search for meaning goes on, *Spiked*, 5 (1–5 September). Available at: www.spiked-online.com.

Furedi, F. (2007), The only thing we have to fear is the culture of fear: how human thought and action are being stifled by a regime of uncertainty, *Spiked*, 4 (1–15 April). Available at: www.spiked-online.com.

Garland, D. (2001), *Culture of Control: Crime and Social Order in Contemporary Society*, Oxford: Oxford University Press.

Giddens, A. (1990), *The Consequences of Modernity*, Cambridge: Polity Press.

Giddens, A. (1991), *Modernity and Self Identity: Self and Society in the Late Modern Age*, Cambridge: Cambridge University Press.

Giddens, A. (1998), *The Third Way: The Renewal of Social Democracy*, Cambridge: Polity Press.

Giddens, A. (2000), *The Third Way and its Critics*, Cambridge: Polity Press.

Glass, N. (2003), Surely some mistake, *Education Guardian* (5 January): 8.

Guardian (2003), Taliban captives should go home say rights groups (5 March): 5.

Guardian (2005), Lawyers criticise house arrest plan (27 January): 5.

Guardian (2006), Sure Start harms children who need it most (16 June).

Guardian (2007a), UK terror detention limit is longest of any democracy (12 November): 1.

Guardian (2007b), Yesterday in Parliament – control orders, *Guardian Unlimited*.

Guardian (2007c), Big rise in dangerous criminals reoffending while on probation (23 October): 4. Available at: www.politics.guardian.co.uk.

Guardian (2007d), Phillip Lawrence killer wins appeal against deportation to Italy (21 August): 2.

Heywood, F., lman, C. and Means, R. (2002), *Housing and Home in Later Life*, Buckingham: Open University Press.

Hubbard, P. (2003), Fear and loathing at the multiplex: everyday anxiety in the post industrial society, *Capital and Class*, 80: 51–75.

Hudson, B. (2000), *Human Rights, Public Safety and the Probation Service: Defending Justice in the Risk Society*, Bill McWilliams Memorial Lecture Imprint (28 June), Oxford: Blackwell Publishing.

Hudson, B. (2001), Punishment rights and difference: defending justice in the risk society. In K. Stenson and R. Sullivan (eds), *Crime Risk and Justice*, Cullompton: Willan Publishing, pp. 144–73.

Kampfner, J. (2004), *Blair's Wars*, London: Free Press.

Kemshall, H. (1997), Sleep safely: crime risks may be smaller than you think, *Social Policy & Administration*, 34, 4: 465–78.

Kemshall, H. (2002), *Risk, Social Policy and Welfare*, Buckingham: Open University Press.

Kemshall, H., Mackenzie, G., Wood, J., Bailey, R. and Yates, J. (2005), *Strengthening Multiagency Public Protection Agreements (MAPPAS)*, Development and Practice Report 46, London: Home Office.

Landers, K. (2009), Obama to shut Guantanamo Bay (23 January). Available at: http://www.abc.net.au/am/content/2008/s2472857.htm

Lupton, D. and Tulloch, J. (2000), Theorising fear of crime beyond the rational-irrational, *British Journal of Sociology*, 36, 2: 317–34.

Marchant, G. (2001), The Precautionary Principle: an 'unprincipled' approach to biotechnology regulation, *Journal of Risk Research*, 4, 2: 143–57.

Matthews, R. and Pitts, J. (2001), *Crime, Disorder and Community Safety*, London: Routledge.

Morgan, R. and Newburn, T. (2007), Youth justice. In M. McGuire, R. Morgan and R. Reiner (eds), *The Oxford Handbook of Criminology*, 4th edn, Oxford: Oxford University Press.

Muncie, J. (1999), Exorcising demons: media politics and criminal justice. In B. Franklin (ed.), *Social Policy, the Media and Misrepresentation*, London: Routledge.

Mythen, G. (2004), *Ulrich Beck: A Critical Introduction to the Risk Society*, London: Pluto Press.

O'Malley, P. (2000), Risk societies and the government of crime. In M. Brown and J. Pratt (eds), *Dangerous Offenders*, London: Routledge.

Raco, M. (2002), Risk, fear and control: deconstructing the discourses of New Labour economic policy, *Space and Polity*, 6, 1: 25–47.

Ring, P. (2003), Risk and UK pension reform, *Social Policy & Administration*, 37, 1: 65–82.

6, Perri and Peck, E. (2004), Modernisation: the ten commitments of New Labour's approach to public management, *International Journal of Public Management*, 7, 1: 1–18.

Smiljanic, N. (2002), Human rights and Muslims in Britain. In B. Spalek (ed.), *Islam, Crime, and Criminal Justice*, Cullompton: Willan Publishing.

Sparks, R. (1992), *Television and the Drama of Crime: Moral Tales and the Place of Crime in Public Life*, Buckingham: Open University Press.

Thomas, P. (2002), Legislative responses to terrorism. In P. Scraton (ed.), *Beyond September 11th: An Anthology of Dissent*, London: Pluto Press.

Tonry, M. and Doob, A. N. (eds) (2004), *Youth Crime and Youth Justice: Comparative and Cross National Perspectives. Crime and Justice: A Review of Research*, 31, Chicago: University of Chicago Press.

Van Swaaningen, R. (2002), Towards a replacement discourse on community safety. In G. Hughes, E. McLaughlin and J. Muncie (eds), *Crime Prevention and Community Safety: New Directions*, London: Sage.

Wiles, P. and Pease, K. (2001), Distributive justice and crime. In R. Matthews and J. Pitts (eds), *Crime, Disorder and Community Safety*, London: Routledge.

Wood, J. and Dupont, B. (eds) (2006), *Democracy, Society and the Governance of Security*, Cambridge: Cambridge University Press.

Young, J. (1999), *The Exclusive Society*, London: Sage.

Zedner, L. (2003), Too much security? *International Journal of the Sociology of Law*, 31: 155–84.

3
Does Difference Make a Difference in Financial Planning for Risk?

Deborah Quilgars, Anwen Jones and David Abbott

Introduction

Over the last two decades, the risk society thesis with its focus on individualization has been privileged over social and cultural theories in attempts to explain how people think about risk in their everyday lives. More recently, some commentators have argued that 'risk cultures' and social group membership may have more of a bearing on determining people's behaviour, reviving and developing Douglas's earlier work on cultural relativity and risk (Tulloch and Lupton 2003; Abbott *et al.* 2006; Tulloch 2008).

However, to date, there have been very little empirical data available to test these theories in real life (Taylor-Gooby 2006). This study sought to investigate whether social and cultural differences along the dimensions of disability, sexuality, faith and ethnicity influence risk perceptions and responses. The research focused on risks associated with financial security and planning, a key social policy focus in recent years and one where the risk society's 'informed citizen' is given centre stage. The policy and risk theories associated with this area are outlined below. The chapter then presents the empirical data from the study and concludes with a consideration of the policy (and theoretical) implications of difference for financial planning.

Financial Planning: Policy and Risk Theories

> More than ever before, people are being asked to make decisions and take responsibility for managing their finances . . . Meanwhile, the comforting arms of the state, and of employers, are steadily being withdrawn. (FSA 2006: 2)

Government policy is increasingly encouraging individuals to plan financially for their short- and long-term future, in so doing attempting to transfer the responsibility for key life-course events away from traditional universal welfare services towards individuals and households (McRae 1995; Quilgars and Abbott 2000; Skinner and Ford 2000). A 'new contract for welfare' between the citizen and the state is presumed, whereby 'wherever possible, people are [privately] insured against foreseeable risks and make provision for their retirement' (Department of Social Security 1998: 2).

This emphasis on individual responsibility and the curbing of state intervention in New Labour's 'third way' approach to welfare derives its intellectual underpinning from the risk society theory originally developed by Beck (1992) and adapted in the UK by Giddens (1991, 1994, 1998). Here, nation states are put under pressure by globalization to modernize their structures and policies so as to better respond to new socio-economic world relations. A process of individualization results, both in terms of shifting responsibilities away from a perceived, constrained state, and in terms of how individuals think and behave. New risks and uncertainties arise, for example, from an increasingly flexible labour market. Individuals are required to become more informed citizens, reflexively reflecting on and reacting to these changes, and the increased array of choices, to create their own biographies. There is a presumption that people are less constrained by the old inequalities and traditions of class and socio-structure, and rather influenced by a myriad of new features of late modern societies. Reflexive individuals become less likely to trust the state and expert advice, relying more on their ability to interpret 'knowledge' within the information society.

Influenced by the risk society thesis, current policy-making tends to assume that people will perceive financial risks in a uniform way and respond 'rationally' to cuts in state welfare by turning to private sector provision (Skinner and Ford 2000). However, research has demonstrated that households have been slow to make this shift and are often poorly prepared for risky events (Quilgars and Abbott 2000; FSA 2002; Sadler 2002; Actuarial Profession 2004). Low levels of financial literacy also challenge the notion of informed consumers (Jones 2005). Policy has acknowledged this latter point, with the Financial Services Authority (FSA) being charged with the task of promoting public understanding of the financial system, including the launch of a national financial capability strategy in 2003. A baseline survey (Atkinson et al. 2006) confirmed varying capability levels, which were influenced by key demographic and socio-economic variables, including age, household type, income, housing and gender. It also noted an association with religion, which it commented was 'hard to explain' (2006: 62).

The FSA survey results were, in the main, unsurprising. A considerable body of research exists that demonstrates that some individuals and groups are less able to plan for, and deal with, contingencies, and that traditional socio-structures continue to shape life experiences (Taylor-Gooby 2001; Glennerster et al. 2004; Cebulla 2007). Ability to afford financial products is the key determinant of take-up for low-income workers (Abbott and Quilgars 2001), with those on benefits most likely to experience financial exclusion (Kempson and Whyley 1999). It is now generally accepted that the risk society thesis has largely ignored the continuing influence of structure in late-modern society (Lupton 1999). More recently, risk theorists have also begun to question whether the risk society has also understated the potentially enduring impact of cultural processes that affect both perceptions and responses of groups of people within society. Douglas's work (1985, 1992) highlighted how different groups of people within the same culture may frame and understand risk differently according to symbolic and shared assumptions held by particular social groups. Lash (1993) also subsequently suggested that reflexivity is influenced by other social factors such as subcultural group membership and lifestyles. Tulloch and Lupton (2003) have more recently highlighted the role of 'risk cultures' that are developed at a local level, and influenced by factors such as gender, age, occupation, nationality and sexuality.

However, empirical studies that explore the possible relationship between social group membership or difference and risk are few and far between (Abbott *et al.* 2006; Taylor-Gooby 2006). Yet some, mainly small-scale policy-related research suggests that different groups may perceive and respond to risks differently due to both structural issues associated with specific, often disadvantaged, positions in society and cultural and lifestyle influences derived from membership of a social group with its attendant values and norms. For example, financial planning may be influenced by religious and cultural attitudes to money among some minority ethnic and faith groups, while low incomes may also be a restriction (Whyley *et al.* 1997; Collard *et al.* 2001; Pilley 2003). Disabled people face particular risks and obstacles in relation to financial planning, given more limited access to the labour market than their non-disabled peers and increased risk of experiencing poverty (Burchardt 2003). Gay men and lesbians may face discrimination in the workplace and in accessing financial services (Collinson 2003; Keogh *et al.* 2004), and societal and family responses to sexuality may lead people to place greater reliance on friendship and social networks than family links (Heaphy *et al.* 2003).

This study began with a hypothesis that risk discourses may be influenced by difference and that the risk society does not adequately describe responses to risk. If substantiated, this has important policy, as well as theoretical, implications for future approaches to risk.

Research Approach

A qualitative research approach was chosen in order to explore the meaning given to risk and financial planning among respondents. A total of 80 interviews were conducted across four groups of interest in 2005/6: disabled people (people with physical impairments as well as people with learning disabilities); people from different faiths (Muslims and Christians); people who identified as lesbian, gay or bisexual; and people from diverse black and minority ethnic backgrounds.

Individuals were recruited using a professional recruiting company, with quotas set to ensure representation of both genders and different socio-economic backgrounds. All respondents were working and between the ages of 25 and 50. Interviews were conducted in two areas (Bristol and Leeds) with broadly similar labour markets and populations, including significant numbers of people from black and minority ethnic backgrounds.

Three main areas of inquiry were pursued: first, the role of finance in people's everyday lives, most particularly their attitudes to work and money;

how and whether financial risks were perceived; and whether and how they planned financially for risk eventualities. Purposively, issues of difference were not the main focus of discussion (to elicit whether these issues arose naturally) although participants were aware that they had been recruited because of their membership of a certain social group.

A semi-autobiographical approach to interviewing was utilized, with the substantive issues of work and income located within a discussion of people's everyday lives. The interviews tended to last between 1.5 and 2 hours. The conversations were digitally recorded with the consent of group members. The recordings were transcribed and analysed using the qualitative software system, MaxQDA. A grounded theory approach (Taylor and Bogdan 1984) was used in the analysis.

Below, the findings from the interviews are outlined, first with respect to the meaning that respondents gave to the role of work and money in their lives, second, their perceptions of any risks to their financial security, and third, their approaches to financial planning.

The Role of Work and Money in People's Lives

A number of themes on the role of work and money were common across the groups. First, the importance of work for its provision of an income was strongest among those on lower incomes. Second, respondents often talked about the need to attain a work–life balance, and a work–home balance was also emphasized by many female respondents (particularly in the faith and ethnicity groups, where a traditional gender division of labour was quite common). Third, many respondents spoke about having chosen particular jobs to fulfil a vocation (and to reflect people's value systems) and/or achieve job satisfaction. Sometimes jobs offered comparatively low salaries, but people were generally happy to sacrifice luxury items and financial benefits to achieve this. Finally, analysis revealed that the meaning of money varied considerably between respondents but there were more similarities between groups than differences – within any one group, respondents described approaches to money from cautious to carefree and everything in between.

However, there were a number of important distinctions evident in the accounts of social groups on some issues. Disabled people's relationship with the labour market was often a more complex one than that of non-disabled respondents. Many (though not all) were constrained by the type of job they could undertake, and some had faced retraining after the onset of disability. People with learning disabilities found it very difficult to access jobs and usually received low wages. Work was also particularly crucial for many disabled respondents as this was associated with independence, providing a vital foothold to an ordinary life. Few of the disabled respondents linked work explicitly with financial security.

Being gay, lesbian or bisexual did not seem to have a particularly prominent effect on approaches to work and money. A couple of people explained that they had chosen to work in the public sector as it was hoped this would be a more tolerant setting. However, respondents were unsure whether their sexuality exerted an impact on their attitudes to money. A few people explained that they did seem to conform to gay stereotypes in placing a high value on lifestyle factors such as 'living well' and 'looking good', but others did not feel that such a link existed. Respondents also challenged whether there was such a thing as a 'pink pound'.

> *'I think there's a lot of pressure within the community to look good and wear the right labels and to have the latest gadgets or gizmos and bigger purchases. And that's all thrust upon you by people who think that there is a pink pound and that we all have massive disposable incomes.'* (Sexuality group)

A dominant theme in Asian and/or Muslim male respondents' accounts was that the main purpose of work was to make money to be able to support their family. A number of respondents explained that this reflected the values that were more broadly held within the Asian community where working hard for the family was expected. It was also evident that people thought it important to work long hours in order to save, to pay off mortgages early, and to reinvest money in other properties and/or businesses. Job satisfaction was often of relatively minor importance. However, Asian and/or Muslim women often remarked that they would have preferred their husbands to spend less time at work and more time at home.

> *'It's a means to an end ... there are a lot of mouths to feed. I dare say if I didn't have a family it probably wouldn't happen, no ... I just find it a bit boring ... Know what I mean, it's not a challenge. But at the end of the day, I just look at the wage packet that I pick up at the end of the week and pay for the mortgage.'* (Faith group – Muslim)

Attitudes towards debt also appeared to be more pronounced among some of the faith and/or ethnicity respondents, most specifically Muslims. People tended to say that they or their partner 'did not like' debt or servicing debt by paying interest. Only a couple of respondents directly attributed this to Shari'ah law. None of those who had a mortgage had a Shari'ah-compliant product but a few people said they were trying to pay the mortgage off as quickly as possible to avoid paying interest for too long, while others preferred to borrow money from family members. Others talked about other family members who did observe Shari'ah law.

The meaning of money was also quite distinct among people with a faith, most particularly Christians. There was a firmly held belief that money belonged to God rather than individuals. This had two implications: it meant that money was placed in people's trust, bringing with it a responsibility to use it wisely and not to waste it. Because of this, some respondents explained that this meant that money was not something they felt they should worry about, on principle. In addition, money was not only something that one 'received' (from work and other sources) but it was also something that one should 'give away'. This is not necessarily to say that people without a faith do not give, but that giving has a specific cultural meaning within a faith. Most said they gave money to charity, friends or relatives, and a smaller number tithed a proportion of their income to the church. The act of giving was also understood as a contract with God to the extent that by giving one may also expect to receive money or gifts in kind as needed.

'I genuinely do feel that I only have what I have because I am blessed, that actually my money is God's . . . I have a responsibility to use it properly and I give a certain amount away on a regular basis and I also do on ad hoc kinds of things as well because it is not actually mine to be precious about.' (Faith group – Christian)

'I shouldn't be worrying about money, I mean that's quite, you know, Jesus said, "Don't worry".' (Faith group – Christian)

'Cos in our faith it says give to charity, I always, and I'm always giving to charity . . . if you give to the poor God gives you more in that sense, and that's my theory really, you know. I give to the poor and I'm surviving.' (Faith group – Muslim)

Perceptions of 'Risk' to Financial Security

As with previous research, it was clear that most respondents perceived the labour market as generally more risky now than in previous decades (Quilgars and Abbott 2000; Tulloch and Lupton 2003; Abbott *et al.* 2006). Nonetheless, when thinking about their own position, the majority of people did not see job loss as a key risk to their household. Some respondents felt relatively secure in their present jobs, particularly within the public sector. However, more typically, people perceived that any risks were manageable ones for a number of reasons. First, many felt 'work-secure' (Quilgars and Abbott 2000), if not job-secure, that is, they were confident that they would be able to find another similar job quite easily, or at worst within a different, albeit lower-paid sector. While most respondents did mention health problems as a possible risk to financial security, they also largely presumed that their health was a constant.

'So I'm not worried about, I mean they're always having restructures at work . . . First one's a bit daunting and then you just realize it's just run of the mill . . . you can always go back and get a temp job somewhere else or do, you know, it's not a big deal, you can talk, you can walk, you've got your arms and legs.' (Ethnicity group – Black Caribbean)

Second, people talked about having other things to fall back on at a time of job loss, including the earnings of a partner as well as specific financial resources. A minority appeared to have worked hard to try and make themselves financially secure, including a number of Muslim respondents who had paid off their mortgages or had small mortgages. More generally, housing equity was seen by many as a cushion to possible future financial difficulties, echoing other studies that suggest that home-ownership makes people feel secure (Jones *et al.* 2007).

'I feel financially secure. And I think probably it comes with purchasing the house . . . I just keep thinking, if anything happens or if push comes to shove I'll just sell the house, use that money to look after me if I'm ill or whatever . . . and that's why I don't worry about pensions, I sort of look at that as a pension.' (Ethnicity group – Black Caribbean)

Some respondents did perceive a moderate risk to their financial security but explained that this was acceptable given the positive benefits that arose from being self-employed or the choice of a particular area of work. The risk itself was not experienced as positive, like some risks may be, e.g. pursuit of dangerous sports or physically risky jobs (Fincham 2007, for example); however, the fact that respondents had elected to take this risk appeared to militate against its potential impact.

A minority of respondents identified the impact of potential job or income loss as a significant risk. Usually this was associated with particularly poor labour market positions. In addition, for some, the experience of a loss of income in the past (to them or their family) meant they were more aware of possible future risks (cf. Cebulla 2007). Others felt that risks were compounded in a number of areas.

'Oh I do, I do [worry]. Firstly because I am self-employed . . . an employer wouldn't be able to help me. And secondly, I've got a large family and thirdly I am financially very committed you see.' (Faith group – Muslim)

However, in contrast to the other groups, there was widespread identification of risks around work and money for the disabled respondents. Some explained they were simply in quite precarious jobs, sometimes reflecting their more marginal place in the job market. There was also an overriding concern centred around the impact of health on people's ability to work, particularly for people who had become disabled more recently. Some also explained that it was generally more difficult to be flexible within the labour force – *'there's a whole gamut of jobs that you couldn't do because you're not physically able to.'* Most crucially, many anticipated worsening health in the future arising from the progressive nature of their condition. Whilst retirement was a concern across the social groups, this appeared to be a particular worry for some disabled respondents.

'There's not much distance between you being okay and then how quickly it can change. There's a vulnerability that I'm much more conscious of.' (Disability group)

'I worry about the future. I worry about money. I worry about how I'm going to be in, please God if I live, another 10 years' time. If I'm like this, what'll I be like in 10 years?' (Disability group)

People with learning disabilities identified a specific risk to their financial security of financial exploitation. This reflected a lack of control over their financial resources, with support staff often in charge of their finances and them having to request money for specific needs, as well as more general risks of people taking advantage of them.

> '*I think you go very careful who you talk to about your money and say how much is in your account. People might not be so very trusting as I found out.*' (Disability group)

Interestingly, changes to welfare benefits were not identified as a risk to the maintenance of income security. Most respondents did not identify benefits as being relevant to them in terms of maintaining an income. Disabled people, in contrast, were often already dependent on some benefits. However, despite media coverage at the time of possible attempts to reform and restructure Incapacity Benefit (now confirmed), only one respondent said that threats to social security benefits were a risk and source of worry.

While poor health was seen as a heightened risk in the disability group, relationship breakdown was only mentioned (unprompted) as a specific risk within the sexuality group. One person thought this reflected the more fickle approach to relationship formation within some parts of the gay community. Others felt that societal structures still did not support same-sex relationships to the same extent, adding to the potential impact of relationship break-down. Some had experienced financial difficulties on splitting up with a previous partner, which had led to them placing a greater emphasis on keeping finances separate to avoid such risks in the future. Other recent research has shown that cohabiting couples make similar preparations to protect themselves against the risk of relationship breakdown (Lewis and Sarre 2006), suggesting that the responses of the sexuality group may accord with mainstream developments. It is possible that other groups, for example faith and ethnicity respondents, have more confidence in traditional structures such as marriage.

> '*I think there is a different agenda with being gay – certainly when you are in a partnership, the partnership perhaps isn't as secure initially because of the gay world and how fickle it is . . . so that makes you very guarded as regards to money and finance and maybe you take out financial restrictions. I would be very protective. Regardless if I move in with somebody or I buy a house with somebody, I would always have my own property in case something goes wrong, because we don't have any other security blanket of children and things like that.*' (Sexuality group)

One of the strongest findings of the research was the potential protective factor that faith may provide against the fear of risks. A common theme among the faith respondents, particularly Christians, was that a personal belief appeared to mitigate the feelings of risk. A number of Christians gave examples of past experiences which made them think that God was 'taking care' of them, or they had a belief that whatever happened in the future, God would provide and things would turn out all right in the end.

'I don't think having a faith makes me less likely to get run over by a bus or anything like that . . . I don't think "Well I'm a Christian so therefore I'm less likely to be, to have to face stuff". I just don't think I fret about this side of life so much.' (Faith group – Christian)

'I just naturally think, "Oh God will take care of that, Jesus will make sure that's right".' (Faith group – Christian)

'In society's eyes, I'm not financially secure . . . But it boils down for me to faith again, that I've never been without a job when I wanted one. And even when it's come to, say the eleventh hour to pay a bill or whatever, it's always got paid . . . I'm not worried.' (Ethnicity group – Black Caribbean)

In addition, a few of the respondents in the disability group recognized a heightened risk to their financial security, but explained that their belief in the social model of disability meant they conceived these risks as being a result of society's disabling attitudes and structures. This made them less likely to worry about these risks. Here, as with faith, a protective factor appeared to arise from assigning responsibility externally, rather than adopting an individualized approach. A few disabled people also explained that they worried less about finances *because* they had learnt that life was outside their control.

'You can't plan to be blind, you can't plan to be in a wheelchair. When it happens you have to deal with it. I've had to deal with it and now I'm ready for anything else that happens because my mind's set that way. Finances will take care of themselves at the end of the day.' (Disability group)

Financial Planning for Risk

There was widespread recognition across respondents in all groups that, in principle, it was important to plan financially for some risk eventualities, particularly for older age and retirement. Most people felt that there was simply no other option but to plan privately if possible, explicitly recognizing the retrenchment of the welfare state.

'We've recently decided that we've got to plan. If we have to go without things we have to go without things because I'd rather have something when I'm a bit older, to be able to enjoy myself when I get to retirement. And I think you've got to plan. People are living longer, the government can't afford to keep paying what it pays now.' (Sexuality group)

Alongside this, there were varying degrees of belief in the importance of individual responsibility. Some respondents held quite strong views about deserving and undeserving groups, with a concern that some people abused the welfare system. This idea was particularly prominent in Christian accounts. It may also contribute to an understanding of why Christians explained that they still planned despite being sometimes less afraid of potential risks (see previous section).

> 'There are many people who can't work because they are ill, be it physical or mental illness and they need to be looked after but there are people who . . . put it on, they are scroungers.' (Faith group – Christian)

> 'I suppose I've always been a great believer in the saying, "God helps those who help themselves", it's no good praying asking God for help if you haven't done your best to help yourself.' (Faith group – Christian)

Sometimes the belief in individual responsibility and the state system existed together – this appeared to be the case for many Asian and Muslim respondents, who placed a high value on self-reliance at times of financial hardship but were also the most likely to say that they thought they *should* be able to depend on the state as they had contributed into the system. Respondents in the disability group appeared to have the strongest support for state welfare provision, partly reflecting their past and/or possible future reliance on benefits. Nonetheless, most disabled respondents believed in a mixed economy of welfare and were reluctant claimers.

> 'I think if you have worked all your life, you have paid your taxes and you do find yourself in a situation where you're unable to work because of health or whatever, you should be able to feel comfortable for that time [of claiming] and not feel guilty, not feel bad.' (Disability group)

The commonly held belief in individual, or at least mixed, responsibility did seem to influence people's overall attitude towards planning. Only a minority of people believed that there was no point in planning financially. Most people did plan to some extent (if they could afford to) and/or said that they would do more if they had more money. Most people who did not plan or only planned a little simply could not afford to do more. However, while respondents often firmly believed in the merits of planning, they often had an equally strong belief in the importance of quality of life. With the possible exception of Asian men (see above), many respondents were searching for a work–life balance. There were also competing priorities for household financial planning, for example helping out extended family, particularly key among the ethnicity group.

Some respondents did, however, appear more relaxed than others about planning. Young people across the groups tended towards this attitude, although most realized that they would have to start planning sooner or later. Enjoying life was placed at quite a premium, although very few said that they were reckless with their spending. There was also sometimes a gender division in planning responsibilities and attitudes. Some disabled people felt that spending was actually the most rational way to proceed given their possible worsening health or shorter life expectancy. However, this did depend on the type of disability or health conditions, with a few people saying the opposite – that they had become more prudent rather than less since becoming disabled.

'I suppose because of my health I'm a bit more carefree because at any point I'm thinking, health goes, I've gone. So I might as well spend it while it's there and not worry about next week.' (Disability group)

'Since being on the sick we've been very prudent with money, we've learnt how to buckle our belts and stuff like that.' (Disability group)

Some planning was complicated by a mistrust or confusion about financial products and advice. Respondents in all groups mentioned this to some extent, though it was a particular issue for disabled people. Some of the mistrust was born of experience of occasions when insurances had not paid out or people had been excluded from taking certain products out. People with learning disabilities did not feel they possessed the information that would enable them to understand financial decision-making. There were also a few specific instances where lesbian, gay or bisexual respondents had also had difficult experiences with financial products.

'There is more you could do – like increasing my pension . . . Yes I've got the money to do it but it's just the hassle . . . half a dozen people coming around, all supposedly independent advisors, coming up with completely different companies that you should be going for.' (Sexuality group)

'It's got to be explained to me in plain English. I don't want all this small print, you know.' (Disability group)

Similar methods of planning were mentioned across the groups, including savings, equity, pensions and insurances. Most saw reliance on family and friends as a last-resort safety net – different ethnic groups did not place any greater emphasis on this despite the importance of extended families. Lesbian, gay and bisexual respondents were no less likely to talk about relying on family despite other research that might suggest that this support may be less available to gay people. Two approaches to planning did, however, emerge as particularly important to certain groups. First, Asian and/or Muslim respondents tended to prioritize reducing debts as quickly as possible, enabling them to save later in life (see above). Respondents explained these attitudes were culturally transmitted within Asian communities rather than being explicitly faith-based.

'It's heavily indoctrinated within Asian community, parents really do put it down to the kids – to save and not be too frivolous.' (Faith group – Muslim)

Second, some faith respondents spoke about 'living within their means' – both as a preventative function (that is, not over-spending to avoid too much debt) and as a strategy to cope should income be reduced in the future.

'But we're happy, we would happily take pay cuts, I'd take a pay cut and do my job, that wouldn't be an issue as long as we can pay the mortgage, you know, we don't, it would be easy to cut back if we needed to.' (Faith group – Muslim)

29

Conclusion

The central hypothesis of this research was that the risk society thesis insufficiently explains the framing and response to risk for many groups in society (Jones *et al.* 2006). This does not mean that some elements of the risk society thesis do not still hold. There was some evidence of individualization in terms of an intention and willingness to plan (possibly more so than in earlier studies – Quilgars and Abbott 2000). There was widespread recognition that one can no longer rely on the state (with varying levels of belief in state support evident) and a tendency to see any failure to plan as a result of their own choices and actions (Mythen 2004; Zinn 2004). There was also some evidence of personal risk reflexivity with people reflecting on a number (though not all) of potential risks and developing their strategies to respond to this (Pidgeon *et al.* 2006). Trust in private provision was low, often following past experiences (Cebulla 2007), as well as exclusions from provision.

In terms of current policy, there was evidence that an emphasis on financial capability is not misplaced as many respondents found financial advice and/or products confusing. However, a much more complex picture emerged as to the reasons why people might not always plan quite as policy (and theory) predicts, with both mainstream – and social group-specific – cultural reference points emerging as important. For example, respondents were often prepared to balance risk of greater insecurity in the workplace, or a lower salary and a subsequent inability to plan as extensively for the future, with other values – most notably a work–life balance. Younger people in our study were more likely to cite this work–life balance, or values alternative to work, as important (cf. Devadason 2007). As suggested by Lash, reflexivity was revealed to be 'multilayered and . . . understood in relation to a sweep of cultural practices and behaviours' (Mythen 2004: 147).

Most centrally, the research revealed that risk perceptions and responses were influenced by difference in a number of ways. First, disabled people faced much more constraint than any of the other groups in making choices about work, security and planning. While the creation of a more flexible labour market may offer new opportunities (in both highly paid, specialist sectors and lower-paid, part-time jobs) to some in society (Jones *et al.* 2006), disabled people in the study did not feel the 'luxury' of a range of job choices should their current job end. At the same time work was an important platform for access to independence and an important sense of citizenship, contribution and identity – in some ways work meant more to this group than to others. However, they felt the most precariously placed group – excluded on the whole from market options which might insure against risk and uncertain as to how future health issues would affect their security and well-being in old age. Other research in this area confirms that these constraints and concerns are very real (Howard 2002; Watson *et al.* 2005), and how disabled people face higher day-to-day living costs than their non-disabled peers (Smith *et al.* 2004), with the impact of this tending to be cumulative, so that disadvantage and dependency increase over time (Zarb 1999). So while policy is rightly focused on helping disabled people enter and stay in the labour market (PMSU 2005), not enough is known about the barriers that they face to planning in the medium and long term for financial security, and about built-in policy disincentives to planning for old age (Morris 2003).

People with learning difficulties, meantime, have barely reached first base with autonomy over their own money (mostly from benefits), let alone opportunities to plan for their futures or access the world of work (Williams *et al.* 2003). The barriers to work and control over money are highlighted in recent policy reports (Department of Health 2007; Joint Committee on Human Rights 2008), but change is slow. While the move towards people with learning difficulties accessing an individual, personalized budget instead of using congregate services will lead to people with learning difficulties being more in control of their money (Department of Health 2006), it is unclear how people with learning difficulties will be supported to make choices about how they plan their financial affairs and futures.

The role of difference was found to be more determining in some areas than has previously been documented – particularly in terms of the role of faith. Attitudes towards money and resisting debt among faith respondents stood out more sharply than among other groups. Clark and Lelkes (2008) also found that, in common with the Christians here, faith can provide a 'buffer' for coping with risky life events such as job loss. At the same time, the current study found there are incentives to plan derived from a highly developed sense of individualized responsibility and a focus on living within one's means. Only a few of the Muslim respondents talked about Shari'ah-compliant products; however, almost all Muslims expressed a dislike of debt and interest. Khan and Bhatti (2008) have highlighted the growth in Islamic banking and financial products; however, it may be that religiosity is more important than religion (Voas 2007). There is a view that Muslims are more culturally or ethnically Muslim rather than observant and that many have adapted religious rules to a more Western lifestyle (Mirza *et al.* 2007). The findings on faith challenge the presumption within the risk society that fate or destiny is no longer a feature of modern societies.

In some areas, the impact of difference was not always as strong as predicted by existing literature. For example, the impact of the 'pink pound' was challenged and lesbian, gay and bisexual respondents often struggled to find links between their approaches to financial planning and sexuality. In addition, we did not uncover significant differences in relation to ethnicity (as opposed to where ethnicity cross-cut with faith/religion) and risk perception and planning. Explicit racial discrimination did not appear to inform respondents' experiences of risks, although some respondents did speak about the need to work hard to prove themselves and challenge 'stereotypes'.

Overall, the research revealed two elements of difference that impacted on risk perceptions and responses. First, there were structural factors that placed constraints on people's ability to plan financially, including access to financial services and the labour market (and therefore income effects) (Abbott *et al.* 2006). Second, some social groups also held culturally embedded attitudes that affected perceptions, and sometimes behaviour. Here, the impact of culture is likely to be influenced by the extent to which people subscribe to particular social groups and affiliated 'identities'. For example, it is probable that practising Christians will subscribe to some of the beliefs identified to a greater extent than people who describe themselves as Christians but do not practise the religion. Quantitative research is needed to test this further. However, where culture is deeply embedded, it may be retained despite movement away from specific practices (for example, attitudes towards debt among some of the Muslim respondents).

Social policy does tend to acknowledge the role of structural constraints, although the longer-term implications of positions are not always taken into account. However, to date policy has tended to ignore the potential impact of more culturally determined assumptions (with the possible exception of faith-based financial products). Without explicit recognition of difference, some social groups may risk further marginalization, compared to other groups where social group cultural values may actually support risk responses.

Theories of risk inevitably tend to polarize the different approaches to understanding uncertainty. Real life is inevitably more complex: individuals behave rationally and irrationally, as highly reflexive individuals and more traditional constrained agents, and as members of mainstream and particular social groups. They do so at different times and places, and sometimes at the same time giving rise to seemingly contradictory accounts. Compromises inevitably emerge as individuals try and balance work and the rest of life, and a present and future standard of living. The nature of mortality means that people can never be expected to make accurate predictions as to their future. A combination of group membership (class/income-based and social/cultural group-based value systems), along with individual predisposition, is what accounts for people's real life decisions. Despite a plethora of risk literature, further research is still required to understand under what circumstances each of these competing factors wins over other factors (Zinn and Taylor-Gooby 2006), and importantly, the points at which real life undermines policy.

Acknowledgements

The research for this chapter was funded by the UK Economic and Social Research Council under the Social Contexts and Responses to Risk (SCARR) Network (coordinated by Peter Taylor-Gooby, University of Kent).

References

Abbott, D. and Quilgars, D. (2001), Managing the risk of unemployment: is welfare re-structuring undermining support for social security? In R. Edwards and J. Glover (eds), *Risk and Citizenship: Debates and Issues*, London: Routledge, pp. 111–25.

Abbott, D., Quilgars, D. and Jones, A. (2006), The impact of social and cultural difference in relation to job loss and financial planning: reflections on the risk society, *Forum: Qualitative Social Research*, 7, 1.

Actuarial Profession (2004), *Consumer Understanding of Risk*, London: Actuarial Profession.

Atkinson, A., McKay, S., Kempson, E. and Collard, S. (2006), *Levels of Financial Capability in the UK: Results of a Baseline Survey*, London: Financial Services Authority.

Beck, U. (1992), *Risk Society: Towards a New Modernity*, London: Sage.

Burchardt, T. (2003), *Being and Becoming: Social Exclusion and the Onset of Disability*, CASE Report 21. Available at: http://sticerd.lse.ac.uk/Case

Cebulla, A. (2007), Class or individual? A test of the nature of risk perceptions and the individualization thesis of risk society theory, *Journal of Risk Research*, 10, 2: 129–48.

Clark, A. and Lelkes, O. (2008), Religion 'linked to happy life'. Available at: http://news.bbc.co.uk/1/hi/health/7302609.stm

Collard, S., Kempson, E. and Whyley, C. (2001), *Tackling Financial Exclusion: An Area-based Approach*, Bristol: Policy Press.

Collinson, P. (2003), Much pride but a lot of prejudice, *The Guardian* (26 July).

Department of Health (2006), *Our Health, Our Care, Our Say: A New Direction for Community Services*, Cm 6737, London: Department of Health.

Department of Health (2007), *Valuing People Now: From Progress to Transformation*, London: Department of Health.

Department of Social Security (1998), *A New Contract for Welfare: Partnership in Pensions*, London: Stationery Office.

Devadason, R. (2007), Constructing coherence: young adults' pursuit of meaning through multiple transitions between work, education and unemployment, *Journal of Youth Studies*, 10, 2: 203–21.

Douglas, M. (1985), *Risk Acceptability according to the Social Sciences*, New York: Russell Sage Foundation.

Douglas, M. (1992), *Risk and Blame: Essays in Cultural Theory*, London: Routledge.

Financial Services Authority (FSA) (2002), *Financing the Future: Mind the Gap! The Implications of an Ageing Population – Key Findings and Proposed Actions*, London: FSA.

Financial Services Authority (FSA) (2006), *Financial Capability in the UK: Delivering Change*, London: FSA.

Fincham, B. (2007), 'Generally speaking people are in it for the cycling and the beer': bicycle messengers, subculture and enjoyment, *Sociological Review*, 55, 2: 189–202.

Giddens, A. (1991), *Modernity and Self Identity*, Oxford: Polity Press.

Giddens, A. (1994), *Beyond Left and Right*, Cambridge: Polity Press.

Giddens, A. (1998), *The Third Way: The Renewal of Social Democracy*, Cambridge: Polity Press.

Glennerster, H., Hills, J., Piachaud, D. and Webb, J. (2004), *One Hundred Years of Poverty and Policy*, York: Joseph Rowntree Foundation.

Heaphy, B., Yip, A. and Thompson, D. (2003), The social and policy implications of non-heterosexual ageing, *Quality in Ageing*, 4, 3: 30–5.

Howard, M. (2002), *Not Just the Job: Report of a Working Group on Disabled People Using Personal Assistance and Work Incentives*, York: Joseph Rowntree Foundation.

Joint Committee on Human Rights (2008), *A Life Like Any Other? Human Rights of People with Learning Disabilities*, London: Stationery Office.

Jones, A. (2005), Financial education and poverty prevention in the UK. In A. Jones and U. Reifner (eds), *Financial Education and Poverty Prevention in Europe*, Hamburg: IFF, pp. 241–55.

Jones, A., Abbott, D. and Quilgars, D. (2006), Social inequality and risk. In P. Taylor-Gooby and J. Zinn (eds), *Risk in Social Science*, Oxford: Oxford University Press, pp. 228–49.

Jones, A., Elsinga, M., Quilgars, D. and Toussaint, J. (2007), Home owners' perceptions of and responses to risk, *European Journal of Housing Policy*, 7, 2: 129–50.

Kempson, E. and Whiley, C. (1999), *Kept Out or Opted Out? Understanding and Combating Financial Exclusion*, Bristol: Policy Press.

Keogh, P., Dodds, C. and Henderson, L. (2004), *Working Class Gay Men: Redefining Community, Restoring Identity*, London: Sigma Research.

Khan, M. and Bhatti, M. (2008), Development in Islamic banking: a financial risk-allocation approach, *Journal of Risk Finance*, 9, 1: 40–51.

Lash, S. (1993), Reflexive modernisation: the aesthetic dimension, *Theory, Culture and Society*, 10: 1–23.

Lewis, J. and Sarre, S. (2006), Risk and intimate relationships. In P. Taylor-Gooby and J. Zinn (eds), *Risk in Social Science*, Oxford: Oxford University Press, pp. 140–59.

Lupton, D. (ed.) (1999), *Introduction: Risk and Socio-cultural Theory: New Directions and Perspectives*, Cambridge: Cambridge University Press.

McRae, H. (1995), There's a bit of Sting in all of us, *The Independent*, 19 October.

Mirza, M., Senthikumaran, A. and Ja'far, Z. (2007), *Living Together Apart: British Muslims and the Paradox of Multiculturalism*, London: Policy Exchange.

Morris, J. (2003), *Barriers to Independent Living: A Scoping Paper Prepared for the Disability Rights Commission*, London: DRC.

Mythen, G. (2004), *Ulrich Beck: A Critical Introduction to the Risk Society*, London: Pluto Press.

Pidgeon, N., Simmons, P. and Henwood, K. (2006), Risk, environment and technology. In P. Taylor-Gooby and J. Zinn (eds), *Risk in Social Science*, Oxford: Oxford University Press, pp. 94–116.

Pilley, C. (2003), *Immigrants and Financial Services: Literacy, Difficulty of Access, Needs and Solutions*, Hamburg: Institut für Finanzdienstleistungen (unpublished).

Prime Minister's Strategy Unit (PMSU) (2005), *Improving the Life Chances of Disabled People*, London: PMSU.

Quilgars, D. and Abbott, D. (2000), Working in the risk society: families' perceptions of, and responses to, flexible labour markets and the restructuring of welfare, *Community, Work and Family*, 3, 1: 15–36.

Sadler, R. (2002), *Medium and Long-term Retail Saving in the UK: A Review*, London: HM Treasury.

Skinner, C. and Ford, J. (2000), *Planning, Postponing or Hesitating: Understanding Financial Planning*, York: Centre for Housing Policy.

Smith, N., Middleton, S., Ashton-Brooks, K., Cox, L., Dobson, B. and Reith, L. (2004), *Disabled People's Costs of Living: 'More than You Would Think'*, York: Joseph Rowntree Foundation.

Taylor, S. and Bogdan, R. (1984), *Introduction to Qualitative Research Methods: the Search for Meaning*, New York: John Wiley.

Taylor-Gooby, P. (2001), Risk, contingency and the third way: evidence from BHPS and qualitative studies, *Social Policy & Administration*, 35, 2: 195–211.

Taylor-Gooby, P. (2006), Social and public policy: reflexive individualization and regulatory governance. In P. Taylor-Gooby and J. Zinn (eds), *Risk in Social Science*, Oxford: Oxford University Press, pp. 271–87.

Tulloch, J. (2008), Culture and risk. In J. Zinn (ed.), *Social Theories of Risk and Uncertainty: An Introduction*, Oxford: Blackwell, pp. 138–67.

Tulloch, J. and Lupton, D. (2003), *Risk and Everyday Life*, London: Sage.

Voas, D. (2007), Does religion belong in population studies? *Environment and Planning*, 39: 1166–80.

Watson, D., Williams, V. and Wickham, C. (2005), *A Valued Part of the Workforce? Employment and Disabled People*, Sussex: SEQUAL.

Whyley, C., Kempson, E. and Herbert, A. (1997), *Money Matters: Approaches to Money Management and Bill-paying*, London: Policy Studies Institute.

Williams, V., Tarleton, B., Watson, D. and Johnson, R. (2003), *Nice Job – If You Can Get It: Work and People with Learning Difficulties*, Bristol: Norah Fry Research Centre, University of Bristol.

Zarb, G. (1999), What price independence? In M. Turner (ed.), *Facing Our Futures*, London: National Centre for Independent Living.

Zinn, J. (2004), Health, risk and uncertainty in the life-course: a typology of biographical certainty constructions, *Social Theory and Health*, 2, 3: 199–221.

Zinn, J. and Taylor-Gooby, P. (2006), Risk as an interdisciplinary research area. In P. Taylor-Gooby and J. Zinn (eds), *Risk in Social Science*, Oxford: Oxford University Press, pp. 20–53.

4

The Great Cut: The Support for Private Modes of Social Evasion by Public Policy

Rowland Atkinson

Introduction

The city has long been seen as a space of learning through encounters with difference and its implications in developing social empathy. It is also the site within which the consequences of inequality may be seen and felt, as public spaces and institutions generate meetings across the social spectrum (Sennett 1990, 1996). For Young (1999) the consequences of social exclusion are public disorder, crime, and their impact on a broadening range of socio-economic groups over time. This unsightliness of poverty, its unacceptability and uncomfortable provocation in the observer, is a theme that takes us back to the very origins of social policy reform and its earliest exponents. Empirical research by writers like Rowntree and Booth was an act of knowing through seeing, both as progressive individuals, but ultimately as work underpinning the actions of states who thereby better knew their subjects (Scott 1998). When writers like Riis (1890/1997) charted how the 'other half' lived it was the poor who were being made visible to a more comfortable and benignly unknowing class that, even while resident in the same city, could not 'see', empathize and thereby act on these abject social conditions. For Riis to *see* such problems was to acknowledge their presence *as* problems. Poverty and difference thereby provided corrective and salutary punctures in the comfortable insulation of affluence, with problems like homelessness and poverty seeing periodic rediscovery and temporary, yet concerted, responses.

In this chapter I suggest that a combination of private residential decisions and directions in housing and urban policy have yielded dramatic feedback effects on urban social and political systems. The persistence and, in some cases, deepening of social exclusion, the clustering of poverty and locking-in of social pain into places that are socially and spatially distant from comfort (Bourdieu 1999; Dorling and Reese 2003) hold out the prospect of diminished imperatives for public and political intervention. In other words, the spatial distribution of social inequalities is critical in influencing not only the relative experience of social problems, but also in generating propensities to reform and public action because of the relative invisibility of social problems. In earlier formulations of this relationship (see particularly Galbraith 1958) the role of public intervention and fiscal policies was, at least in part, to prevent an emerging disjuncture between privatized affluence and public squalor. This meant that social costs of allowing public investment in social problems to falter would tend to create negative externalities that were demo-cratic in their impact on a range of groups, almost regardless of their wealth.

The central assertion in this chapter is that affluence increasingly confers the ability to evade the negative externalities and public squalor produced under contemporary patterns of socio-spatial polarization. This 'cut' between the problems and responsibilities of citizens is also supported by the designs and unintended consequences of housing and urban policy frameworks – policies that buttress private choices for social disaffiliation and insulation from fear and risk. This meshing of private strategies of social evasion, based on perceptions of danger, and public interventions that spatially contain a subsistent welfare client group (Denney 2005), creates longer-term risks that the political and social propensity to deal with social problems is curtailed since it no longer has the kind of feedback effects that previously touched the lives of the affluent:

> Where social capital and cooperation is undermined, due to factors like inadequate housing provision, other consequences ripple out. For example, lifestyles become more privatised. Many services and facilities that were widely provided through communal cooperation or state agencies are replaced by private markets or disappear entirely . . . Defensive expenditures increase and avoidance behaviour is practiced by more affluent people; private security services, private transport and 'fortified' houses appear on the scene. The city itself develops harder divisions and edges. Spatial segregation intensifies. (Berry and Hall 2002: 20)

It would now appear that entire socio-spatial circuits enable the tendency, through technologies (such as SUVs and premium transportation networks) and spaces (gated communities, gentrified neighbourhoods, shopping malls, private schools and services), to evade places and people seen to be too risky or confronting. Such places and circuits have become all the more alluring as public discourses focusing on fear and the relative risks of poorer and deviant groups have become the keynote of contemporary life (Furedi 2002; Bauman 2006). If the visibility and impacts of the poor provided the traditional periodic imperative to policy forays, the social ecology of today's cities high-lights their capacity to hardwire indifference and policy stasis by allowing places and groups to be out of sight and of lowered public cost. In this chapter I refer to this dual process as 'the great cut', the emerging twin project of:

1. the evasion of public costs associated with exclusion and poverty by the state and its supporting constituencies; and
2. the related and circuitous evasion of poverty and exclusion by the affluent.

As conceptions of risk have multiplied so have they become more attached to individuals and their responsibilities as sovereign subjects (Beck 1992). In the context of specific cities danger itself has been more firmly attached to deviant others in deviant places whose responsibilization is sought as the means to a moral vision of the good citizen, underwritten by punitive codes and sanctions. Vulnerability within familial and household units also drives projects focused on personal and community safety. This has notably produced a particular 'stickiness' of socio-economic positions into place, and to places which form a hierarchy of taste and class positions (Burrows and Ellison 2004), to say nothing of senses of relative spatial danger and safety. In societies of growing inequality these patterns of segregation have provided a notable mosaic of social worlds that more rarely collide within the daily pattern of urban social life. As low resources consign residents of social housing to a predominantly static and contained daily life-world, so have rising real incomes for the 'included' allowed both more mobile and concealed trajectories which often weave close by, yet remain hidden from view (Graham and Marvin 2001). As writers like Massey and Denton (1996: 409) have noted:

> In the social ecology now being created around the globe, affluent people increasingly will live and interact with other affluent people, while the poor increasingly will live and interact with other poor people. The social worlds of the rich and poor will diverge.

As segregation has been further fuelled by a polarized income distribution (Dorling and Rees 2003) and the clustering of socio-tenurial positions (particularly related to the geography of social housing), higher-income groups have attempted to avoid other groups more emphatically as danger in public media and political discourses dominate (Garland 2001). Policy-makers continue to ponder the intransigence of 'poor areas' to successive area-based interventions, often without sensing that a system which allocates resources so inequitably, within the generally fixed parameters of housing supply and tenure, will continue to do little other than reproduce a patchwork of poverty and relative affluence (Cheshire 2007).

Central to this chapter is an attempt to understand how emerging patterns of individual and private choices, around spatial and social separation, have been reinforced by public policy actions operating in a broader climate of social trepidation and fear. I begin by setting out what I mean by the idea of the counterpart city and the role of this conceptual device as a means of understanding the impact of processes now shaping many towns and cities. In the two sections that follow I focus on the role of national urban and housing policy directions in England and argue that these have publicly supported diversity while *de facto* tending to amplify the effects of private choice, developer-led aversion to the 'risk' of diversity as well as the disconcerting containment and criminalization of poverty. Finally I return to the idea of the counterpart city and the great cut through a consideration of the way in which social policy can be linked to the socio-spatial structure of urban systems – that an increasing escape by high- and middle-income households from the negative effects of poverty reasserts the relevance of segregation, whose consequences may include diminished calls for social reform by such groups.

38

The Counterpart City: The Broken Mirror of Urban Social Life

The pedestrian journey between Waterloo Station and the South Bank centre used to be punctuated by passing below the railway arches between the station and riverside arts district. A small group of homeless people had mended and made-do with this cubby hole, lighting small fires in winter, pinning up sack-cloths to create a semblance of privacy, sustained by 'spare change' from passers-by. With the remodelling of the South Bank in the late 1990s, this small interstitial space was sealed and integrated into a seamless path through which commuters and consumers of the arts would no longer have their days sullied or interfered with by those desperate enough to occupy such a vulnerable spot. An IMAX cinema later prevented rough sleepers from gathering in the underpass of a nearby roundabout, thereby similarly designing out the misery and desolation that had hung on there.

Boddy's (1992) early charting of the changing streetscapes of the United States has now become a familiar story of the rise of bland 'non-places' wherein consumption has triumphed over more diverse street life and the exclusion of poorer and problematic groups from these places. The hostility of projects of urban governance to difference and abject poverty, such as those marking out New York and Los Angeles in the early 1990s (Smith 1996; Flusty 2001), has changed the public life of cities from one in which participation was conferred, albeit on uneven terms, to a landscape splintered into the micromanaged spaces of public, private and hybrid forms of ownership and control (Graham and Marvin 2001). An important effect of this tendency towards the privatization of public space through such means as gated communities, business improvement districts and the collecting of poverty in areas of residualized public housing has been to change the dynamics of cities as both residential, economic and political entities – to become, in a sense, machines of separation more than they were once collective or municipal entities. As the secured, consuming and leisured city has grown up under terms of more entrepreneurial forms of governance, so has the deprived, impaired and stigmatized city been stage-managed into a penumbra whose undesirable qualities are often hidden (Atkinson and Helms 2007).

Our sense of cities stems from a focus on that which is, so to speak, above ground, or socially visible. We also know that outside these spaces of convention and consumption are places and cultures that lie in darkness – a city made up of the socially excluded, the poor, the despairing, the damaged and the suffering. The systemic production of inequalities is complemented by the functionings of social and private housing markets that tend to condense poverty into poor places of low amenity. We know, for example, that patterns of social and tenurial segregation have been broadly stable and resistant to programmes espousing greater social mix over the past two decades (Meen *et al.* 2005). Similarly, the most recent evidence on negotiations for planning gain and tenure diversity in new housing development also highlights how private developers sometimes seek to reduce commitments, particularly in relation to social housing (Burgess and Monk 2007).

These socio-economic imperatives are now more clearly bolstered by a considerable policy agenda on disorder that connects urban revitalization and social inclusion to criminal justice and anti-social behaviour policies and which locates these problems in deprived and social rented estates (Atkinson and Helms 2007). It is equally clear that political discourses of fear and vulnerability have brought into sharper relief a new set of connections between risk, policing, renewal and housing policies. A nexus has thereby opened between economic development, crime and housing/area-based poverty, the outcome of which appears to be a sharper contrast between areas of 'respectability' and those in decline. This counterpart city is the opposite, or resistant space, to the conventional or 'typical' experience of urban places. Such spaces and their poorer residents permeate the urban around a socio-spatial bifurcation amplified by welfare systems, private housing wealth and the effects of poor places on the life chances of their residents.

This underbelly urbanism of our counterpart cities does not reflect the city above – the mirror of public life and self represented by public street life has often been replaced by opacity in which poverty and desperation are out of sight, even when close by. Down below, walled out, walled in, have been cast those who will not or cannot join the ranks of the included, the normal and the consuming. Toth's (1995) 'mole' people live in the underground spaces of New York, shunning contact with mainstream society and shielding their vulnerabilities in an underworld which, though apparently dangerous, was perceived to be a sanctuary by its anxious residents. The issues raised here are extensions of much older concerns in urban sociology. For example, Zorbaugh's (1929) study *The Gold Coast and the Slum* highlighted how places of wealth and poverty in Chicago were effectively, though a stone's throw away from each other, parallel universes. While the city is a place of encounter with difference it is equally clear that what might be considered the project of affluent life courses is in many ways an attempt to be distinct, and distant, from this broader and disconcerting mass.

Within these broad tendencies the growth of fortified and protected residential neighbourhoods has been notable, particularly so in North America (Low 2003) and South Africa (Landman 2004), though such gated 'communities' are well-established in many British towns and cities where empirical research has shown the presence of nearly a thousand such places (Atkinson *et al.* 2005). This is significant in pointing towards urban physical forms that set in stone the often separated pathways of high- and low-income groups. Such places now more clearly solidify social divisions within our built environments.

While place clearly matters to the wealthy residents of such spaces, as the expression of class position, it also affects the life chances of residents, not least in the way that ghettoized poverty may serve to contain the less well-off. Evidence on the links between where we live and life chances has been expressed by the idea of area, neighbourhood or poverty effects. Living in a poor area may have an independent and measurable influence on the opportunities and outcomes of residents. In short, it is worse to be poor in a poor area than in one that is more socially diverse (Atkinson and Kintrea

2001). For writers like Wilson (1997) such problems can be partially attributed to the lack of local role models.

Critically, the social composition of neighbourhoods appears to add problematic outcomes to the already poorer life chances of deprived residents. While this literature is too complex to engage with in any detail here (for an excellent review, see Ellen and Turner 2003) the key is that who we live among, and in which configurations of public services and environments, may impact on possibilities for personal development that add to the effects of key independent variables such as class, gender and ethnicity. In other words, place matters and, for low-income households it may matter even more for how well parents and their children do over time. In many ways this is the old fear of the ghetto writ large – that poverty may be reproduced across generations as well as containing pockets of existing deprivation.

The link between people and place has been noted by the recent work of Mike Savage and his colleagues (2005). They find that where we live is critical in defining personal identities, and, to this extent, people in general appear to live outside common frames of class reference. In this sense we can further understand the centrality of where we live to opportunity structures. That this is well understood by social actors is demonstrated time and again by the search for safety (and the elision of this quality with 'better' neighbourhoods), for 'good' schools, and the exclusion of various forms of social pollution. In terms of housing markets, social inequalities are played out as the search to optimize these local attributes, with the ultimate effect of squeezing and out-bidding lower-income groups into places that lack these qualities. Of course it is these attributes that, in many ways, existing area-based policy initiatives (ABIs) in the UK and elsewhere seek to bolster by compensating for market failure and by creating amenity and opportunity. Yet such efforts have still tended not to be able to do this sufficiently to compensate for the broader social and economic forces described so far.

Locking Poverty into Place: Housing Policy as Social Centripetalism

A key feature of public housing in the UK and other Western countries has emerged as a diminished stock now plays an exaggerated role in dealing with acute housing need. As stock has been sold off we have witnessed social housing's status shift from one of a more general needs accommodation with a relatively diverse socio-economic character, to a more socially residualized sector. The culture associated with council housing has shifted similarly from one well placed to deal with the needs of a 'respectable' working-class and poor population to one of last resort and the inextricable association with benefit dependency and despair (Ravetz 2001). This fate has similarly been extended and sealed by the locational attributes of the remaining housing stock. For one thing, it has tended to be built, according to the need for economies of scale, either in high- or medium-rise configurations and clustered on cheaper, and thereby low-amenity, land parcels. The kind of area effects that I have already discussed have therefore been a marked feature of the consideration of ways to 'thin out' and socially diversify these places and thus help to boost the life chances of residents.

In combination with fiscal policies which retrenched the socio-economic position and viability of working-class occupations and households, the effect of selling off stock to sitting tenants at significant discounts, while delivering equity to those who could afford it, also split off these new owners and a significant swathe of the stock. The selling of this public good, particularly since capital receipts were not reinvested to offset the reduced capacity to cope with housing need, has had major impacts, while recent reforms have shifted the extent to which this continued and politically unassailable programme is given at such significant discounts (Goodlad and Atkinson 2004). Between 1980 and 2003 this sale of state assets generated 2.1 million sales of council homes and nearly £37 billion in revenue. Meanwhile, the annual share of government expenditure on housing declined from 4 per cent in 1985/6 to 1.7 per cent in 2002/3 (Wilcox 2004).

Social housing has seen a broad shift in governance arrangements and, with the advent of stock transfer, the absolute bulk of development programmes through a shifting of subsidies and management preferences to Registered Social Landlords (RSLs) – publicly accountable, yet able to draw on private finance. This has been seen as a politically acceptable means of keeping a rein on public sector borrowing while advocating a more community-oriented management structure (Gibb 2003). While the roots of the transfer go back to the early 1990s the pace has picked up dramatically in recent years. Among these shifts has been the resulting geography of social housing that I want to emphasize, and its continuing inability to ameliorate the kinds of spatial disadvantage discussed earlier.

A significant result of the shift in state expenditure away from 'bricks and mortar' subsidies in social housing has been the combined erosion of the scale of the sector while leaving new development at low levels. While this picture is currently changing towards proposals for significant investment, the general neglect of housing to date, the 'wobbly pillar' of the welfare state (Malpass 2003), has been reinforced by reduced public spending. However, it is, again, the geography of such new provision which is notable because of the way that it has tended to be locked into areas of relatively high deprivation so that increasingly poor tenants continue to live in areas of general poverty. Housing associations thus compete on the open market for land, with other landlords and investors, and are clearly constrained in their ability to command rents high enough to support the purchase of land in more attractive or socially diverse areas. The result is that even the growing allocation of subsidies is insufficient to address the need to 'pepperpot' development in ways that might further the desegregation of public housing so that it might become a more normalized and a less stigmatized feature of the urban landscape (Atkinson and Kintrea 2002).

Work by Bramley *et al.* (2007) highlights the ways in which the broad spatial patterns of housing development investment by social housing providers has continued to reinforce existing patterns of deprivation. As figure 1 shows, significantly more public housing is developed in more deprived areas. The effect of such investment has been to build new social housing in precisely

Figure 1

The location of social housing investment in relation to area poverty

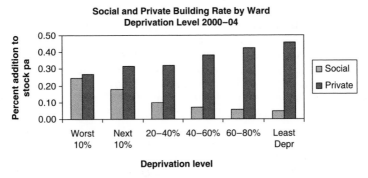

Source: Bramley *et al.* (2007).

those locations already characterized by extensive stigmatization, exclusion, poor service provision and the attendant 'area effects' which may be transmitted via neighbourhood social and environmental infrastructures. More worryingly, the full social potential of such investment is diminished by these features, reproducing the problems associated with poor and mono-tenure areas that a more equitable distribution of such resources might help to counter. Social housing also faces the significant and, under current funding regimes, impossible tasks of (1) tackling social exclusion by focusing on the needs of the poorest and most desperate in order to ration access, while (2) being mandated by government to take on the role of opening up opportunity by promoting access to various forms of opportunity. Even under the most recent, and undoubtedly significant, announcements relating to social housing growth over the coming decade these processes are unlikely to be countered if the location of such development is ignored.

Housing policy, conceived in this way, has been responsible in large part for creating *centripetal spaces* in which the 'weight of the world' (Bourdieu 1999), of poverty and exclusion locked into place, have restrained and disadvantaged the poor. Table 1 distils the key policy arrangements and their effects in this regard. We have seen that these socio-spatial effects and their consequences are strong, even when considered in isolation from the relationship between social housing, workplace incentives and fiscal policies which have similarly served to lock poverty into poor places. Such places have generated the growing sense of a world apart from an 'included' or mainstream society. In short, the effect of seeking to reduce social exclusion by focusing only on need and not on a broadened role for social housing has further isolated those with least resources in already stigmatized areas and extended the scale and concealment of the counterpart city. Such policies have been presided over by political administrations of all colours, and the effect of this has been to keep mobilized and politically articulate constituencies safe from the now significant associations with disorder and anti-social

Table 1

Housing policies and their centripetal effects: poverty contained within deprived spaces

Areas of housing policy and practice	Primary effects	Secondary effects
• Multi-agency working and emphasis on anti-social behaviour	• Containment and social interdiction	• Criminalization of youth in primarily deprived social rented neighbourhoods
• Geography of public housing provision and investment	• Segregation of public housing stock	• Area effects – reproduction of poverty, fatalism, inward-looking and territorial value systems
• Housing and related benefit payments	• Passivity and exclusion of welfare recipients	• Relative incentives toward stasis in deprived neighbourhoods, via inflexible payment practices
• Housing development	• Relative ghettoization of public housing development	• Ineffectiveness of planning gain to produce greater social diversity in new developments
	• Structural avoidance of public housing commitments	• Segregation of new communities by income

behaviour that permeate media and popular political representations of the social rented estate or scheme (Dean and Hastings 2000).

The Courting of a New Urban Middle Class: Urban Policy as Social Centrifuge

If public housing has tended to receive, contain and maintain the excluded, urban policy has acted in complementary ways, by supporting a socio-spatial bifurcation between affluent/included groups and poorer households, and the pushing of the latter to the edges of urban areas. Thus poverty, I argue, is shifted outward into spaces that are away from of the conceptual range and daily pathways of more affluent households. In general, then, urban policy frameworks have acted to 'spin' poverty outwards to the urban margins by tending to lock out or otherwise disenfranchise the deprived from city cores. To flesh out what might at first appear to be a rather unusual argument I want to focus on the way in which the bundle of policies addressing the spatial unevenness of urban economic development and disadvantage has, to date, tended to nurture the role of the market by supporting housing consumption activities and spaces of consumption in these locales. The effect of this has been to broadly gentrify urban cores, cement property equity growth and exclude lower-income households to peripheral areas, regardless of their tenure.

The urban 'renaissance', envisaged as the grand rebirth of British urbanism, has arguably done well on its own terms. The blueprint provided by Lord

Rogers's Urban Task Force report (1999), espoused a design-led strategy modelled on European urbanism which emphasized density, good-quality design and mixed commercial and residential uses. Combined with a strong national economy and a broader re-setting of geographies of commercial investment, this vision achieved much as strong land-use planning arrangements under the Urban Development Corporations continued to engineer new neighbourhoods and central districts. These stressed high-end uses, and the desire to recapture the lost middle class of, particularly regional, British cities that has undoubtedly created significant challenges and a loss of social diversity (Champion and Fisher 2004). Writers like Lees (2003) emphasized that much of the Rogers vision could be read as a 'gentrifiers' manifesto' and that the result has been the creation of central city spaces saturated with riverfront high-rise and high-cost apartments alongside a commercial revitalization that, while desirable to many, did little to address housing shortages or the diversity of commercial infrastructure and work economies that might more effectively integrate lower-income and workless households.

A key strand of the urban renewal of the past decade has been a proliferation of area-based interventions set up to ameliorate poverty in concentrated forms. The flagship programme here, the New Deal for Communities, followed the work of the prime minister's Social Exclusion Unit, crossing a wide variety of policy domains including health, crime, unemployment and education, among others. Such plans continue a history of expenditure targeted in order to address the kind of area effects discussed earlier. If stigma and lack of economic opportunity and other public service provision were failing excluded and ghettoized communities, the rationale seemed both laudable and potentially effective. Yet, these policy frameworks appear to have (a) maintained poorer neighbourhoods at the bottom of the urban hierarchy through their continued social housing stocks, and (b) displaced the functions of low-rent, low-cost or social housing districts to new locations as these areas are gentrified or shifted by patterns of new investment and more affluent households. Further examples are provided in table 2, where the range of significant urban policy instruments is briefly highlighted. In general the key effect of these arrangements has been the spatial stigmatization of poverty as an anti-risk/disorder agenda has more firmly attached itself to these spaces. Gentrification and displacement have followed in those quarters where demand was to be stimulated, the Housing Market Renewal areas being the clearest case in point. In all cases these programmes have done more to condemn and challenge the symptoms of urban malaise, poverty and structural decline than to soften and tackle their causes.

All of this is to provide only a crude snapshot of a complex system of provision and intervention. Yet while much of the broader modernization of government envisaged by the Blair administration was designed to address the silo mentality and mutually exclusive operation of central government departments, the efficacy of these programmes has been more uncertain. A clear example of this is the way in which the planning system has tended to respond to developer-led initiatives which have continued to push for products aimed at the upper end of the market and, the mirror of social housing investment, sought land parcels devoted to mono-occupation by

Table 2

Urban policies and their centrifugal effects: poverty excluded to margins of urban systems

Areas of urban policy and practice	Primary effects	Secondary effects
• Urban renaissance and related objectives	• Emphasis on urban design and repopulation of cores	• Residential gentrification – affluent ghettos • General exclusion or absence of affordable and social housing provision
• Area-based renewal programmes	• Conjunction of renewal activities with policing and community safety interventions	• Potential criminalization/exclusion of low-income areas • Positive effects relating to life-chance outcomes
• Housing market renewal programme and Urban Development Companies	• Exceptional planning without consultation • Commodification of public housing areas • Demolition of 'unpopular' housing	• Displacement of low-income households • Marginal gentrification of neighbourhoods affected

higher-income owners. While the ethos of the British planning system has long been to try and create socially diverse areas, it has often been weak in the face of local planning authority discretion and developer pressure to create boundaries and products that often seek to move away from social diversity outlined in the new *Planning Policy Statement 3* (Housing Development) (Department of Communities and Local Government 2006). In short, the tendency has been to fight at both ends of the spectrum, for diversity in affluent and deprived neighbourhoods, but while being subject to the market realities of these contexts. It is also important to remember that there are valid criticisms of the kind of desegregation that might stem from dispersal and mix whereby such actions may actually further conceal social problems:

> Dispersing public tenants is advantageous because it takes attention away from crime, high unemployment, poverty and other social problems experienced by a particular sector of the population. However, in reality, the situation is paradoxical because disadvantaged public tenants will still exist but be rendered less visible through dispersal. (Arthurson 2002: 255)

The effect of these shifts has been to produce an agenda led by private sector interests, bemoaned by Lord Rogers, among others, for producing the kind of nondescript and over-priced product that has flooded central city markets. It is also surely a perverse outcome to the current public flavour of policy pushing for social diversity and strong communities, that we have seen the rise of significant numbers of gated communities (Atkinson *et al.* 2005) that have created spaces of seclusion from the negative externalities and overhead of poverty in urban areas. Critically, these bubbles of security have further engendered the sense that urban risks and beachhead gentrification have been managed by the locking out of risky populations through the creation of security as a club realm to which consumers are granted privileged access and a haven from the kind of dangerous public realm seen to lurk outside such neighbourhoods (Crawford 2006). As Graham and Marvin (2001) argue persuasively,

> local and international real estate interests seem to be intent on packaging together larger and larger luxury spaces of seduction or secession for the more affluent groups whilst, at the same time, they work harder to secure such spaces from incursion, or, perhaps more important, the threat of incursion, from the new urban poor. (Graham and Marvin 2001: 227)

This raises another crucial element of the broader thesis of this piece; this relates to the longer-term impact of affluence when it is separated from its social counterpart and counterpart spaces. An important element of this move to seclude and socially insulate comes from another turn in urban and housing policies which become inflected or, more specifically, criminalized through an emphasis on producing order, reducing anti-social behaviour and otherwise disciplining and responsibilizing citizens in areas of disorder that are synonymously linked to public housing (Atkinson and Helms 2007).

Writers like Flint (2006) have keenly pursued this agenda, showing how social housing management practices have been made complicit in a broader politics of conduct, which has been enforced effectively along tenurial lines – discipline effected through tenancy sanctions or other powers, such as that of the Anti-Social Behaviour Order (ASBO). As with Young (1999), we can see how the social has been 'made simple' through a sound-bite political culture that has come to haunt socially excluded constituencies. Such places, characterized *in extremis* by the social rented estate (or 'worst neighbourhoods' as it was put by the then Department of the Environment, Transport and the Regions), have been portrayed as primary sites of disorder – requiring both the disciplining of already economically disadvantaged groups, and the action of already damaged communities in exerting control over their most unruly elements. The nexus described earlier, between economic development, crime and housing/poverty, has thus been bolstered by action within the urban policy circuit and undergirded by an actuarial politics of policing and disorder management that has sought to make predictable urban public and residential spaces.

In its most recent formulation key urban policy strategies have focused on the creation of *sustainable communities*. This plan has stressed the need to accommodate new households in the south-east while restructuring neighbourhoods lacking 'demand' in the north. The latter nine Housing Market Renewal areas allocated to this agenda have pursued the general removal of those populations remaining in these areas, often blighted by crime, which has deterred investment and new residents. Such policy programmes are breathtaking in their arrogance in the face of earlier exegeses relating to the social costs of demolition and community displacement and in seeking more economically active citizens. The aspirations of developers for new land to redevelop and of local authorities and their councillors to remake and be rid of the social overhead represented by existing residents has been a rather shameful consequence of the diagnosis of market failure (Cameron 2003) in areas actually containing significant swathes of public housing itself set up to combat market failure (see table 2).

Urban policies, even while complex in their manifold implementation, have engineered a significant rebirth of the cores of the British urban system in ways that have privileged the insulation of affluence as a means of civilizing and displacing the disorderly. As fears of anti-social behaviour and crime have become embedded in daily understandings of the constitution of urbanism, it has become more publicly legitimate to engage in plans that effectively dislocate urban poverty. New developments have led to *de facto* ghettoization as new housing has tended not to include provision for either mixed incomes or tenure. This gentrification of central city living and the opening of further and unfettered opportunities for capital investment have, unsurprisingly, sought to disengage from an agenda that might include those groups who have been portrayed by politicians and the media as generally mad, bad or dangerous to encounter. Commentators like Boyer (1996) have argued that the effect of this increase in social insulation from deprivation will lead to the further criminalization of poorer groups where a 'retreat into privatized "zones" enhances the view of the city as a site of deprivation and dysfunction' (1996: 152). The overall impression is, then, of a series of agendas running parallel and which have been ineffective in producing the kind of diversity that might begin to reintegrate, desegregate and destigmatize areas of social renting or concentrations of poverty as well as offering more substantive routes out of the kind of fear and insecurity seen to permeate urban lifestyles more generally.

Conclusion: The Great Cut, the Evasion of Risk, Social Contact and Political Responsibility

My preceding observations lead me to a broader conclusion about the links between the social structure of cities and the nature of contemporary social politics. I want to suggest that the changing flows of social encounter and mutual insulation between the broad strata of included and excluded in cities today suggests two mutually reinforcing processes. First, that housing and urban policies have worked with urban property markets in ways that have tended to reinforce a pattern of segregation and disaffiliation by the affluent and that this has spatially dislocated the excluded to peripheral and interstitial spaces. Second, that the consequences of such a spatial 'cut' and social disconnect between diverse social groups has become a central project of affluence which seeks to disentangle itself both from the fiscal overhead of deprivation and its negative externalities. Critically, it is fear of social difference and the desire for social insulation from otherness and harm that mediates these forces and consequences. As policies have facilitated the desires of an enlarged and increasingly affluent constituency, it is these fears that have fuelled and legitimized actions that seek to manage and contain poverty into capsular spaces.

The idea of a great cut expresses a new-found capacity for social and political elites to advance projects of welfare retrenchment and the avoidance of social responsibility because of the growing invisibility of a counterpart city of the excluded that can be skirted, through both public and private strategies of evasion. As social empathy is diminished by the withdrawal of the affluent from urban public spaces, into SUVs, gated communities and gentrified enclaves, it seems possible that the public squalor that was previously supposed to be the cost of a selfish private affluence can be minimized, even while fear itself remains all-pervasive.

If such problems are concealed by spatial distance, by residing in bubble neighbourhoods, then the prospects for greater public involvement may be bleak. The general picture assembled here suggests the creation of a social and spatial split, but one that is also highly complex in its particularized trajectories. It is not simply true that people on high incomes don't come into contact with lower incomes, or vice versa. Yet what does appear to be happening is that it is now more easy to insulate ourselves, particularly insofar as this is related to our income or wealth, from the stark visibility of social problems. That this is also supplemented and bolstered by often disturbing public interventions into such visibility is all the more worrying. The removal of the street homeless (Smith 1996), the outlawing of begging and curfews for the young (Mitchell 1997) highlight such programmes. Yet the banality of socio-spatial sanctions like ASBOs in the UK (Flint 2006), business improvement districts and community safety strategies facilitates subtle approaches to the management of conduct in which there has been a devolution of discretion to what may sometimes be hostile local political actors or administrations seeking the displacement, rather than resolution, of visible local disorder or incivility.

The second key point to emerge from these discussions relates to the longer-term social impacts that local social homogeneity may produce. For some time the area effects debate has focused on the costs to the poor of living in ghettoized and thus concentrated poverty. However, absent from such debates has been the way in which affluent cultures and congregations may be implicated in the long-run reproduction of circuits of privilege, largely outside the viewpoints of those excluded from the social systems, institutions and sites within which this 'included' class operates. The opacity and separated quality of circuits of affluence and relative deprivation are important in considering the ramifications of the mutual invisibility of the poor and the rich. These processes are supported by states, local and central, mediating the aspirations of middle England through the mobilization of social housing agencies in a 'criminalized' urban and social policy agenda.

Sennett (1996) and others have argued that the essential value of the street is its ability to help construct and understand identities of difference, but what happens when public space is turned into an interdictory and excluding space (Flusty 2001) which seeks, through design and policing, to exclude those who are seen as illegitimate non-consumers? The emerging recruitment of social anger by politicians has been a marked feature of policies targeting the synonymy of disorder and operating through exclusion in political discourse and popular imagination.

Finally, it is worth considering this social and spatial split as sowing the seeds for a further ratchet effect in the articulation of agendas around social problems which vilify and contain disorderly non-constituencies of the excluded. As emerging research on Russia's billionaire children suggests, the effect of total seclusion is naivety and isolation, which may also produce a singular lack of empathy with those living outside the gates of their own privileged compounds. As social problems withdraw from the view of the growing ranks of middle- and high-income households, so too does an appreciation of their causes diminish. The public squalor that J. K. Galbraith so eloquently described as the negative corollary of private affluence can now be circumvented or remade, like the railway arch at the South Bank, as a counterpart city that rests out of the sight and minds of the affluent – failing to provoke us to action or shame at its existence.

An interaction between the gears operating between housing and urban policy, mediatized crime and spectacle and political systems, has amplified the need to cast off of a geography of exclusion – a counterpart city that is largely outside the lived urban experience of the majority. Not only has public policy exaggerated the effects of private residential choices, in some cases it has sought to displace, contain and otherwise cloak the presence of the poor and the desperate. These socio-political and spatial forces have furthered the sense of well-being and success for those groups moving through circuits around home, education and leisure that are at least partially disconnected from the kind of social distress that is congealed into marginal space.

All of this suggests the need to maintain cities in which difference is confronting. The importance of such encounters is twofold: first, because political empathy and understanding may be spurred by such exchanges – the argument of citizenship; second, growing income inequalities and their attendant social conditions should not be enclosed such that affluence is left unchallenged – the related argument of communal obligation. The key argument of this chapter is that both of these widely held value positions may have been eroded by the capacity of individuals and urban systems to generate profound social indifference and disregard.

In a climate, or culture, of fear, the decision to withdraw into safety is not irrational, but its effect is to reinforce a spatial and social bifurcation in which a kind of post-social contract has emerged within which space and its social ordering is deeply implicated – the great cut. An emerging urban politics, based on personal ambition and self-interest, subtly leaves the counterpart city as a space interwoven into the life of the city and yet bypassed, stepped around and otherwise ignored as the place of personal deficiencies and un-contemplatable personal trajectories that are too painful to consider, given their ability to challenge the satisfaction of the included.

References

Arthurson, K. (2002), Creating inclusive communities through balancing social mix: a critical relationship or tenuous link? *Urban Policy and Research*, 20, 3: 245–61.

Atkinson, R. and Helms, G. (eds) (2007), *Securing an Urban Renaissance? Crime, Community and British Urban Policy*, Bristol: Policy Press.

Atkinson, R. and Kintrea, K. (2001), Disentangling area effects: evidence from deprived and non-deprived neighbourhoods, *Urban Studies*, 38, 12: 2277–98.

Atkinson, R. and Kintrea, K. (2002), A consideration of the implications of area effects for British housing and regeneration policy, *European Journal of Housing Policy*, 2, 2: 1–20.

Atkinson, R., Blandy, S., Flint, J. and Lister, D. (2005), Gated cities of today? Barricaded residential development in England, *Town Planning Review*, 76, 4: 417–37.

Bauman, Z. (2006), *Liquid Fear*, Cambridge: Polity Press.

Beck, U. (1992), *Risk Society: Towards a New Modernity*, London: Sage.

Berry, M., with Hall, J. (2002), *New Approaches to Expanding the Supply of Affordable Housing in Australia: An Increasing Role for the Private Sector*, Melbourne: Australian Housing and Urban Research Institute.

Boddy, T. (1992), Underground and overhead: building the analogous city. In M. Sorkin (ed.), *Variations on a Theme Park: The New American City and the End of Public Space*, New York: Hill and Wang, pp. 123–53.

Bourdieu, P. (ed.) (1999), *The Weight of the World: Social Suffering in Contemporary Society*, Cambridge: Polity Press.

Boyer, C. (1996), *Cybercities: Visual Perception in the Age of Electronic Communication*, New York: Princeton Architectural Press.

Bramley, G., Leishman, C., Kofi-Karley, N., Morgan, J. and Watkins, D. (2007), *Transforming Places: Housing Investment and Neighbourhood Market Change*, York: Joseph Rowntree Foundation.

Burgess, G. and Monk, S. (2007), *How Local Planning Authorities Are Delivering Policies for Affordable Housing*, York: Joseph Rowntree Foundation.

Burrows, R. and Ellison, N. (2004), Sorting places out? *Information Communication and Society*, 7, 3: 321–36.

Cameron, S. (2003), Gentrification, housing redifferentiation and urban regeneration: 'going for growth' in Newcastle upon Tyne, *Urban Studies*, 40, 12: 2367–83.

Champion, T. and Fisher, T. (2004), Migration, residential preferences and the changing environment of cities. In M. Boddy and M. Parkinson (eds), *City Matters: Competitiveness, Cohesion and Urban Governance*, Bristol: Policy Press.

Cheshire, P. (2007), *Are Mixed Communities the Answer to Segregation and Poverty?* York: Joseph Rowntree Foundation.

Crawford, A. (2006), Policing and security as 'club goods': the new enclosures? In J. Wood and B. Dupont (eds), *Democracy, Society and the Governance of Security*, Cambridge: Cambridge University Press, pp. 111–38.

Dean, J. and Hastings, A. (2000), *Challenging Images: Housing Estates, Stigma and Regeneration*, Bristol: Policy Press.

Denney, D. (2005), *Risk and Society*, London: Sage.

Department of Communities and Local Government (2006), *Planning Policy Statement 3 (PPS3): Housing*, London: HMSO.

Dorling, D. and Rees, P. (2003), A nation still dividing: the British census and social polarisation 1971–2001, *Environment and Planning A*, 35: 1287–1313.

Ellen, I. and Turner, M. (2003), Do neighborhoods matter, and why? In J. Goering and J. Feins (eds), *Choosing a Better Life? Evaluating the Moving to Opportunity Social Experiment*, Washington, DC: Urban Institute, pp. 313–38.

Flint, J. (2006), *Housing, Urban Governance and Anti-social Behaviour: Perspectives, Policy and Practice*, Bristol: Policy Press.

Flusty, S. (2001), The banality of interdiction: surveillance, control and the displacement of diversity, *International Journal of Urban and Regional Research*, 25, 3: 658–64.

Furedi, F. (2002), *Culture of Fear: Risk-taking and the Morality of Low Expectation*, London: Continuum.

Galbraith, J. K. (1958), *The Affluent Society*, New York: Mariner Books.

Garland, D. (2001), *The Culture of Control: Crime and Social Order in Contemporary Society*, Oxford: Oxford University Press.

Gibb, K. (2003), Transferring Glasgow's council housing: financial, urban and housing policy implications, *European Journal of Housing Policy*, 3, 1: 89–114.

Goodlad, R. and Atkinson, R. (2004), Sacred cows, rational debates and the politics of the right to buy after devolution, *Housing Studies*, 19, 3: 447–63.

Graham, S. and Marvin, S. (2001), *Splintering Urbanism: Networked Infrastructures, Techno-logical Mobilities and the Urban Condition*, London: Routledge.

Landman, K. (2004), Gated communities in South Africa: the challenge for spatial planning and land-use management, *Town Planning Review*, 75, 2: 151–72.

Lees, L. (2003), Visions of 'urban renaissance': the urban task force and the urban White Paper. In R. Imrie and M. Raco, *Urban Renaissance? New Labour, Community and Urban Policy*, Bristol: Policy Press.

Low, S. (2003), *Behind the Gates: Life, Security, and the Pursuit of Happiness in Fortress America*, London: Routledge.

Malpass, P. (2003), The wobbly pillar? Housing and the British postwar welfare state, *Journal of Social Policy*, 32, 4: 589–606.

Massey, D. and Denton, N. (1996), *American Apartheid: Segregation and the Making of the Underclass*, Cambridge, MA: Harvard University Press.

Meen, G., Gibb, K., Goody, J., McGrath, T. and Mackinnon, J. (2005), *Economic Segregation in England: Causes, Consequences and Policy*, Bristol: Policy Press.

Mitchell, D. (1997), The annihilation of space by law: the roots and implications of anti-homeless laws in the United States, *Antipode*, 29, 3: 303–35.

Ravetz, A. (2001), *Council Housing and Culture: The History of a Social Experiment*, London: Routledge.

Riis, J. A. (1890/1997), *How the Other Half Lives*, Harmondsworth: Penguin.

Savage, M., Bagnall, G. and Longhurst, B. (2005), *Globalization and Belonging*, London: Sage.

Scott, J. C. (1998), *Seeing like a State: How Certain Schemes to Improve the Human Condition Have Failed*, New Haven, CT: Yale University Press.

Sennett, R. (1990), *The Conscience of the Eye: The Design and Social Life of Cities*, New York: Norton.

Sennett, R. (1996), *Flesh and Stone: The Body and the City in Western Civilization*, New York: Norton.

Smith, N. (1996), *The New Urban Frontier: Gentrification and the Revanchist City*, London: Routledge.

Toth, J. (1995), *The Mole People: Life in the Tunnels beneath New York City*, Chicago: Chicago Review Press.

Urban Task Force (1999), *Towards an Urban Renaissance*, Norwich: Stationery Office.

Wilcox, S. (2004), *UK Housing Review*, Coventry: CIH/CML.

Wilson, W. J. (1997), *When Work Disappears: The World of the New Urban Poor*, New York: Vintage.

Young, J. (1999), *The Exclusive Society: Social Exclusion, Crime and Difference in Late Modernity*, London: Sage.

Zorbaugh, H. (1929), *The Gold Coast and the Slum: A Sociological Study of Chicago's Near North Side*, Chicago: University of Chicago Press.

5

Risk and Public Protection: Responding to Involuntary and 'Taboo' Risk

Hazel Kemshall and Jason Wood

Introduction

The spectre of the invisible predatory paedophile in our midst is a powerful and frightening one that has captured the imagination of public, media and policy-makers alike (Kemshall 2003; Kitzinger 2004). This 'monstrous' offender has framed much of contemporary penal policy to high-risk offenders (see Kemshall 2008; Thomas 2005, for a full review), although it is increasingly recognized that this is somewhat out of proportion to the numbers of such offenders actually under community supervision. Kitzinger (2004) has commented extensively on this distortion and notes how the media framing of child sexual abuse as located almost exclusively in the alien 'Other', 'stranger-danger' has influenced the framing of policy and legislation. This framing has resulted in an over-emphasis upon the 'men in dirty macs' rather than the danger present in many families (Kitzinger 2004: 129), an emphasis that is repeated in court. The paedophile is always defined as an 'outsider' (Cross 2005: 290) – a rather more comfortable thought for those on the inside. Most policy and procedures are geared towards detecting and controlling this outsider, resulting in overwhelming shock and blame when children are harmed by those charged with their care (e.g. Victoria Climbie – Laming 2003).

The impact of the 'risk agenda' on penal policy can be measured by the volume of legislation (some seven major Acts in 12 years), and the extensive systems and processes designed for its management (Kemshall 2003; Nash 2006). The impact on key criminal justice agencies has also been significant, with a 'sea change' in the role and responsibility of the Probation Service and a tighter focus on risky offenders for the police (see Kemshall 2003 for a full review). The resulting 'public protection industry' is now extensive, and has led to an 'escalating vocabulary of punitive motives' (Welch *et al.* 1997: 486) in which ever harsher penal policies against the dangerous are advocated, a situation Sanders and Lyon (1995) have described as 'repetitive retribution'. This retribution has largely crystallized in the sex offender and most notably the paedophile (Kitzinger 2004; Thomas 2005), but has been accompanied by seepage to other offenders and offence types, notably violent offenders, those deemed to have a 'dangerous severe personality disorder' and, following the Criminal Justice Act 2003, robbery.

Public protection is also a sensitive and contentious issue, attracting much media and political attention since its inception in the early 1990s (Kemshall 2003). Public protection and risk management failures elicit public scrutiny and blame, resulting in the dismissal of staff and occasionally Home Secretaries. It is also characterized by public anxiety, fear, distrust of experts and intense media scrutiny (Kitzinger 2004). Risk management failures provide a constant reminder that protection cannot be guaranteed and the failure to honour the promise brings both policy-makers and professionals tasked with its delivery into disrepute. The erosion of public confidence and trust is corrosive, fuelling further anxiety and greater demands for protection, and paradoxically more failure (Kitzinger 2004: 148–57).

In this context, it is also important to note that 'involuntary' and 'taboo' risks are both less acceptable to the public and are open to distortion and inflation (see the seminal work by Slovic 1987, 1992, 2000; and the Royal Society Study Group 1992).

Involuntary risks imposed by others are seen as less tolerable, and can provoke extreme outrage, for example the reaction of residents on the Paulsgrove estate who believed paedophiles had been housed locally and who subsequently attacked the homes of suspected paedophiles (some of whom were not) (Denney 2005; Nash 2006).

Lack of trust in local professional experts and a perception of being 'dumped on' were important factors in precipitating public reaction (Nash 2006; see also Kemshall and Maguire 2003). The situation was exacerbated by the *News of the World* 'name and shame' campaign in which hundreds of sex offenders were 'outed', and the paper's call for a Sarah's Law following the murder of Sarah Payne by Roy Whiting, a sex offender on the register (see Silverman and Wilson 2002 for a full review).

Mary Douglas's now famous work *Risk and Blame* (1992) explores in detail the role of taboo risks in constructing 'outsiders' and more importantly in consolidating the collective. Risk allocates blame and:

> Blaming is a way of manning the gates and at the same time of arming the guard. News that is going to be accepted as true information has to be wearing a badge of loyalty to the particular political regime which the person supports. (Douglas 1992: 19)

For Douglas contemporary risk taboos are linked to a 'rhetoric of retribution and accusation against a specific individual' (see Lupton 1999: 47), in this case the sex offender, and by extension all offenders (Garland 2001). The 'Criminology of the Other' has been extensively theorized (notably Garland 2001; O'Malley 2004a, 2004b), with Garland arguing that it is a

> criminology that trades in images, archetypes, and anxieties, rather than in careful analyses and research findings. In its deliberate echoing of public concerns and media biases, and its focus on the most worrisome

threats, it is, in effect, a politicised discourse of the collective unconscious, though it claims to be altogether realist and 'commonsensical' in contrast to 'academic theories'. In its standard tropes and rhetorical invocations, this political discourse relies upon an archaic criminology of the criminal type, the alien other. Sometimes explicitly, more often in coded references, the problem is traced to the wanton, amoral behaviour of dangerous offenders, who typically belong to racial and cultural groups bearing little resemblance to 'us'. (2001: 135; see also Boutellier 2000; Matravers 2005; Young 2007)

Contemporary images of the criminal other include 'hoodies', paedophiles, and various 'monsters in our midst' (Simon 1998). The spectre of the 'Other' justifies increasingly anticipatory measures. That is, early identification of risk and preventative measures to stop those risks occurring. At the extreme this can mean preventative sentencing for high-risk offenders such as Indeterminate Public Protection Sentences (IPPS), or the use of measures against offenders such as Sexual Offender Prevention Orders (SOPOs) requiring only civil standards of proof.

A key policy response has been the development of techniques and processes to make the invisible (usually sexual) offender more visible through the creation of registers, community notification, information-sharing databases such as VISOR (Violent and Sex Offenders Register), and the Multi-Agency Public Protection Arrangements (MAPPA) developed for their assessment and management. The next section explores the critical factors in the rise of public protection before returning to an exploration of the potentially distorting impact of 'taboo' paedophile risks on the systems created for the community management of high-risk offenders.

Critical Factors in the Public Protection Trend

The Criminal Justice Act (1991) was the first to reframe the role of probation to 'protect the public from serious harm' (Home Office 1990: 2), resulting in public protection becoming the key driver for probation work, replacing its traditional social work values (Kemshall 2003). While probation had always shifted according to broader penal policy, the demise of the rehabilitative ideal in the 1970s, together with increasing questions about the effectiveness of the service as a criminal justice intervention, led to new probation principles.

The CJA (1991) was to be superseded and expanded by a series of legislative and policy developments throughout the 1990s that would continuously reshape the role of probation towards a correctional service. This period saw the service characterized by 'risk aversion, enforced repositioning and blame avoidance' (Kemshall 2003: 85). Two of these legislative developments, the Criminal Justice and Court Services Act (2000) and the Criminal Justice Act (2003) influenced the development of MAPPA discussed later in this chapter.

While the contextual reasons for these changes are numerous, there are arguably two significant strands for discussion here. The first was the changing debate around involuntary and taboo risks in the public, political and media discourse. The second was the development of the 'new penology'. Both developments amount to a 'punitive turn' in aspects of criminal justice policy.

The public, political and media discourse

Throughout the 1990s, key 'cultural shifts' occurred in the public discourse concerning 'dangerousness' and in particular, the notion of involuntary risk (Nash 2005). These shifts were located around a changing political climate that was mirrored by increasing media attention on dangerousness, and in particular the predatory paedophile (Kitzinger 1999). Sensitivity to the seemingly rare and dangerous risks was heightened, with studies revealing the extent of child sexual abuse (e.g. Cawson *et al.* 2000), and the inadequacy of criminal justice responses across the spectrum (Prior *et al.* 1997). These studies challenged conventional wisdom insofar as they revealed not only the true extent of prevalence, but the varying types of offence and their degrees of severity (Grubin 1998). Despite apparent complexity, the media focus on dangerous strangers superseded discussion around, for example, the high proportion of sexual offences that occur within the family. Public safety and security from the 'unknown' dangers mirrored a wider, growing insecurity associated with the now well documented 'rise of risk' (Kemshall 2003; Nash 2005). The result: a dominant policy focus on the exclusion and distancing of offenders characterized as monsters and 'Others' (Kemshall and Wood 2007b).

Key incidences of grave crime were seen to be more systemic and preventable than previously argued. Politicians of the time utilized key, high-profile cases to inform their proposed law and order reforms (Williams 2005). The political context in the UK was particularly important in shaping this discourse. In the early 1990s, the Labour Party ideologically positioned itself as a 'tough' law and order party: a key component of a remodelling exercise in order to become electable (Raynor and Vanstone 2007).

The murder of two-year-old James Bulger in 1993 by two young people provided a context in which the 'politics of punishment' (Wallis 1997) would be played out. As Cohen notes: 'at the time of the Bulger murder about 70 children aged under five were being killed each year' (2003: 5). Children responsible for murder represented a small and static number, with their crimes being 'random and idiosyncratic' events from which it was hard to draw inferences about the condition of 'wider society' (Cohen 2003: 5). The response by media and politicians might have been measured in the sense that they recognized the strangeness of the crime. Rather, the then opposition home affairs spokesperson, Tony Blair, suggested that the convicted killers Thompson and Venables 'personified the state of a feral nation' (Cohen 2003: 6). This key case set in motion a series of political debates about the extent to which law and order needed reform. With every charge from the Opposition, the Conservative government proposed more punitive responses to crime, targeted usually at 'undesirable' others (Cohen 2003: 15).

Such 'extraordinary cases' are central to debates about the risk management of sex offenders. The murder of Sarah Payne in 2000 resulted in the development of MAPPA and increased media calls for greater public disclosure and awareness of the location of sex offenders (Kemshall and Wood 2007b), a proposal resisted by public protection professionals (Wood and Kemshall 2007). The example offered an interesting parallel: public protection through MAPPA embodied a more restrictive and punitive model of community management, cementing the notion that offenders are in fact 'evil and intractable', while excluding the public from participating in their own vengeance through vigilantism (see Kemshall and Wood 2007b).

The murders of Holly Wells and Jessica Chapman precipitated the Bichard Inquiry in 2004 that led to reforms to the sharing of information about potentially dangerous offenders. In the USA, it is common even for legislation to adopt the name of the victim, symbolizing the importance of certain victims in shaping law (Williams 2005) – with 'Megan's Law' the case in point.

In more general terms, victims increasingly became central to policy decisions about crime and punishment (Williams and Goodman 2007). This was manifested in greater rights, protections and case involvement for 'actual' victims (see for example, the Victims Charter in 1990 and guidance issued by the Home Office 2003a) but also increasingly more abstract victim 'groups', evidenced by notions of community protection. Here, the focus was on the wider public and their collective status as potential victims. Despite the relatively low incidence of actual risk of harm:

> Political parties were parading their tough credentials, anxious to appease the press. Little was done to represent the real nature of the risk to an increasingly aware and concerned public. (Nash 2005: 18)

The national debate impacted upon local arrangements with increasing statutory guidance and standardization of practice (cf. Maguire *et al.* 2001; Kemshall *et al.* 2005). Rather than vesting trust and independence within professional groups, the criminal justice system itself became more centralized with politicians both 'responding to and aggravating public concern about crime' through systematic punitive policy-making (Raynor and Vanstone 2007: 68).

A complex relationship of anxiety inflation ensued with the media, politicians and the public cyclically setting the punitive agenda. Rather than seeing this as mere media influence, a process of cultural reproduction was under way (Anderson 2006) that translated risk from something abstract and rare to something that criminal justice agencies should 'do something about' (Nash 2005).

This relationship between the media, public and politicians together with a reframing of the 'victim' in the public protection debate contributed to a more punitive approach to managing involuntary risk. The question remains as to whether its focus on 'stranger danger' is the most effective.

The new penology and the community protection model

The second and interrelated contextual shift was marked by the rise of a 'new penology' of risk and actuarial justice (Feeley and Simon 1992, 1994). This has been well documented elsewhere (see Kemshall 2003 for a review) but is revisited in summary here. A marked decline in confidence in liberal crime management strategies, together with economic pressures on crime management and concern about how to manage the most dangerous and habitual offenders, led to a focus on risk management over and above rehabilitation (see, for example, Garland 2001). In relation to the management of sex offenders, this manifested itself in increasing convictions, new post-custody licence conditions that imposed restrictions, curfews and the community management of sex and other dangerous offenders (Kemshall and Wood 2007a). In addition, the emphasis on risk assessment came to the fore with increasing measures to calculate likelihood, imminence and seriousness of reoffending. Technical and actuarial methods were promoted as consistent tools to facilitate this process, and the prominence of inter-agency working in risk management represented the bifurcation of the Probation Service (Kemshall 2003).

Emblematic of this punitive turn was the development of community punishment and risk management strategies that sought to contain risk. Termed the 'community protection model' by Connelly and Williamson (2000), public protection agencies manage offenders through restrictions, conditions, sanctions and enforcement. The assumptions inherent in this model are extensively discussed by Kemshall and Wood (2007b).

Responding to Involuntary and 'Taboo' Risk: The Rise of MAPPA Risk Management

MAPPAs epitomize community protection in practice, and the Criminal Justice and Court Services Act (2000) sections 67 and 68 placed a responsibility upon police and probation to

> establish arrangements for the purpose of assessing and managing risks posed in that area by –
>
> a) relevant sexual and violent offenders, and
> b) other persons who, by reason of offences committed by them (wherever committed), are considered by the responsible authority to be persons who may cause serious harm to the public. (Section 67 (2) CJCS 2000)

The Criminal Justice Act 2003 strengthened these arrangements (see particularly sections 325–327) and facilitates closer working between prisons, probation and police. It also places a 'duty to cooperate' upon agencies such as housing, social services, health authorities and youth offending teams (see Kemshall and Wood 2007a for a full review).

By October 2007 there were 30,416 registered sex offenders in England and Wales (Ministry of Justice 2007). This represented a 1.44 per cent increase on the preceding year. It should be noted that the cumulative effect of adding people to the register each year inevitably means that fewer are leaving the register than are joining it – resulting in predictably higher numbers. The total number of offenders managed by MAPPA in October 2007 was 48,668. These included violent as well as sexual offenders. Of these, 1,249 'critical few' offenders were managed at level 3 MAPPAs (Ministry of Justice 2007).

In essence, MAPPAs are meant to concentrate on the 'critical few' in order to subject them to greater scrutiny and more intensive management (Home Office 2001, 2002). The critical few is an operational term, and relates to very high-risk offenders (as defined by the Probation Service risk assessment tool OASys), and those deemed to require very intensive risk management at level 3 of MAPPA.[1] However, there are a number of difficulties with the operation of the 'critical few'. The concept has proved elastic in practice (Kemshall et al. 2005), and the range of offenders actually covered by MAPPA is quite wide and comprises: Category 1, Registered sex offenders; Category 2, Violent and other sex offenders; Category 3, Other offenders (see MAPPA Guidance, Home Office 2003b, paragraphs 52–57, pp. 16–17; 2004). The 2003 guidance attempted to refine the definition and criteria for the critical few, recognizing that inconsistency of definition had been a problem (Department of Health 2002), and added the following:

Although not assessed as high or very high risk, the case is exceptional because the likelihood of media scrutiny and/or public interest in the management of the case is very high and there is a need to ensure that public confidence in the criminal justice system is sustained.

An offender on discharge from detention under a hospital order.

An offender returning from overseas (whether immediately following their release from custody or not).

An offender having been managed as medium or even a low risk in the community . . . comes to present a high or very high risk as the result of a significant change of circumstances. (Home Office 2003b, 2004: paragraphs 116–117, p. 36)

In essence, this introduction of a 'catch-all' extended rather than qualified the category of the 'critical few'.

Correct identification of the critical few has also proved problematic, prone to a precautionary principle approach in which the absence of evidence of a risk does not necessarily mean low risk, and a 'better safe than sorry' approach is taken (see research by Maguire et al. 2001; Kemshall et al. 2005). MAPPA, particularly in the early days of operation, has been prone to inflation and the principle that cases should be managed at the lowest level possible has been hard to operate consistently. MAPPA is also a large and resource-intensive system for the prevention of a potentially small risk. In 2006/7, the number of serious further offences (SFOs) committed by offenders managed at level 2 or 3 (the 'critical few') was 83 or just over half a percentage point of all cases (Ministry of Justice 2007). This represents a very low reconviction rate for this group.

This is a rather large 'sledgehammer to crack a nut'. It is also notable that those offenders categorized as medium-risk are in fact the most likely to commit a 'further serious offence', i.e. to commit a serious offence of harm while the subject of probation/parole supervision (NPS 2005a). In 2006, this ran at 80 per cent of all SFOs (NPS 2005b; HMIP 2006). Risk is not necessarily located in the 'critical few' but in the mid-range of cases, many of which do not come under MAPPA. This difficulty has led to the Chief Inspector of Probation recommending that 'risk of harm is assessed in all cases' (HMIP 2006). However, this rather undermines a system based upon risk levels and intended to ration resources on the basis of risk of harm.

As evaluation systems and techniques are embryonic it is difficult to establish with certainty the extent to which risk has been prevented by the MAPPA system (or would simply not have occurred anyway), although recent research would indicate significant levels of 'good practice' with high-risk offenders (Kemshall *et al.* 2005; Wood and Kemshall 2007). It is also important to note that sexual offending actually constitutes 0.9 per cent of all police recorded crime, and serious sexual crime such as rape forming about *one-quarter* of that 0.9 per cent (Dodd *et al.* 2004). The number of children abducted, sexually assaulted and subsequently killed by a stranger has remained fairly constant since the 1940s at about 6–8 children per year (Soothill 2003), although media coverage and public perception of this risk would suggest otherwise (Kitzinger 2004; Thomas 2005). The media and penal policy pre-occupation with sexual offenders has been out of proportion to their occurrence in the general offending population, and is in marked contrast to the number of violent offenders supervised in the community and subject to MAPPA (currently at 14,883, a figure which includes 'other sex offenders'). Violent offenders have been a rather late policy discovery, given impetus by the SFO by Damien Hanson resulting in the murder of John Monckton (HMIP 2006).

Similarly, the Probation Service supervised approximately 200,000 offenders in the community, of which 0.36 per cent committed a SFO during 2004/5 (NPS 2005a). In considering sexual and violent crime more generally, Tonry has argued that 'there is nothing in English crime trends to suggest why violence generally, or dangerous offenders, should be regarded as worsening problems' (2004: 134), and he concludes that: 'the tabloid version of reality is the one in which the government prefers to operate' (2004: 124).

The operation of MAPPA can also produce perverse incentives in the management of risk. The HMIP inspection on MAPPA (HMIP 2005) asked the important question 'what does MAPPA contribute to the work of frontline staff?' Interestingly, staff saw MAPPA as a source of support, a forum for sharing responsibility as well as information, and a way of garnering additional scarce resources such as accommodation or surveillance (HMIP 2005: 40) – advantages echoed in recent research (Wood and Kemshall 2007). This suggests a certain function for MAPPA in sharing risk responsibilities, and reducing anxiety for case managers rather than in managing risk *per se*, a situation which Lieb has described as 'joined-up worrying' (Lieb 2003). There is also evidence that MAPPA is used to access resources in difficult (although not always risky) cases (Kemshall *et al.* 2005). The perverse incentive to overuse MAPPA strains resources, and the Inspection report also noted that a lack of resources was diminishing the impact of MAPPA, particularly on surveillance and police home visits to sex offenders, and found that planned unannounced visits to the homes of sex offenders actually took place 10 per cent less than originally planned (HMIP 2005: 41). Perversely, the system set up to monitor high-risk offenders, and particularly sex offenders, cannot meet its objectives as expectations continue to outstrip resources.

The concern with public, political and media anxiety with sex offenders in the community has resulted in an overemphasis in most MAPPA areas on restrictive conditions (Wood and Kemshall 2007). Restrictive conditions are those conditions attached to supervision orders or licences which restrict where an offender can go or live, what they can or cannot do, who they must not approach or contact. For example, a sex offender may have a restriction against using certain leisure facilities (e.g. swimming pools), approaching local schools, and may have a condition to reside in a certain place (e.g. a probation hostel). Offenders can also be made the subject of a curfew to restrict their activities at certain times of the day or night when they are known to be more risky (e.g. when children either enter or leave school). These conditions restrict the opportunity to commit offences and to 'groom' victims. Monitoring, surveillance and control procedures are those which provide a 'watching eye' over the offender, usually used to monitor compliance with restrictive conditions, to monitor grooming activities and to gain further information on networks and criminal activities. These procedures can include electronic or satellite tracking, CCTV and police observation.

However, restrictive conditions can sometimes have an adverse effect. The HMIP thematic report on sex offenders (HMIP 2005) noted sex offenders subject to restrictions prohibiting them from living in proximity to schools and parks resulted in social isolation, distance from their own families and support networks, and lack of reintegration. Lack of integration has been seen as a significant factor in the re-offence rates of sex offenders (Wilson *et al.* 2000; Wilson 2003; Wilson and Picheca 2005; Wilson *et al.* 2005; Bates *et al.* 2007), and there is potential for some risk management interventions to exacerbate rather than reduce risk. This housing policy can also result in sex offenders being accommodated together in a small geographical area, inadvertently fuelling paedophile networks (Levenson and Cotter 2005). Such resettlement often takes place in deprived and impoverished communities least able to manage the risks in their midst (Kemshall 2003), fuelling the type of resentment and anger exhibited at Paulsgrove, reducing trust in professionals, and eroding the credibility of experts (Kemshall and Maguire 2003; Nash 2006). In effect, without consultation, those with the least resources are exposed to the 'ultimate neighbour from hell' (Kitzinger 1999). This in itself can quickly bring the risk management system designed to protect the public into disrepute (Kemshall 2003; Kemshall and Maguire 2003), and refocuses public attention on the involuntary and taboo risks in our midst.

Regulating Sex Offender Risk

While comprising a number of different agencies (some of whom are Responsible Authorities and some who only have a 'duty to cooperate'), MAPPA can be understood as

> more than the sum of its constituent parts, a supra or hybrid institution with its own protocols, rules and procedures. Knowledge production

and processing are the key activities of panel work, and the key objective of panel work is the constitution and reproduction of networks of surveillance. (Kemshall and Maguire 2003: 192)

A key issue is how this supra institution of risk management can be regulated appropriately. Hood, Rothstein and Baldwin define risk regulation as: 'governmental interference with market or social processes to control potential adverse consequences to health' (2001: 3). Based on this definition, MAPPA can be understood as a risk regulation regime. MAPPA both provides risk regulation (in this case of sex offenders) and also requires appropriate regulation of its own activities.

MAPPA is also illustrative of a further risk management trend, that is, the tendency for the state to demand greater risk regulation and audit of risk systems while at the same time distancing itself from the day-to-day management of risk (Hood et al. 2001; Kemshall 2003; Rose 1996). Risk regimes are by no means uniform, with variations in attitudes to risks and their regulation across nation states (for example differing attitudes across Europe to the export and import of beef during the BSE crisis), and indeed differences between policy domains *within* the same country (Hood et al. 2001). A notable example is the differing attitudes of the UK government to genetically modified foods, in which it has not adopted a particularly precautionary approach (on occasion quite the opposite), and to sex offenders, where a precautionary principle has dominated. These risks share some similarities: they both engender public disquiet, they are both seen to be pervasive and insidious, and to some extent their future impact is unknowable and potentially incalculable. Interestingly, different policy and regulatory approaches have been applied to them. The approach to sex offender risks has been characterized by anticipationism and high levels of intrusion (Kemshall 2003). These differences in regulatory approach do not necessarily reflect differing levels or frequency of risk. As Hood et al. point out, traditionally car emissions have been more tightly regulated than smoking although the latter claims more lives (2001: 7). Anticipationism subtly changes traditional probabilistic risk thinking to a preoccupation with 'worse case scenarios' and possibilistic thinking focused solely on 'what if' the worst happens and the spectre of risk management failures (see Furedi, this volume). This type of thinking permeates risk regulation regimes and distorts them towards defensive policies and strategies (Kemshall 2008).

Greater transparency has been seen as a central and recurring recipe for 'better regulation' and as exposure to the unexamined processes in public services (Hood et al. 2001: 147-8). It is possible to distinguish differing levels of response to this demand for greater openness, from complete compliance without distortion through to bounded institutions that exhibit strong tendencies towards secrecy to the point that it is impossible to exert external controls (2001: 149-50). A realistic position is more common: Hood et al. define this as a 'staged retreat' where agencies will respond to calls for transparency with a series of phases and steps. Changes observed include: a greater transparency in procedures for information gathering and standard setting; wider public participation in some or all of these components;

and heightened accountability in terms of obligation on the part of those managing risks (see Hood *et al.* 2001: 151).

Accountability within multi-agency partnerships has been identified as problematic by various commentators (most notably Crawford 1998, and Harrison *et al.* 2003), with concerns about ill-defined roles and responsibilities for each partner, lack of a shared understanding about collaborative working, and lack of accountability between partners, and lack of accountability to any body or organization outside the partnership arrangements. This can raise issues of accountability for the delivery of risk management – how are other agencies and workers held to account, and what sanction can reasonably be imposed if risk management is compromised? (Maguire *et al.* 2001; Kemshall *et al.* 2005).

However, in public protection partnerships (and other risk arenas) the requirement for transparency has resulted in, among other measures, attempts to engage the public in 'arms-length' oversight (e.g. through the lay advisers), joint information-sharing protocols between stakeholders and partners, and the production of annual reports detailing effectiveness and reporting mechanisms to central government released annually into the public domain. This takes place within a cultural bias in criminal justice which leans towards reduced transparency, justified by an assumption that any increase will hinder the management of risk (for example, by causing vigilante action) (Hood *et al.* 2001: 157; Kemshall 2003).

Drawing on the work of Hood *et al.* (2001; also Hood *et al.* 1999; Hood and Rothstein 2001); and other commentators (notably Douglas 1985; Horlick-Jones 1998; Morris 2000; Rothstein 2003a, 2003b) the distinctiveness of sex offender risk can be attributed to the following:

- Media salience and an 'exponential growth in press coverage' (Hood *et al.* 2001: 93; see also Kitzinger 2004; Soothill and Walby 1991).
- Nimbyism, spilling over to public outrage and vigilante action if such a risk is perceived to be imposed on communities. This is linked to the taboo nature of the risk, and to what Slovic has labelled a 'dread risk', a risk that is potentially uncontrollable and resulting in high harm and possibly death (1987, 1992).
- Low trust in experts (Banks 2004), particularly of professional competence to manage risk effectively, and in the systems and processes created by professional experts to manage risk (Douglas 1992; Kemshall and Maguire 2003; Power 1997, 2007). Hood *et al.*, for example, contrast public expectations of a rigorous risk management system with a subsequent media and public perception of a rudimentary and failing system. This can be exacerbated where professionals are seen to be operating for their own self-interest (Lowe 1993), or where targets, rationing of services and workload take precedence over quality (Le Grand 1997).
- Low public participation and engagement in the regulatory regime, often in contrast to the high expectations of participation and engagement that the public holds (Hood *et al.* 2001). The public's perception and experience of exclusion, particularly when coupled with imposed risks, can lead to outrage and lack of confidence (the Paulsgrove reaction is the key example – Nash 2006).

Figure 1

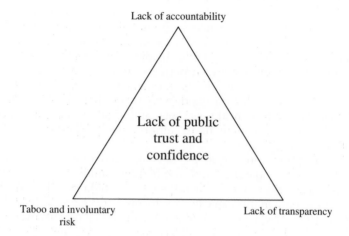

Lack of accountability

Lack of public
trust and
confidence

Taboo and involuntary   Lack of transparency
risk

- Low transparency and low public accountability. This can result in public perceptions of secrecy, anxiety and doubt about the adequacy of the system to offer the protection demanded, and closed systems can result in higher rates of error (Pidgeon *et al.* 2002).
- The risk is a 'dread risk' without any potential benefits for the public. Furedi (this volume) explores the current policy response to 'dread risks', most notably terrorism, and the culture of vulnerability it fosters.
- The risk is targeted almost exclusively at a vulnerable group (i.e. children). Again Furedi (this volume) argues that current state responses to risk can be characterized by their concern with vulnerability or 'exposure to risk' and the perceived lack of resilience on behalf of the public to cope and manage such risks. This is clearly played out in the arena of sex offender risks.
- One instance of failure can bring the whole system of risk management into disrepute.

This places the regulation of sex offender risks (and MAPPA as a key mechanism of that regulation) in a difficult position, summed up by figure 1.

Despite assurances from politicians, senior policy-makers and leading practitioners, MAPPA and the statutory regulation of sex offenders is in a no-win situation, in which it is constantly responding to failures and having to emphasize increasingly punitive and restrictive measures to engender public confidence. In effect, this ratchets up the public protection promise beyond the resources available to deliver it (Kemshall 2003; Nash 2006).

Are there any alternative regulatory mechanisms that might engender public confidence and overcome some of the issues outlined above? Enhancing the level of public participation and engagement has been seen as key to increasing public confidence in risk regulation regimes (Hood *et al.* 2001; Royal Society Study Group 1992) and in reducing system error (Pidgeon *et al.*

2002). While the government has resisted calls for a UK version of Megan's Law (see Wood and Kemshall 2007), and community notification in the USA has not been linked to a reduction in sexual offences (Finch 2006), other processes for engaging the public have been pursued with some success, the most notable being Circles of Support and Accountability (COSA).

COSA grew out of negative public reaction to the release of a sex offender into the community, and perceptions that formal supervisory mechanisms could neither successfully reintegrate sex offenders nor guarantee public safety (Wilson 2003, 2007; Wilson and Picheca 2005; Wilson et al. 2005, 2007a). It has its roots in faith-based communities agreeing to form circles of support and accountability around a sexual offender, offering support, monitoring and vigilance. The approach takes a broadly restorative and reintegrative approach to sexual offending, and seeks to improve community safety through the successful reintegration of sex offenders into the community (Wilson et al. 2007a; for a detailed description of COSA see: Correctional Service of Canada 2002; Wilson and Picheca 2005). This model has been adopted in the USA, the UK, the Netherlands, South Africa, and Bermuda, and has been promoted for its effectiveness in reducing sex offender recidivism, with 70 per cent lower recidivism than offenders in a matched sample. In the three instances of sexual recidivism the re-offences were of less severity, thus achieving a harm reduction function (Wilson et al. 2007b: 333). Data, both in Canada and the UK, are beginning to indicate that COSA can achieve greater effectiveness for higher-risk offenders (Wilson et al. 2007b). The model is also advocated for its usefulness in reducing public anxiety and outrage about the location of sex offenders (Wilson 2003), and in engendering public confidence in the work of professionals (Bates 2005). In the UK context[2] volunteers work alongside professionals from the MAPPA and contribute to the management of MAPPA cases (Bates et al. 2007). These processes increase the level of public participation, knowledge and scrutiny in the work of MAPPA and in the supervision of sex offenders generally. COSA, in particular, places responsibility on to local residents for the management and safety of the sex offender, and also makes the work of professionals more transparent.

Other broader, reintegrative approaches to the management of sex offenders emphasize public participation and engagement. Leisurewatch,[3] for example, provides a helpful and concrete response to sexual offender grooming behaviours, and actively engages the public in safely managing sex offenders within their own communities. Leisurewatch targets sites where children are likely to gather and to be potentially targeted by sex offenders and aims to safeguard leisure sites (e.g. swimming pools) and more recently shopping centres. The purpose of Leisurewatch is to enable staff to spot potentially dangerous behaviour and empower them to make safe challenges to customers/users; and to promote an observant and vigilant image for the site which is off-putting to sex offenders and reassuring to the public (adapted from: www.derwentinitiative.org.uk/leisurewatch.htm).

Fear of crime often presents as an intractable problem, spawning a 'fear of crime industry' (Lee 2007). However, in the area of sex offenders and MAPPA it is crucial to distinguish between the management of risk and

65

the management of public fear and anxiety. MAPPA was created to do the former, but can easily be distorted by policy and political concerns to do the latter. This is not to argue that public fears and anxieties are either 'unreal', 'irrational' or illegitimate. On the contrary this indicates that there is a political, policy and practice role for more public engagement on these issues. For example, the Cosgrove Report in Scotland strongly argued for public awareness and public education campaigns to allay public fears on sex offending as part of a broader strategy on sexual offending (Cosgrove 2001). Such campaigns emphasize that not all sex offenders are monsters and incapable of change, and outline those treatment programmes that work (although campaigns are not without some difficulties, see Kemshall 2008 for a full review). Interestingly, following a recent campaign, The Derwent Initiative found that awareness went up by 20 per cent, and that a number of participants in the programme disclosed that they or a relative had been affected by sexual abuse (TDI 2007) – again, illustrating the point that sex offenders are not invisible 'monsters in our midst' but people we know and are often related to. There is also a role for a more critical exploration of public anxieties about sexual offending – to what extent are these fears real, or are they a policy myth, distorted by political responses to media coverage? (Kitzinger 2004; Wood and Gannon 2008).

These kinds of initiatives extend accountability outwards to local communities and the wider public, rather than relying entirely on internal reporting and audit mechanisms. They also serve to close the gap between public and experts, a gap that is problematic in most risk regulation (Lupton 1999; Hood et al. 2001; Royal Society Study Group 1992), and in the arena of crime risks can result in significant public inflation of risk (see Kemshall 1997 for a full review).

Conclusion

These initiatives indicate some potential to strengthen both transparency and accountability, offering concrete ways to engage the public in the management of traditionally involuntary and taboo risk. As such, they may remove the 'dread' from the risk, and provide some sense of 'risk realism'. In turn, there is opportunity for concrete and pragmatic ways to enable and equip the public to deal with the involuntary risk in their midst. Public engagement is fundamental to the appropriate regulation of this risk, and to gaining both public confidence and policy accountability.

Involuntary risk is not going away. Aspirations for zero risk found within the community protection model will inevitably result in risk management failure, and consequent erosion of public confidence and trust. Alternative approaches move us from risk management systems based upon exclusivity and defensiveness to those characterized by inclusivity and engagement. Alternative risk management and risk regulation regimes for sex offenders are embryonic. However, there is potential for risk management to be effectively strengthened by a more sustained public involvement (Kemshall and Wood 2007b). These approaches deserve further development and empirical evaluation.

Notes

1. Level 1 management is carried out by a single agency; level 2 management is through local inter-agency arrangements but does not usually require the intensive management of the formal MAPPA procedures.
2. See, for example, the Quakers' pilot scheme in Thames Valley and Hampshire: www.restorativejustice.org.uk/?RJ_%26amp%3B_the_CJS:Circles_of_Support_%26amp%3B_Accountability
3. Leisurewatch is a project developed by the The Derwent Inititative (TDI) (www.derwentinitiative.org.uk).

References

Anderson, A. (2006), Media and risk. In G. Mythen and S. Walklate (eds), *Beyond the Risk Society: Critical Reflections on Risk and Human Security*, Maidenhead: Open University Press, pp. 114–31.

Banks, S. (2004), *Ethics, Accountability and the Social Professions*, Basingstoke: Palgrave.

Bates, A. (2005), Evaluation. In *Circles of Support and Accountability in the Thames Valley: The First Three Years April 2002–March 2005*, London: Quaker Communications.

Bates, A., Saunders, R. and Wilson, C. (2007), Doing something about it: a follow-up study of sex offenders participating in Thames Valley circles of support and accountability, *British Journal of Community Justice*, 5, 1: 19–42.

Boutellier, H. (2000), *Crime and Morality: The Significance of Criminal Justice in the Post-modern Culture*, Dordrecht: Kluwer Academic.

Cawson, P., Wattam, S. and Kelly, G. (2000), *Child Maltreatment in the United Kingdom: A Study of the Prevalence of Child Abuse and Neglect*, London: NSPCC.

Cohen, N. (2003), *Pretty Straight Guys*, London: Faber and Faber.

Connelly, C. and Williamson, S. (2000), *Review of the Research Literature on Serious Violent and Sexual Offenders*, Edinburgh: Scottish Executive.

Correctional Service of Canada (2002), *Circles of Support and Accountability: A Guide to Training Potential Volunteers. Training Manual 2002*, Ottawa, ON: Correctional Service of Canada.

Cosgrove, Lady (2001), *Reducing the Risk: Improving the Response to Sex Offending. Report of the Expert Panel on Sex Offending*, chaired by Lady Cosgrove, Edinburgh: Scottish Executive.

Crawford, A. (1998), *Crime Prevention and Community Safety: Politics, Policies and Practices*, London: Longman.

Cross, S. (2005), Paedophiles in the community: inter-agency conflict, news leak and the local press, *Crime, Media and Culture*, 1, 3: 284–300.

Denney, D. (2005), *Risk and Society*, London: Sage.

Department of Health (2002), *Safeguarding Children: A Joint Chief Inspectors' Report on Arrangements to Safeguard Children*, London: DoH.

Dodd, T., Nicholas, S., Povey, D. and Walker, A. (2004), *Crime in England and Wales 2003/2004*, Home Office Statistical Bulletin, London: Home Office.

Douglas, M. (1985), *Risk Acceptability according to the Social Sciences*, London: Routledge.

Douglas, M. (1992), *Risk and Blame*, London: Routledge.

Downes, D. and Morgan, R. (2007), No turning back: the politics of law and order into the millennium. In M. Maguire, R. Morgan and R. Reiner (eds), *The Oxford Handbook of Criminology* (4th edn), Oxford: Oxford University Press.

Feeley, M. and Simon, J. (1992), The new penology: notes on the emerging strategy for corrections, *Criminology*, 30, 4: 449–75.

Feeley, M. and Simon, J. (1994), Actuarial justice: the emerging new criminal law. In D. Nelken (ed.), *The Futures of Criminology*, London: Sage, pp. 173–201.

Finch, K. (2006), *Megan's Law: Does It Protect Children?* London: NSPCC.

Garland, D. (2001), *The Culture of Crime Control: Crime and Social Order in Contemporary Society*, Oxford: Oxford University Press.

Grubin, D. (1998), *Sex Offending against Children: Understanding the Risk*, London: Home Office.

Harrison, R., Mann, G., Murphy, M., Taylor, A. and Thompson, N. (2003), *Partnership Made Painless: A Joined-up Guide to Working Together*, Lyme Regis: Russell House Publishing.

HM Inspectorate of Probation (HMIP) (2005), *Managing Sex Offenders in the Community: A Joint Inspection on Sex Offenders*, London: Home Office.

HM Inspectorate of Probation (HMIP) (2006), *An Independent Review of a Serious Further Offence Case: Damien Hanson and Elliot White*, London: HMIP.

Home Office (1990), *Crime, Justice and Protecting the Public: The Government's Proposals for Legislation*, Cm 965, London: HMSO.

Home Office (2001), *Initial Guidance to the Police and Probation Services on Sections 67 and 68 of the Criminal Justice and Court Services Act 2000*, London: Home Office.

Home Office (2002), *Further Guidance to the Police and Probation Services on Sections 67 and 68 of the Criminal Justice and Court Services Act 2000*, London: Home Office.

Home Office (2003a), *A New Deal for Victims and Witnesses*, London: Home Office.

Home Office (2003b), *MAPPA Guidance: Protection Through Partnership*, London: Home Office.

Home Office (2004), *MAPPA Guidance: Protection Through Partnership (Version 1.2)*, London: Home Office.

Home Office (2007), *MAPPA – the First Five Years: A National Overview of the Multi-Agency Public Protection Arrangements 2001–2006*, London: Home Office.

Hood, C. and Rothstein, H. (2001), Risk regulation under pressure: problem solving or blame-shifting? *Administration and Society*, 33, 1: 21–53.

Hood, C., Rothstein, H., Spackman, M., Rees, J. and Baldwin, R. (1999), Explaining risk regulation regimes: exploring the 'minimal feasibility response' hypothesis, *Health, Risk and Society*, 1, 2: 151–66.

Hood, C., Rothstein, H. and Baldwin, R. (2001), *The Government of Risk*, Oxford: Oxford University Press.

Horlick-Jones, T. (1998), Meaning and contextualisation in risk assessment, *Reliability Engineering and System Safety*, 5: 79–89.

Kemshall, H. (1997), The dangerous are always with us: dangerousness and the role of the Probation Service, *VISTA*, 2, 3: 136–53.

Kemshall, H. (2003), *Understanding Risk in Criminal Justice*, Maidenhead: Open University Press.

Kemshall, H. (2008), *Understanding Responses to 'Dangerousness': The Management of High Risk Offenders*, Maidenhead: Open University Press.

Kemshall, H. and Maguire, M. (2003), Sex offenders, risk penality and the problem of disclosure to the community. In A. Matravers (ed.), *Sex Offenders in the Community, Managing and Reducing the Risks*, Cullompton: Willan Publishing.

Kemshall, H. and Wood, J. (2007a), High-risk offenders and public protection. In L. Gelsthorpe and R. Morgan (eds), *Handbook of Probation*, Cullompton: Willan Publishing, pp. 381–97.

Kemshall, H. and Wood, J. (2007b), Beyond public protection: an examination of community protection and public health approaches to high risk offenders, *Criminology and Criminal Justice*, 7, 3: 203–22.

Kemshall, H., Mackenzie, G., Wood, J., Bailey, R. and Yates, J. (2005), *Strengthening the Multi-Agency Public Protection Arrangements*, London: Home Office.

Kitzinger, J. (1999), The ultimate neighbour from hell: media framing of paedophiles. In B. Franklin (ed.), *Social Policy, Media and Misrepresentation*, London: Routledge.

Kitzinger, J. (2004), *Framing Abuse: Media Influence and Public Understanding of Sexual Violence Against Children*, London: Pluto Press.

Laming, Lord (2003), *The Victoria Climbie Inquiry*, London: Crown Copyright.

Available at: www.victoria-climbie-inquiry.org.uk/finreport/finreport.htm (accessed 16 March 2007).

Lee, M. (2007), *Inventing Fear of Crime: Criminology and the Politics of Anxiety*, Cullompton: Willan Publishing.

Le Grand, J. (1997), Knights, knaves or pawns? Human behaviour and social policy, *Journal of Social Policy*, 26, 2: 149–69.

Levenson, J. S. and Cotter, L. P. (2005), The impact of the sex offender residence restrictions: 1,000 feet from danger or one step from the absurd? *International Journal of Offender Therapy and Comparative Criminology*, 49, 2: 168–78.

Lieb, R. (2003), Joined-up worrying: the Multi-Agency Public Protection Panels. In A. Matravers (ed.), *Sex Offenders in the Community*, Cullompton: Willan Publishing, pp. 207–18.

Lowe, R. (1993), *The Welfare State in Britain since 1945*, London: Macmillan.

Lupton, D. (1999), *Risk*, London: Routledge.

Maguire, M., Kemshall, H., Noaks, L. and Wincup, E. (2001), *Risk Management of Sexual and Violent Offenders: The Work of Public Protection Panels*, London: Home Office.

Matravers, A. (2005), *Managing Modernity: Politics and the Culture of Control*, Abingdon: Routledge.

Ministry of Justice (2007), *National Statistics for Multi-Agency Public Protection Arrangements (MAPPA)*, *Annual Reports 2007*, London: Ministry of Justice.

Morris, J. (2000), *Rethinking Risk and the Precautionary Principle*, Oxford: Butterworth.

Nash, M. (2005), The Probation Service, public protection and dangerous offenders. In J. Winstone and F. Pakes (eds), *Community Justice: Issues for Probation and Criminal Justice*, Cullompton: Willan Publishing.

Nash, M. (2006), *Public Protection and the Criminal Justice Process*, Oxford: Oxford University Press.

National Probation Service (NPS) (2005a), *Learning Points Derived from Serious Further Offence Full Reviews*, London: NPS.

National Probation Service (NPS) (2005b), Probation Circular PC 82/2005, *Monitoring of Risk of Harm*, London: National Probation Service.

O'Malley, P. (2004a), The uncertain promise of risk, *Australian and New Zealand Journal of Criminology*, 37, 3: 323–43.

O'Malley, P. (2004b), *Risk, Uncertainty and Government*, London: Glass House Press.

Pidgeon, N., Kasperson, R. and Slovic, P. (eds) (2002), *Social Amplification of Risk and Risk Communication*, Cambridge: Cambridge University Press.

Power, M. (1997), *The Audit Society*, Oxford: Oxford University Press.

Power, M. (2007), *Organized Uncertainty: Designing a World of Risk Management*, Oxford: Oxford University Press.

Prior, V., Glaser, D. and Lynch, M. A. (1997), Responding to child sexual abuse: the criminal justice system, *Child Abuse Review*, 6: 128–40.

Raynor, P. and Vanstone, M. (2007), Towards a correctional service. In L. Gelsthorpe and R. Morgan (eds), *Handbook of Probation*, Cullompton: Willan Publishing.

Rose, N. (1996), Governing 'advanced' liberal democracies. In A. Barry, T. Osborne and N. Rose (eds), *Foucault and Political Reason*, London: UCL Press.

Rothstein, H. (2003a), Neglected risk regulation: the institutional attenuation phenomenon, *Health, Risk and Society*, 5, 1: 85–103.

Rothstein, H. (2003b), *Precautionary Bans or Sacrificial Lambs? Participative Risk Regulation and the Reform of the UK Food Safety Regime*, CARR Discussion Paper no. 15, London: ESRC Centre for Analysis of Risk and Regulation, London School of Economics.

Royal Society Study Group (1992), *Risk: Analysis, Perception and Management*, London: Royal Society.

Sanders, C. R. and Lyon, E. (1995), Repetitive retribution: media images and the cultural construction of criminal justice. In J. Ferrell and C. Sanders (eds), *Cultural Criminology*, Boston, MA: Northeastern University Press.

Silverman, J. and Wilson, D. (2002), *Innocence Betrayed: Paedophiles, the Media and Society*, Cambridge: Polity Press.

Simon, J. (1998), Managing the monstrous: sex offenders and the new penology, *Psychology, Public Policy and Law*, 4, 1: 452–67.

Slovic, P. (1987), Perceptions of risk, *Science*, 236: 280–5.

Slovic, P. (1992), Perceptions of risk: reflections on the psychometric paradigm. In S. Krimsky and D. Golding (eds), *Social Theories of Risk*, Westport, CT: Praeger.

Slovic, P. (2000), *The Perception of Risk*, London: Earthscan.

Soothill, K. (2003), Serious sexual assault: using history and statistics. In A. Matravers (ed.), *Sex Offenders in the Community: Managing and Reducing the Risk*, Cullompton: Willan Publishing.

Soothill, K. and Walby, S. (1991), *Sex Crime in the News*, London: Routledge.

The Derwent Initiative (TDI) (2007), *Tackling Sex Offending Together*, Newcastle upon Tyne: TDI.

Thomas, T. (2005), *Sex Crime: Sex Offending and Society*, Cullompton: Willan Publishing.

Tonry, M. (2004), *Punishment and Politics: Evidence and Emulation in the Making of English Crime Control Policy*, Cullompton: Willan Publishing.

Wallis, E. (1997), A new choreography: breaking away from the elaborate corporate dance. In R. Burnett (ed.), *The Probation Service: Responding to Change*, Oxford: Probation Studies Unit, Oxford University.

Welch, M., Fenwick, M. and Roberts, M. (1997), Primary definitions of crime and moral panics: a content analysis of experts' quotes in feature newspaper articles on crime, *Journal of Research on Crime and Delinquency*, 34: 474–94.

Williams, B. (2005), *Victims of Crime and Community Justice*, London: Jessica Kingsley.

Williams, B. and Goodman, H. (2007), Working for and with victims of crime. In L. Gelsthorpe and R. Morgan (eds), *Handbook of Probation*, Cullompton: Willan Publishing.

Wilson, R. J. (2003), Risk, reintegration and registration: a Canadian perspective on community sex offender risk management, *ATSA Forum*, 15.

Wilson, R. J. (2007), Out in the open, *Community Care* (19–25 April): 36–37.

Wilson, R. J. and Picheca, J. E. (2005), Circles of support and accountability: engaging the community in sexual offender risk management. In B. K. Schwartz (ed.), *The Sexual Offender*, vol. 5, New York: Civic Research Institute.

Wilson, R., Stewart, L., Stirpe, T., Barrett, M. and Cripps, J. E. (2000), Community based sexual offender management: combining parole supervision and treatment to reduce recidivism, *Canadian Journal of Criminology*, 42: 177–88.

Wilson, R. J., Picheca, J. E. and Prinzo, M. (2005), *Circles of Support and Accountability: An Evaluation of the Pilot Project in South-Central Ontario* (Research Report R-168), Ottawa, ON: Correctional Service of Canada.

Wilson, R. J., Picheca, J. E. and Prinzo, M. (2007a), Evaluating the effectiveness of professionally-facilitated volunteerism in the community based management of high-risk sexual offenders: Part One – Effects on participants and stakeholders, *Howard Journal*, 46, 3: 289–302.

Wilson, R. J., Picheca, J. E. and Prinzo, M. (2007a), Evaluating the effectiveness of professionally-facilitated volunteerism in the community based management of high-risk sexual offenders: Part Two – A comparison of recidivism rates, *Howard Journal*, 46, 4: 327–37.

Wood, J. and Gannon, T. (2008), *Public Opinion and Criminal Justice*, Cullompton: Willan Publishing.

Wood, J. and Kemshall, H., with Maguire, M., Hudson, K. and Mackenzie, G. (2007), *The Operation and Experience of Multi-Agency Public Protection Arrangements*, London: Home Office.

Young, J. (2007), *The Vertigo of Late Modernity*, London: Sage.

6

Social Policy beyond Fear: The Globalization of Strangeness, the 'War on Terror', and 'Spaces of Wonder'

Chris Rumford

Introduction

This chapter explores themes which, in a bout of recent writing and theorizing, have been placed, unsatisfactorily in my view, under the rubric of 'fear', a term which it would seem has become indispensable to social scientists attempting both to characterize the times we live in ('liquid fear') and to explain the tensions between our securitized forms of governance and the insecurities and anxieties experienced in everyday life. However, accounts of fear offer only partial explanations of an important dimension of contemporary policy responses to uncertainty and apprehension. This chapter seeks to place the 'strangeness' of (and in) the world at the centre of accounts of collective insecurity and examines the role of globalization in increasing this sense of strangeness, with particular reference to the strangeness of emerging political spaces, some of which, it is argued, have become 'spaces of wonder'.

At the core of the chapter is the argument that a focus on the politics of strangeness can provide valuable ways of understanding policy choices and governance strategies not matched by the literature on fear, even those accounts which examine the ways in which fear is increasingly used as an organizing principle for governing social relations. For example, according to Robin (2004) it is insufficient to view fear as simply an emotion: it is best thought of as a 'political tool, an instrument of elite rule or insurgent advance, created and sustained by political leaders or activists who stand to gain something from it' (Robin 2004: 16). A similar conclusion is reached by Huysmans, writing about the securitization to which anxieties about immigration in Europe often give rise, who talks of the 'politics and administration of fear' and the way it provides opportunities for a particular mode of governance. For Huysmans, 'fear is not simply an emotion that security framing instigates in social relations. It is first of all an organizing principle that renders social relations as fearful' (Huysmans 2006: 54).

Useful as these formulations are, what is neglected in the current concern with fear, anxiety, apprehension and trepidation is the sense of wonder that dramatic, devastating or traumatic events can provoke. In such cases the world becomes a strange and unfamiliar place in which standard reference points have been erased and a new logic of cause and effect seems to be at work. In sociological terms, sudden and dramatic changes to the world can lead to acute anomie, to employ a Durkheimian phrase, a situation in which old rules and established norms no longer apply. Former Prime Minister Tony Blair's repeated assertions that the events of 9/11 changed the world, a world which no longer 'makes sense' in conventional terms can be interpreted as responses to the anomie which characterizes a world in which the old rules no longer apply but new ones have yet to emerge. The idea of anomie goes some way to explaining the normlessness which characterizes uncertain times, but in the recent sociological literature the failure of social mechanisms for dealing with the collective fear resulting from devastating events has tended to be explained in terms of 'cultural trauma' (Alexander *et al.* 2004). As I have argued elsewhere (Rumford 2008) such approaches place too much emphasis on re-establishing the *status quo ante* and fail to grasp the transformative potential inherent in an encounter with 'spaces of wonder'.

'Spaces of wonder', made manifest (either discursively or territorially) by processes of globalization, have an unsettling, destabilizing or disorienting effect in the sense that they are difficult to comprehend or assimilate into existing understandings of political topography, to the extent that they inspire awe or wonder in those trying to apprehend them. For example, the response by the US authorities to the devastation caused in and around New Orleans by Hurricane Katrina was seen by many not only as totally inadequate but almost unbelievable in the context of the resource mobilization of which the world's most powerful nation state is capable (or believes itself to be capable). The devastation of New Orleans, the tardiness and inadequacy of the response, the breakdown of law and order that ensued, and the fortitude of many who suffered there as a result were truly awe-inspiring and produced the mixture of strangeness and wonder to which I am alluding. Similarly, the events of 11 September 2001 are illustrative of the disorientation which can accompany the emergence of 'spaces of wonder', a disorientation which stemmed not so much from the attacks of 9/11 themselves, but from the revelation that the United States lacked the capacity to 'manage' globalization to the extent hitherto assumed. In this respect, the language of the *9/11 Commission Report* is instructive: 'To us, Afghanistan seemed very far away. To members of al-Qaeda, America seemed very close. In a sense, they were more globalized than we were' (quoted in Devji 2005: 1). At the moment of the attack on the twin towers, globalization was no longer a 'given', and the world no longer a familiar place.

It is argued that new opportunities for governance (and perhaps also political opposition, although this is not pursued here) accompany the emergence of these spaces of wonder, particularly where political actors are capable of rendering the strangeness of 'spaces of wonder' in very familiar and reassuring terms. By looking at 'spaces of wonder' rather than the politics of fear, it is argued that we can better understand important dynamics of contemporary governance. To this end the chapter examines three 'spaces of wonder': (1) 'the world', made more uncertain and threatening by accounts of the global nature of terror; (2) the UK's borders, which according the government are now located 'offshore' and controlled remotely from the UK; and (3) 'global borderlands' where the separation between good and evil, civilization and barbarism is regulated. Before we can proceed to look at these examples it is necessary to establish what is meant by 'strangeness', how it is related to processes of globalization, and its implications for the governance of 'spaces of wonder'

Globalization and Strangeness

In addition to alerting us to the 'oneness of the world', accounts of globalization have also made it possible to view the world as a more uncertain and strange place. This is because at the heart of social science understandings of globalization lies a paradox. At the same time as generating an awareness that the world is a single place and encouraging actors to rethink their place in relation to the world as a whole (Robertson 1992), globalization can also provoke a sense that the world is larger, more complex, and more threatening and dangerous than was hitherto the case. In other words, globalization both compresses the world, and, paradoxically, brings its great size into focus. While we are increasingly conscious of the compactness of an increasingly interconnected world in ways that bring the globe within the grasp of all individuals, we are also cognizant that the flows and mobilities constitutive of globalization processes constitute a threat to the integrity of our familiar (nationally constituted) communities, as a result of which much economic and political decision-making is removed from democratically elected polities, and the individuals that constitute them.

The idea that globalization has undermined the familiar territoriality of a world of nation states has become well established in the social science literature on globalization (Sassen 1991). For example, McGrew (1995: 52) writes that 'processes of globalization are transforming the very foundation of world order, by reconstituting sovereign statehood and reordering international political space'. Similarly, Harvey holds that globalization has 'undermined older material and territorial definitions of place' (quoted in Eade 1997: 8). A range of contributions have bolstered this view, from the more apocalyptic accounts associated with the idea that globalization has led to the 'annihilation' of space, to advocates of 'network society' who see mobilities and flows as being indifferent to territorial boundaries, and the deterritorialized sovereignty of Hardt and Negri's *Empire* (2000). In all of these approaches the emphasis is very much on the transformed spatiality of the world rather than the strangeness of it, even in accounts where attention is drawn to the link between global connectivity and 'the concomitant rise in the danger of "strangers" in the modern world' (Robertson 2007: 404). In other words, the vast majority of accounts of the transformation of spatiality in a world of connectivity focus on the new spaces created by globalization and the flows and mobilities thought to energize them, rather than the processes by means of which our familiarity with those spaces is undermined and the strangeness and unpredictability – unknowability, even – of the world has increased. But this under-researched realm of the strangeness of the spaces of globalization

Chris Rumford

is an important one, it is argued, and the focus of attention here. If globalization makes and re-makes the world, it also makes the world increasingly strange.

In a recent discussion of securitization and the 'open society', Roland Robertson draws attention to the link between increasing global connectivity and 'the concomitant rise in the danger of "strangers"'. For Robertson, in his now famous formulation, globalization is best understood as both the increasing interconnectedness of the world coupled with the realization that this is the case (Robertson 1992). Both elements of the equation are equally important as 'increasing global consciousness runs in complex ways, hand in hand, so to speak, with increasing connectivity' (Robertson and White 2007: 56). One dimension of the global connectivity–global consciousness nexus is the way in which globalization results in the institutionalization of difference leading to increased strangeness. We live in a world in which distance is said to have died but it is still one 'in which there are many barriers and borders being erected by individuals, communities, societies, regions, and civilizations against "strangers"' (Robertson 2007: 404–5). For Robertson, alterity, or strangeness, is the flipside of securitization, and social cohesion is sustained through the invocation of the threatening 'Other'. In other words, strangeness – the radical and threatening difference associated with the Other – is exacerbated by processes of globalization which are perceived as throwing open the doors to the world and leaving us unprotected from threats that come from beyond previously secure borders. The result is that 'we live in a world in which we are encouraged to believe in more and more dangers, and an increasing number of "protections" are offered to help us' (Robertson 2007: 406). These 'protections' include 'everyday' or DIY forms of securitization: installing CCTV, consuming training on how to survive terrorist attacks,[1] living in gated communities, and driving SUVs, which may make us feel more secure but will also increase our awareness of alterity. All of this chimes with what Furedi (2004) terms the 'cultivation of vulnerability', which renders us powerless and passive in the face of perceived threats. In addition, the 'democratization of surveillance' means that 'we are all spies now' (Robertson 2007: 408) and the upshot is that 'we are constrained to be suspicious of all others', thereby cranking alterity up another notch. The result is that 'the problem of strangeness is becoming institutionalized' (Robertson 2007: 409) and part of the global fabric of our everyday lives. Globalization thus creates the sense that we are living in an open and networked world and, at the same time, increases our perceptions of the threats inherent in such an 'open' world. Our response to this is to create at a local level what we no longer believe the nation state to be capable of or committed to: our collective security. In short, the increasing securitization of our lives exacerbates our sense of alterity: the world is rendered unfamiliar and is full of strangeness.

Balibar (2006: 3) pursues similar themes but focuses more on the role of borders in the construction and reproduction of strangeness in Europe. He writes: 'increasingly it is the working of the border, and especially the difference between geopolitical, economic and security borders and mere administrative separations, which constitutes, or "produces" the stranger/foreigner as social type' (2006: 4). In other words, some types of borders are more important than others in producing strangeness – and the borders he has in mind constitute what he terms 'the Great Wall of Europe', 'a complex of differentiated institutions, installations, legislations, repressive and pre- ventive politics, and international agreements which together aim at making the liberty of circulation not impossible but extremely difficult or selective and unilateral for certain categories of individuals and certain groups' (Balibar 2006: 1–2). This border is not conceived at the outer edges of Europe but in fact projected beyond Europe's borders, and component parts of the 'Great Wall of Europe' include the Israeli-built wall dividing the West Bank from Israel and the heavily fortified security fences guarding the Spanish enclaves of Ceuta and Melilla in Morocco. What this means for Europe is that citizens from other member states are no longer 'fully strange' (because the borders that separate them from us are of the 'merely administrative' type) while those from beyond 'the Great Wall of Europe' are constituted as full strangers. ' "Strangeness" and the various conditions referred to by the category of the Stranger are nothing natural, but they are produced and therefore also reproduced' (by borders) (Balibar 2006: 4).

Consideration of the idea of globalization and strangeness has given shape to some key themes which will be developed throughout the rest of the chapter. The first is the way in which globalization is seen to increase the dangerousness of the world, for example the realization that jihadist terror networks are 'more global' than the United States and its allies who seek to neutralize them (Devji 2005), thereby creating the need for a new type of protection (a global 'war on terror'). The second is the recognition that increasing securitization measures, whether at nation-state level or in terms of personal and local initiatives, also works to increase our perception of alterity. The practices of securitization construct the world as dangerous and full of strangeness. The third, following on from this, is the important role of borders in the construction and reproduction of strangeness. Borders have a crucial role in creating the 'spaces of wonder' which not only act as a conduit for increasing strangeness but also provide the context within which the policy responses are framed. The fourth theme is that the strangeness of the world can be appropriated as a tool of governance.

Dangerousness and the Domestication of Terror

We can now consider our first 'space of wonder', the globe itself, or more specifically the uncertain and threatening world (dis)order. One key theme in the political responses of Tony Blair, John Reid and other senior UK politicians to the threat of terrorism in the UK was to emphasize the dangerousness of the post-9/11 world; a world which 'no longer makes sense'. Tony Blair was keen to assert that the world has changed post-9/11, and such a world requires a new style of politics: 'a new world order needs a new set of rules'. What is portrayed as particularly new, as Runciman (2004: 11) points out in his discussion of Blair's politics, is the risk represented by the future (uncertain, unknowable) and the impossibility of being able to fully assess the risk posed by the world's new strangeness. The perceived dangerousness of the world is utilized by politicians and policy-makers to frame responses to the threat of 'global terror'. In Albrecht's terms, 'demonisation has been replaced by the concept and strategy of "dangerisation"' (quoted in Bauman 2004: 56). But dangerousness and 'dangerization' are not merely new words to describe fears, risks and insecurities. In addition to the world order being portrayed as dangerous and unmanageable, and terrorist threats as inevitable and unpredictable, 'dangerization' offers solutions to the problems it identifies.

We can see this more clearly if we examine two policy responses occasioned by a perception of a world of terror and the idea of 'dangerousness' to which this threat has given rise. These policy responses are good examples of how the perception of globalization as the source of threats has led to the need to create novel forms of protection. One example is the 'control orders' introduced to the UK by the Blair government and designed to restrict the freedoms of suspected terrorists (without initiating criminal proceedings). The other is a recent example from the USA, the case of the suspected bombers detained in Chicago in 2006 (six men suspected of plotting to blow up the Sears Tower). Described in news reports as 'home-grown terrorists', the men were suspected of al-Qaeda sympathies (according to the charges brought against them they had 'sworn allegiance to al-Qaeda but had no contacts with it'[2]). After being charged they were refused bail on the ground that, in the opinion of the judge, they posed a danger to society.[3] This news story is of significance not because it deals with the rather odd circumstances surrounding the arrest and detention of suspected terrorists, but because of the rationale used to detain them.

Although they were thought to pose a danger to society by the judge, US government officials quoted by the BBC said, 'they posed no real threat because they had no actual al-Qaeda contacts, no weapons and no means of carrying out the attacks'.[4] Another BBC news story reported that officials said the men 'posed no danger'.[5] The BBC journalists were alert to the fact that US officials were making contradictory statements. One BBC reporter remarked that official statements both confirmed that the alleged plot was not far advanced and the terrorists were 'aspirational rather than operational', at the same time as the US Attorney General saw it as evidence that there exists a heightened possibility of home-grown terror plots.[6] Mr Gonzales said that 'the lack of direct link to al-Qaeda did not make the group any less dangerous . . . Left unchecked these home-grown terrorists may prove as dangerous as groups like al-Qaeda.'[7]

Clearly, those that pose no palpable threat can still be considered dangerous. The 'war on terror' constructs its own temporality, stretching the threat of terror into the distant future. This is because dangerousness is seen as a latent property which may only reveal itself in the future. Judith Butler, in her book *Precarious Life* (Butler 2004: 74–7) makes the point that one line of defence used by the USA for detaining 'enemy combatants' at Guantanamo Bay indefinitely and without the prospect of a trial is that they are 'dangerous people'. Butler argues that the determination of dangerousness is extra-legal and according to the new 'post-political' logic at work in these situations, establishing dangerousness trumps the need to prove guilt. According to Butler, 'a certain level of dangerousness takes a human outside the bounds of law . . . makes that human into the state's possession, infinitely detainable.

What counts as "dangerous" is what is deemed dangerous by the state' (Butler 2004: 76).

There are UK parallels in the response to 'dangerousness'. The much-debated 'control orders', introduced by the Blair government in March 2005 in cases where there is insufficient evidence to prosecute suspected terrorists, are motivated by the same need to construct dangerousness. Control orders replaced emergency laws that were introduced after 9/11 and permitted the indefinite detention of suspects, but were adjudged illegal by the House of Lords in December 2004. The newer control orders are designed to limit the mobility of suspects who to this end are tagged, confined to their homes, and restricted in their communication. Although they are applied to those deemed 'dangerous', the danger that they actually represent has been the subject of much debate. For example, Shami Chakrabarti, director of Liberty (a human rights advocacy group), was quoted by the BBC as saying 'if someone is truly a dangerous terror suspect, why would you leave them at large'.[8]

Moreover, the control orders have themselves been deemed dangerous (to individual liberties), and Britain has been criticized, by the Council of Europe, for introducing this measure. The legality, or otherwise, of control orders is in fact central to an ongoing debate on the contemporary nature of rights and freedoms in the UK. Human rights are no longer sacrosanct (a point to which we will return later in the chapter). Some members of the Labour government portray them as outmoded, brought into being by a Europe in which the memory of 'state fascism' was still fresh (Tempest 2006). In the contemporary context in which a Home Office minister can suggest the introduction of 'a stronger version of control orders which would depart from the European Convention on Human Rights', the status of 'dangerous terror suspect' in both the UK and the USA trumps mere criminality.

The extra-legal status of dangerousness is rightly flagged up by Butler for undermining the rule of law and the quality of democracy which depends upon it. However, the point that I wish to make is of a different nature. Dangerousness – indeed the very language of the fight against terror networks – works to domesticate a global threat and constructs that threat in terms which are familiar and reassuring. What sorts of things are usually described as dangerous? Escaped prisoners, vicious dogs, faulty electrical appliances, freak weather conditions. 'Dangerousness' renders a global threat into familiar and reassuring terms and makes the 'spaces of wonder' constituted by global terror networks explicable, manageable and amenable to policy solutions. The practice of labelling something dangerous is at the same time a strategy to mobilize discourses of security, and to assuage anxieties and trepidation.

Bringing the Offshore Border Back Home

The second 'space of wonder' under consideration is the UK's border and its changing configuration under contemporary conditions of insecurity. The UK border falls into the category of a 'space of wonder' for the same reason as the other two examples considered here, the world-as-global-threat and the global borderlands, because it too can be perceived as strange, unfamiliar and disorientating, lacking familiar reference points, and suggesting a new logic of cause and effect, thereby proving difficult to assimilate into existing worldviews. Many commentators have noted that the nature of borders is changing under conditions of globalization (Balibar 1998; Axford 2006; Rumford 2006). Rather than existing as 'lines in the sand' which delineate sovereign jurisdiction, borders can now take many forms. No longer only physical presences at the edges of a polity working to regulate movement and protect the domestic realm from outside threats, borders can be everywhere and anywhere: 'smart' borders, relying on high-tech biometric technology, or 'remote borders' located away from domestic ports, airports and land frontiers (Amoore 2006). It has become increasingly evident that borders are not only 'at the border': they can be elsewhere too – at airports, in railway stations, in internet cafes, and along the motorway (Walters 2006; Rumford 2007). Security functions associated with bordering have in many cases been privatized – by offloading security checks to airlines and other carriers, for example (Lahav and Guiraudon 2000).

In the UK the approach to bordering has changed significantly in recent years. In a recent publication entitled 'Securing the UK border: our vision and strategy for the future' (Home Office 2007), the UK government takes a far from conventional view of where the UK borders are to be found. No longer is it the goal of border policy to fortify and secure the traditional perimeter (although there is now some domestic political momentum for the idea of a new unified border police force[9]). The approach favoured by the UK is to move the border rather than fortify it in the standard way. The UK prefers to locate its borders 'offshore'. 'The days when border control started at the White Cliffs of Dover are over', in the words of one government spokesperson.[10] According to the 'Securing the UK border' document, 'border control can no longer be just a fixed line on a map . . . we must create a new offshore line of defence, checking individuals as far from the UK as possible'. Moreover, the aim, according to the Immigration Minister Liam Byrne, is to lay the foundation stone for 'offshore borders all over the world'.

According to the Home Office document, offshore borders are designed to combat methods of illegal entry to the UK by exercising tighter controls on the issue of travel visas throughout the world and fining airlines who carry passengers not in possession of the correct documents. An important development is the 'electronic borders' (e-borders) programme. Travellers to the UK will be required to submit full personal details prior to travel, thus allowing the UK authorities to authorize or deny permission to travel at an early stage. In developing offshore and remote borders, the UK relies heavily on the 'e-borders' technology, especially the use of biometric visas and the 'remote control' of passenger carriers. However, the government's problem is that these initiatives do not necessarily increase public confidence that the country's borders are working properly and its population is safe from terrorist attacks, traffickers and illegal immigrants. Smart borders do not have high public visibility, and the government has to be seen to be doing something reassuring. It is within this context that we can understand the August 2007 announcement that immigration officers at Gatwick Airport have been given new uniforms 'to make it clear to people that they are at a UK border'. Home Office minister Tony McNulty said, 'we are determined to improve public confidence in how immigration is managed. Key to this is the creation of highly visible staff at our borders, to deter people who have no right to be here.'

In recent times the effectiveness of the UK's borders has been the subject of much debate, with high-profile cases of illegal immigration, the massive influx of workers from the former Eastern Europe, and the ease with which foreign nationals can 'disappear' into British society, to the fore. The borders have been portrayed as ineffectual and a contributing factor to increased insecurity. At the same time the UK has been investing heavily in 'virtual' borders, a policy for which much success has been claimed (Home Office 2007) but which does little to reassure critics that the government has 'got it right'. It is for these reasons that the 'space of wonder' represented by the UK's offshore border has been subjected to a policy makeover by familiar and reassuring border images; the clear signage at UK airports that confirms that 'you are now at the UK border', and the uniforms worn by officers of the newly created Borders and Immigration Authority. The capacity of these initiatives to fortify the border is questionable: do smart uniforms really 'deter people who have no right to be here'? The suspicion remains that open borders are rather difficult to close, both in reality and through policy 'sleight of hand'. As Bauman (2006: 109) states, 'However many border security guards, biometric appliances and explosive-sniffing dogs are deployed at the ports, borders that have already been thrown open and kept open by and for free-floating capital, commodities and information can't be sealed back and kept sealed against humans.'

One consequence of moving the border offshore is that its visibility decreases at the same time as its effectiveness increases. Reconciling the contradictory faces of the offshore border is difficult to achieve. Nevertheless, the UK government has developed a strategy for doing just this. In a recent Cabinet Office document entitled 'Security in a global hub: establishing the UK's new border arrangements', the government has outlined how it aims to enhance national security while at the same time encouraging the flows and mobilities associated with economic prosperity. To this end it conceives of the border as being both a securitized barrier and an economic gateway: 'The border protects the UK from threats such as organised crime and terrorism, while at the same time facilitates the legitimate movement of goods and people on which our economy depends' (Cabinet Office 2007: 18). Moving the border offshore facilitates the management of risk associated with open borders because it allows strict border controls to be deployed where they are most needed, and at the same time permits the construction of welcoming borders 'at home' designed to reassure bona fide travellers and increase public confidence. In the words of the Cabinet Office document, 'border controls have a part to play in providing reassurance. It is important that border controls are visible and dynamic, and that staff are professional in their appearance and performance' (2007: 28) – in other words, offshore borders to deter criminals and traffickers, smart uniforms to reassure legitimate tourists and entrepreneurs travelling closer to home.

Fighting Nazis in the Global Borderlands

The third 'space of wonder' outlined here is the global borderland, a 'global space' not subject to the rule of law. This is a realm where 'global outcasts' reside, refugees, migrants, asylum-seekers living in a state of 'permanent transitoriness' (Bauman 2007: 37). It is these very qualities that make it highly suitable as a realm of global governance. The global borderland can be appropriated by powerful nation states such as the USA and the UK to pursue forms of exclusion, create barriers to global mobility, and pursue a 'politics of pre-emption' which would be most unthinkable and unacceptable in conventional domestic politics. Global borderlands are the 'spaces of wonder' within which Guantanamo Bay and Abu Ghraib have become possible, and which also allow thousands of 'illegal' immigrants to perish in the Mediterranean and Atlantic while undertaking journeys by sea or in attempts to cross into the EU at the barbed wire fences erected in the Spanish enclaves of Ceuta and Melilla in North Africa. In some places the global borderland resembles the aforementioned 'Great Wall of Europe' (Balibar 2006) designed to keep the unwanted out of Europe. This section will examine one attempt to conduct the 'war on terror' in the global borderlands.

In a speech at Kings College, London, on 20 February 2006, against a background of suspected abuse of Iraqi civilians by British troops, the then Home Secretary John Reid stated that he was not attempting to defend the indefensible. The army must be responsible for maintaining high standards. However, he was concerned with what he saw as a lack of 'balance and fairness towards our troops' who today have to fight on a 'changed and hugely uneven battlefield' (Reid 2006). It should be noted that what starts as a speech defending the actions of British soldiers in Iraq quickly mobilizes the (non-Iraqi) threat of al-Qaeda in order to frame the difficulties that those troops face. Because of media openness and the access of the terrorists to the media, our troops are under greater scrutiny than ever before. 'British troops are forced to operate on what I call "an uneven playing field of scrutiny" . . . there is now asymmetric – uneven – scrutiny of warfare' (Reid 2006).The crux of the matter is that 'it is this uneven battlefield of one-sided scrutiny which has done so much to encourage the perception among our troops that they are increasingly constrained while the enemy is freer than ever to perpetrate the most inhumane practices and crimes' (Reid 2006).

Reid argues his case for not dwelling disproportionately on isolated acts of wrongdoing by British soldiers by appealing to historical experiences of war, and more particularly to familiar oppositions such as good versus evil, and sacrifice versus freedoms, and by invoking 'core' values such as 'fairness' (which becomes counterposed to human rights). The good/evil dichotomy is based on more than a reminder that the enemy are 'beyond the pale' and possess no moral legitimacy, although this is a key motif: 'we' fight for what is right and oppose what is wrong, the adversary 'revels in mass murder' and 'sets out to cause the greatest pain it can to innocent people' (Reid 2006). To bolster the good/evil distinction Reid draws upon the enemy imagery of Hitler and the Nazis to point up the magnitude of the evil which al-Qaeda is capable of, unfettered as it is by any sense of morality: 'it is the rule of law and the virtue of freedom of expression versus barbarism' (Reid 2006).

Another key theme in Reid's speech is that of 'sacrifice versus freedoms', which again resonates with resistance to Nazism. 'Without the wartime generation that made sacrifices to defeat Hitler, we wouldn't have the means to fight this more modern evil' (Reid 2006). The freedoms referred to here are press freedoms, and the sacrifices are those associated with a curtailment of press freedom 'in the national interest', which it is assumed the media were happy to go along with during the Second World War 'in the national interest'. Reid's argument is that al-Qaeda will exploit media images for its own ends; 'it is the media's responsibility to ensure that in reporting the facts . . . it does not fall victim to this campaign' (Reid 2006). The enemy seeks to undermine our public morale by using 'our democratic freedom of speech to destroy our will to fight for our democratic values' (Reid 2006). It is a battle of ideas which, like earlier ideological struggles against communism and Nazism, can be won. In his attempts to mobilize society in the fight against terrorism ('the struggle has to be at every level, in every way and by every single person in this country'[11]) he is drawn to equate the terrorist threat to the UK with the earlier threat of Nazism: 'Britain is living in the most threatening time since the second world war.'

Reid has reiterated the 'war against the Nazis' theme on other occasions. In a talk at a conference on technology he was reported as saying that the technological race to stay ahead of extremists recalls 'innovators of the past' such as Barnes Wallis or Alan Turing during the Second World War. These individuals, Reid said, 'were vital in the technological battle to beat the then enemy, the Nazis, so we must be able to utilise the skills and expertise of all in our society in the battle against terror'.[12] Pursuing another favourite theme, the inappropriateness of human rights legislation in the 'war against terror', Reid states that 'Europe-wide human rights – such as freedom from detention, forced labour, torture and punishment without trial – had been formulated in the wake of state fascism, but were now threatened by what he dubbed "fascist individuals"' (quoted in Tempest 2006).

Another key theme in his Kings College speech is 'fairness' as opposed to human rights, and this links strongly with the previously discussed themes of good versus evil and sacrifice versus freedom. Reid reiterates that British troops go to great lengths to stay within the law, treat people fairly ('even the enemy'). Fairness is built in to military operations; the problem, however, is human rights legislation which 'has improved lives in so many areas' but 'has also sometimes become the convenient banner under which some who are fundamentally opposed to our Armed Forces, or to the government of the day, or to a particular military conflict, have chosen to march' (Reid 2006). This is a problem, states Reid, because in the soldiers' perception 'human rights lawyers and . . . the International Criminal Court are waiting in the wings to step in and act against them' (Reid 2006). They need to know that they operate under British law, not European and international law. Reid opposes 'fairness', an intrinsic decency rooted in the professionalism of an army which 'seeks to inject morality – right and wrong – into the harsh reality of warfare' (Reid 2006), to the idea of human rights, which is portrayed as well-meaning but in reality benefiting the enemy.

Former Prime Minister Tony Blair has also given a clear indication that the struggle against 'global terror' is best fought in the global borderlands. In a speech to the World Affairs Council in August 2006,[13] he stated that success in the battle against global extremism will not come about through force as such, but can be won 'at the level of values' where we can show that 'we are even-handed, fair and just in our application of those values to the world'. In this way, the 'war on terror' becomes domesticated through its translation into a battle over values rather than a war against an enemy which involves killing large numbers of civilians and 'unlawful combatants'. Pursuing this theme Blair states, 'We could have chosen security as the battlefield. But we didn't. We chose values.' The fairness invoked by Blair is both an attempt to deterritorialize the war (thereby exacerbating the global nature of the threat) and to domesticate the struggle by transcribing it within the familiar reference points of war – our decency versus their barbarism – a regular theme of British war movies, for example. Similarly, equating the enemy in the 'war on terror' with the Nazis is another attempt to domesticate strangeness, and the British government is happy to be 'still hunting Nazis' (Mestrovic 1994), this time out of choice, rather than necessity. By conducting the 'war on terror' in the global borderlands (the terrain of values, rather than conflict), it has been given a 'familiar' face; the Nazis are enemies of us all and no one can deny their evil intent or the legitimacy and justness of the struggle against them.

Concluding Comments: From Apprehension to Wonder

This chapter offers an alternative to the idea of fear as a catch-all category for understanding social policy. It is argued that through a critical awareness of 'spaces of wonder' we can better understand the ways in which policy choices are framed in order to reposition global spaces and the disorientating effects that these can have within the vernacular of everyday politics. We have examined attempts to domesticate 'spaces of wonder' through policy responses which seek to take advantage of the power of the global to create experiences of trepidation and anxiety by encroaching upon the normality of everyday existence. Such policies aim to enfold 'spaces of wonder' in discourses of familiarity. In this way the threat of global terror is localized in terms of 'dangerousness', the futuristic 'offshore borders' are 'brought back home' through new signage and smart uniforms, and the sliding standards of human rights occasioned by the 'war on terror' are justified by invoking the struggle against Nazism.

The literature on globalization has long emphasized the interconnectedness and resulting 'oneness' of the world. It has also taught us that globalization can bring negative as well as positive developments; new winners and losers, new patterns of inequality, as well as a new world of threats resulting from environmental degradation and overproduction. What is rarely confronted in the literature is that at the same time as the world is re-made by processes of globalization the world is also becoming increasingly unfamiliar. Global threats have occasioned a range of solutions which themselves have heightened a sense of insecurity and threat. This is true of the nationalisms which seek to defend the authenticity of culture at the same time as portraying that same culture as being under terminal threat from external forces, and it is also true of the gated communities which offer commoditized safety at the same time as working to remind inhabitants that the world beyond the gates is violent, unpredictable and fraught with danger. This chapter has sought to take Robertson's idea that globalization has resulted in an institutionalization of strangeness (Robertson 2007) and used this to explore the ways in which this strangeness or perception of 'stranger danger' has resulted in new opportunities for governance and in new strands of public policy which work to offer 'solutions' to everyday trepidation. To understand these social policies, it is argued, we need to focus less on the 'politics of fear' and more on 'spaces of wonder'.

Notes

1. 'Survival skills for an era of terrorism', Julia Horton, *The Guardian*, 20 August 2007. Available at: http://www.guardian.co.uk/terrorism/story/0,,2152316,00.html
2. 'US fears home-grown terror threat', *BBC News*, 24 June 2006. Available at: http://news.bbc.co.uk/1/hi/world/americas/5112354.stm
3. 'Chicago plot suspects denied bail', *BBC News*, 5 July 2006. Available at: http://news.bbc.co.uk/1/hi/world/americas/5152652.stm
4. 'Chicago plot suspects denied bail'.
5. 'US fears home-grown terror threat'.
6. James Coomarasamy, 'Home front fears in war on terror', *BBC News 24*, 4 June 2006. Available at: http://news.bbc.co.uk/1/hi/world/americas/5108582.stm
7. 'US fears home-grown terror threat'.
8. 'Terror controls "may get tougher"', *BBC News*, 17 October 2006. Available at: http://news.bbc.co.uk/1/hi/uk/6057562.stm
9. In July 2007 Prime Minister Gordon Brown announced that the UK would get a 'unified' border force 'to boost the fight against terrorism'. The new force was planned to bring together officers from the Border and Immigration Agency, Revenue and Customs, and UK Visas in order to create a 'single primary checkpoint' for passport control and customs. After the proposal was criticized for being 'a border force lite without police powers or the incorporation of the transport police' ('UK to get "unified" border force', *BBC News*, 25 July 2007), the prime minister confirmed that the police would in fact have a role ('Brown to confirm role for police in border force', *The Guardian*, 14 November 2007).
10. 'Marriage visa age to rise to 21', *BBC News*, 28 March 2007. Available at: http://news.bbc.co.uk/1/hi/uk_politics/6501451.stm
11. 'Reid makes Nazi terror comparison', *BBC News*, 31 October 2006. Available at: http://news.bbc.co.uk/1/hi/uk/6102508.stm
12. 'Reid makes Nazi terror comparison'.
13. Tony Blair, Speech to the World Affairs Council in Los Angeles, California, 1 August. Available at: http://www.number10.gov.uk/output/Page9948.asp

References

Alexander, J., Eyerman, R., Giesen, B., Smelser, N. and Sztompka, P. (2004), *Cultural Trauma and Collective Identity*, Berkeley: University of California Press.

Amoore, L. (2006), Biometric borders: governing mobilities in the war on terror, *Political Geography*, 25, 3: 336–51.

Axford, B. (2006), The dialectic of borders and networks in Europe: reviewing 'topological presuppositions', *Comparative European Politics*, 4, 2/3: 160–82.

Balibar, E. (1998), The borders of Europe. In P. Cheah and B. Robbins (eds), *Cosmopolitics: Thinking and Feeling Beyond the Nation*, Minneapolis: University of Minnesota Press.

Balibar, E. (2006), *Strangers as Enemies: Further Reflections on the Aporias of Transnational Citizenship*, Globalization Working Papers 06/4, Institute on Globalization and the Human Condition, McMaster University, Canada. Available at: http://globalization.mcmaster.ca/wps/balibar.pdf

Bauman, Z. (2004), *Wasted Lives: Modernity and its Outcasts*, Cambridge: Polity Press.

Bauman, Z. (2006), *Liquid Fear*, Cambridge: Polity Press.

Bauman, Z. (2007), *Liquid Times: Living in an Age of Uncertainty*, Cambridge: Polity Press.

Butler, J. (2004), *Precarious Life: The Powers of Mourning and Violence*, London: Verso.

Cabinet Office (2007), Security in a global hub: establishing the UK's new border arrangements. Available at: http://www.cabinetoffice.gov.uk/upload/assets/http://www.cabinetoffice.gov.uk/publications/reports/border_review.pdf

Devji, F. (2005), *Landscapes of the Jihad: Militancy, Morality and Modernity*, London: Hurst.

Eade, J. (1997), Introduction. In J. Eade (ed.), *Living the Global City: Globalization as Local Process*, London: Routledge.

Furedi, F. (2004), The politics of fear. Available at: http://www.frankfuredi.com?articles/politicsFear-20041028.shtml

Hardt, M. and Negri, A. (2000), *Empire*, Cambridge, MA: Harvard University Press.

Home Office (2007), Securing the UK border: our vision and strategy for the future. Available at: http://www.bia.homeoffice.gov.uk/6353/aboutus/Securing_the_UK_Border_final.pdf

Huysmans, J. (2006), *The Politics of Insecurity: Fear, Migration and Asylum in the EU*, London: Routledge.

Lahav, G. and Guiraudon, V. (2000), Comparative perspectives on border control: away from the border and outside the state. In P. Andreas and T. Snyder (eds), *The Wall Around the West: State Borders and Immigration Controls in North America and Europe*, Lanham, MD: Rowman and Littlefield.

McGrew, A. (1995), World order and political space. In J. Anderson, C. Brook and A. Cochrane (eds), *A Global World? Re-ordering Political Space*, Oxford: Oxford University Press.

Mestrovic, S. (1994), *The Balkanization of the West: The Confluence of Postmodernism and Postcommunism*, London: Routledge.

Reid, J. (2006), We must be 'slower to condemn, quicker to understand' the Forces. Speech given at Kings College, University of London, 20 February. Available at: http://www.mod.uk/DefenceInternet/DefenceNews/DefencePolicyAndBusiness/WeMustBeSlowerToCondemnQuickerToUnderstandTheForcesJohnReid.htm

Robertson, R. (1992), *Globalization: Social Theory and Global Culture*, London: Sage.

Robertson, R. (2007), Open societies, closed minds? Exploring the ubiquity of suspicion and voyeurism, *Globalizations*, 4, 3: 399–416.

Robertson, R. and White, K. (2007), What is globalization? In G. Ritzer (ed.), *The Blackwell Companion to Globalization*, Oxford: Blackwell.

Robin, C. (2004), *Fear: The History of a Political Idea*, Oxford: Oxford University Press.

Rumford, C. (2006), Introduction: theorizing borders, *European Journal of Social Theory*, 9, 2: 155–69.

Rumford, C. (2007), Does Europe have cosmopolitan borders? *Globalizations*, 4, 3: 327–39.

Rumford, C. (2008), Finding meaning in meaningless times: emotional responses to terror threats in London. In A. Closs and N. Vaughan-Williams (eds), *Terrorism and the Politics of Response: London in a Time of Terror*, London: Routledge.

Runciman, D. (2004), *The Politics of Good Intentions: History, Fear, and Hypocrisy in the New World Order*, Princeton, NJ: Princeton University Press.

Sassen, S. (1991), *The Global City: New York, London, Tokyo*, Princeton, NJ: Princeton University Press.

Tempest, M. (2006), Britain facing 'most sustained threat since WWII', says Reid, *The Guardian*, 9 August. Available at: http://politics.guardian.co.uk/terrorism/story/0,,1840482,00.html

Walters, W. (2006), Rethinking borders beyond the state, *Comparative European Politics*, 4, 2/3: 141–59.

7

Fear and Security: A Vulnerability-led Policy Response

Frank Furedi

In an age of insecurity, the response of a community to the threat it faces can play a decisive role in influencing the impact. This is clearly the case in relation to terrorism, where its impact is shaped by the response of a community to it. As one leading academic expert on the subject observes, it is not the terrorist but the sense of vulnerability that in the end influences how society engages with this threat (Freedman 2005: 10). That is one reason why policy-makers and emergency planners appear to be so devoted to the project of promoting the public's resilience. However, official focus on resilience is not confined to the domain of counter-terrorist policy-making. In recent years resilience has been adopted as an all-purpose policy objective for countering any disruptive challenge to everyday life. The UK Cabinet Office's report *Dealing with Disaster* claims that the 'central government's approach to civil contingency planning is built around the concept of resilience' (Cabinet Office Civil Contingencies Secretariat 2003: para. 1.1). The Cabinet Office's Civil Contingencies Secretariat, which was established in 2001, is charged with leading the delivery of 'improved resilience across the government and the public sector' (Cabinet Office 2007). In 2004 under the initiative UK Resilience, the government adopted an approach that embraced what it called 'high-profile risks' such as foot and mouth disease, flooding, avian influenza and a human flu pandemic (UK Resilience 2007).

The promotion of resilience is not confined to countering a small number of dramatic 'high-profile risks'. Government policy-makers advocate the virtues of resilience as a solution to problems in health, education and social policy. For example, the Department for Children, Schools and Families sponsors 'Risk and Resilience Workshops' as part of its Every Child Matters Programme (Every Child Matters 2006). Sure Start also represents the resilience of children as one of its objectives. The government's education campaign against drug abuse is directed towards 'young people and families to promote resilience against drug use' (DirectGov 2007). Policy advisers, think tanks and academics frequently discuss resilience as the solution to the problem of risk. The title of a research project 'Risk and Resilience' run by the Institute of Public Policy Research implicitly points to a taken-for-granted inverse relationship between the two (IPPR 2006). UK Resilience acclaims 'the Government's aim', which is to 'reduce the risk from emergencies so that people can go about their business freely and with confidence' (UK Resilience 2007). As we argue in this contribution, the adoption of resilience as a policy objective is motivated by the belief that society has become vulnerable to a growing range of threats to its security. Paradoxically, the growing usage of the rhetoric of resilience in official discourse is informed by a powerful mood of insecurity that encourages a *vulnerability-led* response to uncertainty (Furedi 2007: ch. 5).

A Concept in Search of Meaning

The growing tendency to frame policy through the medium of resilience has not been matched by greater clarification of the concept. Indeed, the term 'resilience' remains a relatively underdeveloped one. It is frequently used in a metaphor-like manner to describe factors that may protect individuals or communities from risks.[1] The focus on resilience as an antidote to risk informed the discussion around the Civil Contingencies Bill. The importance attached to the promotion of resilience was justified on the grounds of its alleged ability to contain 'risks of disruptive challenge' which 'must where possible be identified, either by considering internal weaknesses or scanning the horizon for external threats' (Cabinet Office 2003: ch. 2, para. 3). In official language the term resilience refers to any institutional or organizational attribute that contributes to the management of risks.

However, although it is claimed that the concept of resilience 'underpins' the Draft Civil Contingencies Bill (Cabinet Office 2003), it is far from evident what are the processes that are captured by this concept. The report offers a very general description of resilience. It is defined as the ability 'at every relevant level to detect, prevent, and if necessary, to handle and recover from disruptive challenges'. It is worth noting that although this key concept is mentioned in the first paragraph of the *Draft Civil Contingencies Bill: Consultation Document*, it is not elaborated in this 96-page report. Indeed, it is evident that UK government officials do not have a single agreed definition of resilience. According to the *Draft Civil Contingencies Bill: Consultation Document* (Cabinet Office 2003), 'resilience is the ability to handle disruptive challenges that can result in crisis'. But after a close examination of this text it is difficult to be sure what exactly is meant by this term (see Denney, this volume). It seems that resilience is used as a synonym for effective emergency planning. Apparently, it is also 'the ability – at every level – to anticipate, pre-empt and resolve challenges into healthy outcomes' and 'the key to resilience is agility'. The reference to 'every level' tends to refer to institutions and organizations associated with emergency planning and the state. Reading between the lines one can easily draw the conclusion that resilience refers to capabilities associated with emergency planning and institutions of the state rather than to communities of people. Take the following account of official thinking by Bruce Mann, Head of the Civil Contingencies Secretariat:

The Civil Contingencies Secretariat, set up in 2001, has sought to promote the notion of 'resilience' – the ability to respond to an emergency, minimise and absorb any damage, and recover. We see this being the responsibility of a 'resilience community' engaging practitioners at all levels – national, regional and local – and involving not just public sector emergency planners and responders, but the private, business, and voluntary sectors as well, in a campaigning partnership to improve preparedness. (Mann 2007)

Mann's orientation is towards institutional capacity and adaptability. From his perspective the 'resilience community' encompasses emergency planners and technocrats but not the public. As we will argue, the tendency to displace the idea of a resilient community of people by a resilience community of experts has important implications for the way that policy-makers regard the role of the public.

The lack of clarity about the meaning of resilience in official documents is not surprising. It mirrors the lack of precision about its usage in expert communications and academic literature. There is no consensus definition of resilience. Matters are not helped by the fact that different academic disciplines and private and public organizations have diverse perspectives about the relevance of resilience and its meaning. Nevertheless, as Kendra and Wachtendorf note, the different literatures tend to associate resilience with an ability to withstand shock (2002: 11). They believe that most conceptions of resilience 'involve some idea of adapting to and "bouncing back" from a disruption'.

Definitions of resilience are often predicated on the agenda of authors. Psychologists have explored resilience from the point of view of the individual's capacity to engage with risk and sometimes treat it as an individual character trait (Waller 2001: 3). In contrast, management theorists tend to regard resilience as the outcome of particular forms of organizational and management styles. According to one account, 'resilience is a fundamental quality of individuals, groups, organizations, and systems as a whole to respond productively to significant change that disrupts the expected pattern of events without engaging in an extended period of regressive behaviour' (Horne and Orr 1998: 31).

The absence of an agreed definition of resilience need not necessarily be a problem. It can often serve as prelude to a debate that can lead to conceptual clarity. It is, however, a problem when such a widely used concept and policy objective is used in a taken-for-granted manner, since there is a danger that it will play the role of a cultural metaphor rather than an analytical concept. The absence of a self-conscious engagement with the analytical status of the concept means that it works mainly as a rhetorical idiom used to signify the desirability of managing risks.

Resilience: Defined by its Absence

Since 9/11 officials in Britain and the United States frequently acclaim the need for cultivating the resilience of the public. For example, one American advocate of the National Resilience Development Act of 2003 stated that 'the importance of improving the psychological resilience of the American population cannot be overstated'. According to him, the goal of this Act was to 'coordinate the efforts of different government agencies in researching, developing, and implementing programs and protocols designed to increase the psychological resilience and mitigate distress reactions and maladaptive behaviours of the American public as they relate to terrorism' (Barnett 2004: 64–5). What's interesting about this statement is that while it goes beyond the usual concern with institutional adaptability and focuses on people's behaviour, it assumes that resilience is not a normal state but the outcome of policies and programmes dedicated to its realization. It is not a condition that exists by itself. On both sides of the Atlantic official policies towards resilience appear to be defined by its absence

Our analysis of official discourse leads us to conclude that experts do not think that resilience can flourish by itself. Officials do not seem to have much faith in the ability of the public to act with resilience. On the contrary, policy-makers tend to assume that the response of the public to an act of terrorism or unexpected risk is likely to be characterized by a mood of vulnerability rather than resilience. As I note elsewhere, political elites often recycle their own uncertainties about the future through attributing to the wider public a fragile and defeatist mentality (Furedi 2007: ch. 1). Its elevated sense of danger is expressed through a lack of confidence in the capacity of the public to deal with a terrorist attack. Gone are the days when the people were regarded as a source of strength. In the twenty-first century policy-makers do not expect people to respond robustly to acts of terrorism. They assume that a terrorist attack is likely to lead to mass panic and the breakdown of social norms and civil behaviour. As US General Tommy Franks warned, a 'massive casualty-producing event somewhere in the western world' could lead American people to 'question our own Constitution and to begin to militarize the country' and to risk the loss of 'what it cherishes most, and that is freedom and liberty' (cited in Mueller 2006: 45).

According to one study, 'the perception of the public as inherently prone to panic in the face of scenarios such as a chemical, biological, radiological (CBR), or mass casualty conventional attack is pervasive' (Sheppard et al. 2006: 220). Another study speculates that the 'United Kingdom might prove to be rather brittle in the face of a CBRN [chemical, biological, radiological or nuclear] attack – there might be a demoralizing sense of defencelessness, particularly if unknown and invisible agents and pollutants are used, and possibly even widespread panic' (Cornish 2007: 3). Ideas about how the public is likely to respond to a terrorist attack have an important influence on the conceptualization of this threat. If emergency planners anticipate public panic they are likely to opt for vulnerability-led policy recommendations.

Emergency planners, politicians and security experts appear to believe that the public is unlikely to possess the resilience necessary to cope with a violent terrorist incident. The apprehension that communities lack the capacity to bounce back and thrive after a such an incident informs government policy. That is why resilience is represented as a kind of protective vaccine injected into the body politic from outside. The everyday official usage of resilience suggests that the term is underpinned by the assumption that resilience is not a phenomenon that can be relied on to flourish by itself. Frequently it is used as a *second-order concept* that is subordinate to the more powerful condition of vulnerability. Academic literature too depicts resilience as a counter-trend to the dominant state – which is that of vulnerability. This point is rarely made explicit, but in most of the discussion around the threat of terrorism, vulnerability is perceived as the norm and resilience is presented as a potential counter-trend against it. The term resilience tends to be used in a way that presupposes the primacy of vulnerability – resilience is the exception, the modifying factor, rather than the defining state (Waller 2001). In many accounts vulnerability is conceptualized as both logically and chronologically prior to resilience. Indeed, resilience is sometimes presented as a phase that is encompassed by a more dominant working of vulnerability: 'while a focus on reducing risk directs attention to mitigating or containing the phenomenon causing harm to a community – whether it be fire, floods, or terrorist attacks – vulnerability encompasses the community's responsiveness and resilience in the face of loss' (Clarke and Chenoweth 2006: 12). According to this model resilience represents a dimension of the response to a pre-existing state of vulnerability. So two academic supporters of the British government's policy focus on vulnerability warn that its initiative 'is likely to be no more than a panacea unless it includes the wider agenda of vulnerabilities' (O'Brien and Read 2005: 354). Vulnerability is presented as the normal condition that makes people susceptible to 'harm and in turn affect[s] their ability to respond and bounce back (resilience), after the disaster' (Cutter 2005: 2).

Vulnerability-led Policy Response

Since 9/11 the predominant approach to threats to security can be described as vulnerability-led. A heightened sense of vulnerability has encouraged an attitude of fatalism, pessimism and a dread of terrorism. There is almost an obsessive desire to represent vulnerability as the sensibility that dominates the public imagination. The reigning paradigm of vulnerability has fostered a climate where terrorism is represented as what Tony Blair described as an 'existential threat'. It is as if the very anticipation of an act of terror serves to expose the wounds of the collective psyche. 'America the vulnerable' summed up the self-diagnosis of many Americans about their circumstances after 9/11. Bush articulated this sentiment in statements that tended to magnify the scale of destruction suffered by the United States as a result of this catastrophe. In numerous post-9/11 speeches he emphasized the gravity of the threat to the US economy and to the American way of life posed by this attack. He also repeatedly stressed that Americans are 'hurting' and feel vulnerable. According to Bush it was the very condition of an open, democratic industrial society that served to render the USA vulnerable to terrorism. He stated:

the characteristics of American society that we cherish – our freedom, our openness, our great cities and towering skyscrapers, our modern transportation systems – make us vulnerable to terrorism of catastrophic proportions. America's vulnerability to terrorism will persist long after we bring justice to those responsible for the events of September II. (cited in Mitchell 2004: 64)

Bush's association of freedom and prosperity with a disposition to vulnerability reveals a radical reversal of the way in which modern, relatively open industrial societies make sense of themselves. In previous times democracy and industrial might were associated with national security. These dimensions of a modern democratic society were seen as a source of strength and flexibility. That these features of American life are now regarded as markers of vulnerability is testimony to an important shift in officialdom's conceptualization of security. Technological innovation and the evolution of an efficient network of cooperation are represented as a source of vulnerability rather than of prosperity and resilience. This point is reiterated by a British analyst who associates the prevailing sense of vulnerability with the 'information revolution' where governments find themselves 'ever more interconnected' with changes that 'reverberate unpredictably – and often chaotically' throughout society' (Edwards 2006: 5). From this perspective change itself is directly responsible for bestowing a sense of vulnerability on society.

What is striking about the threat assessments made by political leaders and their officials is the lack of confidence they have in the resilience of their own institutions and people. Rather than seeing technology and innovation as resources that can be mobilized against terrorism, policy-makers and security analysts interpret them as a source of vulnerability. This point is echoed by academic contributions on the 'risk society'. Writing in this vein, the German sociologist Ulrich Beck claims that 'the terrorist dangers we face expand exponentially with technical progress' (Beck 2003: 260). The same point is asserted by the American sociologist Lee Clarke, who asserts that 'modern organization and technologies bring other new opportunities to harm faraway people' (Clarke 2006: 34). From this standpoint, Western technological power serves to empower the terrorist.

The very fruits of human development and prosperity that were until recently seen as essential for providing society with protection and security have become a source of concern because they have the potential to serve as instruments of terrorist destruction. Numerous contributions on this subject insist that any technology can be transformed into a terrorist weapon. From this perspective a technology has a dual use. It can be used for the purpose for which it was originally designed or it can be turned into a weapon. So a passenger plane can fly people to their destination or be turned into a weapon that can crash into a building. 'Attackers can use the diffusion capacity of our large critical networks and turn them against the target population so that each element of the network (e.g. every aircraft, every piece of mail) now becomes a potential weapon', argues a contribution on the dual use idea (Kunreuther and Michel-Kerjan 2004: 4).

A mature, complex, technologically sophisticated society is often represented as powerless against the actions of small groups of determined individuals. It is as if the relation of power has been reversed to the benefit of those lacking economic and technological resources. Indeed, it is sometimes claimed that it is the success of Western economies that makes them so intensely vulnerable to the threat of terrorism. According to one account, vulnerability is the product of growing complexity and interconnectedness. It states that 'the advantage in this war has shifted toward terrorists'. Moreover, 'our increased vulnerability – and our newfound recognition of that vulnerability . . . makes us more risk-averse, while terrorists have become more powerful and more tolerant of risk'. Consequently, it is claimed that 'terrorists have significant leverage to hurt us' (Homer-Dixon 2002: 12).

A vulnerability-led analysis of contemporary times tends to regard society one-sidedly as a target and people as victims. Such an orientation tends to focus on the task of avoiding losses rather than looking for opportunities for managing uncertainty. *Its defining feature is a powerful sense of vulnerability to risk and an inflated assessment of the threat it faces.* Public pronouncements often take the form of an alarmist oracle. According to one commentary on Blair and Bush's post-9/11 statements, they tended to exaggerate 'the terrorist threat at every level', so that their speeches communicate 'general anxiety and vulner-ability' (Johnson 2002: 215). Vulnerability has turned into the dominant idiom through which the threat of terrorism is represented and experienced. Numerous contributions insist that terrorist risk should be addressed through an analysis of society's vulnerability. After noting how a 'handful of determined individuals' so 'greatly disrupted the world's most powerful nation' on 9/11, Paul Slovic, a leading US expert on risk perception, demanded that 'risk analysis should be supplemented by "vulnerability analysis", which characterises the forms of physical, social, political, economic, cultural and psychological harms to which individuals and modern societies are susceptible' (Slovic 2002: 425). 'I think we haven't paid enough attention to how vulnerable we are to worst case events', argues Lee Clarke (Clarke 2006: 35).

A vulnerability-led response to terrorism is likely to foster a climate that intensifies people's feeling of insecurity and fear. In turn, the search for vulnerabilities invariably leads to the discovery of weaknesses that have the potential to turn virtually any institution in any place into a terrorist target. The steady proliferation of such targets inevitably follows threat assessments that are vulnerability-led. One of the unfortunate consequences of a vulnerability-led response is that virtually every dimension of social life is perceived as a terrorist target. It is as if Western societies have come to think of themselves as sitting ducks living in a state of vulnerability. According to the Office of Homeland Security, 'our society presents an almost infinite array of potential targets that can be attacked through a variety of methods'. It claims that with so many targets the terrorists enjoy 'tactical advantages' since the reduction of vulnerability in one sphere simply encourages terrorists to look for a target somewhere else. 'As we reduce our vulnerabilities in one area, they can alter their plans and pursue more exposed targets', it notes (Office of Homeland Security 2002: vii and 4). With so much of everyday life transformed into a potential target, vulnerability is increasingly experienced as a defining condition of existence. Some analysts recognize that an orientation towards vulnerability may inadvertently help those who are looking for targets to attack. 'Parading our worst fears could encourage the terrorists' desire to acquire unconventional means of attack', writes David Omand, the British government's former Security and Intelligence Coordinator. Nevertheless, he adds that 'the tragic scenes in New Orleans in the aftermath of Hurricane Katrina were a terrifying reminder of the vulnerability to massive disruption of those who live in modern cosmopolitan cities, and of the fragility of the complex systems that support food, water and sewage distribution, medical services, telecommunications and power' (Omand 2005: 111).

As the consciousness of vulnerability dominates the official imagination, threat assessment often acquires the form of worst-case thinking. Instead of asking the question 'what do we know?', opinion-formers opt to speculate and ask the 'what-if question'. As Jenkins argues, 'in present attempts to anticipate and prepare for what terrorists might do next, virtually no scenario is dismissed' (Jenkins 2006: 119). Traditional threat analysis 'assessed an enemy's intentions and capabilities', notes Jenkins, whereas today's 'vulnerability-based analysis identifies a weakness and hypothesizes a terrorist and a worst-case scenario' (Jenkins 2006: 120). One of the principal problems with this approach is that the worst-case scenarios have a habit of migrating from the realm of speculation into the official imagination. They often assume the status of a new cultural norm. 'Often, such a scenario is reified and becomes a threat: it is successively considered possible, probable, inevitable', warns Jenkins. As a result, the threat of terrorism may become inflated as the intentions of terrorist groups become confused with policy-makers' fears. As Jenkins concludes, the 'terrorists' actual capabilities, ambitions blur with our own speculation and fears to create what the terrorists want: an atmosphere of alarm'. In other words, society ends up inadvertently terrorizing itself.

Too often the vulnerability-led approach helps consolidate a mood of helplessness. Such a response can only encourage acts of terror. Bill Durodie has noted that 'assuming far-fetched scenarios and acting as if these were true' has led to a situation where instead of asking 'what if' questions that call for specific evidence there is a shift to 'asking more speculative or anticipatory "What if?" type questions' (Durodie 2005: 46). 'What if they contaminate the milk supply?' 'What if a train carrying nuclear fuel is hijacked?' 'What if a toxic biological substance infects the water supply?' 'What if' thinking encourages speculation which in turn can transform previously untroubled aspects of life into targets. Such thinking distracts attention from the far more productive questions of 'what can' and 'what is likely' to happen.

The Consolidation of 'What If' Thinking

The unprecedented sensitivity of policy-makers to the condition of vulnerability is strikingly reflected in a radically new orientation towards how risks are perceived and managed. The traditional association of risk with probabilities is now under fire from a growing body of opinion that believes that society lacks the knowledge to calculate them. Numerous critics of *probabilistic thinking* call for a radical break with past practices on the ground that in today's uncertain world we simply lack the information to calculate probabilities of high-consequence risks. Environmentalists in particular have been in the forefront of constructing arguments that devalue probabilistic thinking. They claim that the long-term irreversible damage caused to the environment cannot be calculated and therefore a probability-based risk analysis is irrelevant. However, once risk is detached from probabilities it ceases to be a risk. Such a phenomenon is no longer subject to calculation. Instead of risk assessment, the use of intuition is called for.

The emergence of a speculative approach towards risk is paralleled by the growing influence of *possibilistic* thinking. Possibilistic thinking invites speculation about what can possibly go wrong. In our culture of fear, frequently what can possibly go wrong is confused with what is likely to happen (Furedi 2007: ch. 3).

The shift towards possibilistic thinking is driven by a powerful sense of cultural pessimism about society's ability to manage high-consequence risks to its security. The cumulative outcome of this sensibility is the routinization of the expectation of worst possible outcomes. The principal question posed by possibilistic thinking, 'what can possibly go wrong?', continually invites the answer 'everything'. The connection between possibilistic and worst-case thinking is self-consciously promoted by the advocates of this approach. The American sociologist Lee Clarke acknowledges that 'worst case thinking is *possibilistic* thinking' and that it is 'very different' from the 'modern approach to risk', which is 'based on probabilistic thinking' (Clarke 2006: 5). However, he believes that the kind of dangers confronting humanity today require us to expect the worst and demand a different attitude towards risk. He claims that 'modern social organization and technologies bring other new opportunities to harm faraway people'. 'Nuclear explosions, nuclear accidents, and global warming' are some of the examples he uses.

Warning us about 'how vulnerable we are to worst case events', Clarke concludes that 'we ought to prepare for possible untoward events that are out of control and overwhelming' (Clarke 2006: 35).

Politicians and their officials have also integrated worst-case thinking into their response to terrorism and other types of catastrophic threats. Appeals to the authority of risk assessment still play an important role in policy-making. However, the prevailing culture of fear dictates that probabilistic-led risk management constantly competes with, and often gives way to, possibilistic-driven worst-case policies. As an important study of Blair's policy on terrorism notes, he combines an appeal to risk assessment with worst-case thinking. David Runciman, the author of this study, observed that in his response to the threat of terrorism 'Blair relied on expert risk assessment and on his own intuitions'. Runciman added that Blair 'highlighted the importance of knowing the risk posed by global terrorism, all the while insisting that when it comes to global terrorism the risks are never fully knowable' (Runciman 2006: 11). In practice, the co-existence of these two forms of threat assessment tends to be resolved in favour of the possibilistic approach. The occasional demand for a restrained and low-key response to the risk of terrorism is overwhelmed by the alarmist narrative of worst-case scenario.[2]

The swing from probabilistic to possibilistic thinking is closely linked to changing society-wide attitudes and perceptions of the future. Increasingly, the future is perceived as predetermined and independent of present human activities. It is an unknown world of hidden terror. The amplification of threat and of fear is inextricably linked with possibilistic thinking. As Lipschutz, argues, the 'paradox of unknowability' leading to 'worst case analysis' reinforces the 'narratives of fear' of terrorism' (Lipschutz 1999: 17). The future of the world appears to be a far darker and frightening one when perceived through the prism of possibilities rather than probabilities. Probabilities can be calculated and managed and adverse outcomes can be minimized. In contrast, worst-case thinking sensitizes the imagination to just that – worst cases! Clarke acknowledges the contrast between these two ways of perceiving the future. He notes that 'if we imagine the future in terms of probabilities, then risks look safe', but 'if we imagine the future in terms of possibilities, however, horrendous scenarios appear' (Clarke 2006: 42). While it is simplistic and inaccurate to suggest that probability analysis works towards portraying the future as safe, it is definitely the case that worst-case thinking strives to highlight the worst. Possibilistic interpretation of problems works to normalize the expectation of worst possible outcomes and fosters a one-sided and fatalistic consciousness of the future. Why? Because it minimizes the potential for understanding a threat. Since understanding is a precondition for countering a problem, the declaration of ignorance intensifies a sense of impotence, which in turn augments the threat.

Cultivating a Response of Powerlessness to an Act of Terror

Through vulnerability-led policies the sense of powerlessness is cultivated as part of the normal state of being. The positing of people as victims of circumstances reflects Western cultural sensibilities towards the supposed unprecedented uncertainties confronting twenty-first-century society. In this era of uncertainties Western culture nevertheless succeeds in communicating a sense of certainty about the enduring quality of vulnerability. It is remarkable just how prevalent the idea of human powerlessness has become. The emphasis placed on human vulnerability in worst-case scenarios dooms people to the role of helpless victims of circumstances. The deflation in the status of human agency coincides with the inflation of threats such as that of terrorism. In this scenario, the counterposition of the helpless self to the overwhelming force of the external world helps validate the proposition that people lack the power to contain the challenge of terror. As Linenthal recorded in his survey, the Oklahoma bombing was internalized by people; the 'traumatic vision' of the event strongly influenced the public's reaction. This 'traumatic vision' revealed a self that was 'intrinsically weak, passive, seemingly helpless amid the onslaughts of traumatic events' (Linenthal 2001: 92).

The possibilistic orientation to risk signals a fundamental redefinition of the relationship between people and risk. According to this paradigm people do not so much take risks as suffer their consequences. Vulnerable people cannot manage the uncertainties facing them. That is why officials increasingly devise policies to 'support' so-called vulnerable groups, the vulnerable and the recently invented construct of 'vulnerable adults'. According to the official UK definition, a vulnerable adult is someone 'who is or may be in need of community care services by reason of mental or other disability, of age or illness; and who is or may be unable to take care of him or herself, or unable to protect him or herself against significant harm or exploitation' (Lord Chancellor's Department 1997). Here vulnerable adults are represented as biologically mature children who require official and professional support. Reading between the lines it is difficult to avoid the conclusion that policy-makers readily apply such infantilizing assumptions to a wider section of a 'vulnerable society'. The emphasis of this definition is on lack of agency of the vulnerable. It is worth noting that since 1997 there has been a steady expansion of the definition of the vulnerable adult. The Care Standard Act (2000) provides a definition that includes virtually anyone in receipt of regular medical support. A vulnerable adult is someone 'to whom prescribed services are provided by an independent hospital, independent clinic, independent medical agency or National Health Service body'.

Since the mid-1990s, policies are justified on the grounds that they 'support' a particular target group. Policy aims not so much to 'solve' problems as to support otherwise disempowered clients. This is particularly the case with policies that are designed to deal with the vulnerable. The manner in which vulnerability is framed is used to convey the impression that people suffer from vulnerability as a condition of their existence. Their disadvantage is conceptualized as a 'condition people are in, not something that is done to them' (Fairclough 2000: 54–5). It is worth noting that the official definition of the vulnerable adult serves as the point of departure for policy-making in general. So a Better Regulation Task Force Report, *Protecting Vulnerable People*, merely adds 'poverty related vulnerability', 'location related vulnerability', 'technology related vulnerability' and numerous other deficits to the concerns associated with vulnerable adults (Better Regulation Task Force 2000: 9–10). Institutional responses to mental health deficits serve as a model through which policy-makers 'support' other vulnerable groups.

An analysis of UK- and US-based newspapers through the database LexisNexis and the index of *The Times* and *New York Times* indicates that the presentation of vulnerability as an enduring condition is a relatively recent development. It is mainly since the 1990s that groups presumed to deserve economic, social or moral support tend to be described as 'vulnerable' or 'the vulnerable' or 'the most vulnerable'. Government publications on health, education, crime and welfare continually refer to the targets of their policy as 'vulnerable children', 'vulnerable adults' or just as 'the vulnerable'. Such official reports echo the media narrative of vulnerability which conveys a diffuse sense of powerlessness through this term.

The past three decades have seen a steady expansion of people and groups who are defined or who present themselves as vulnerable. In the 1960s and 1970s the term was mainly but very selectively applied to children and the elderly. In the 1980s, ethnic minorities, the homeless, single parents, the mentally ill, people in care and the unemployed were added to this list. A search of UK newspapers indicates that since the 1990s, vulnerability has encompassed the experience of a new range of emotional distress of 'depressed men', 'stressed employees' and 'career women'. In more recent times, young Muslim men, university students, teenagers under pressure to be thin, people addicted to Internet pornography are only a small sample of the ever-growing constituencies who have been characterized as vulnerable (*Observer* 2003). A similar pattern is evident in the United States. By the 1990s the term vulnerable was commonly used to refer to virtually every group facing a difficult predicament. One *New York Times* headline 'We're All Vulnerable Now' illustrates this sensibility (*New York Times* 1998).

The relationship between vulnerability and the wider global threats to human existence is most clearly represented through the concept of being 'at risk'. The conceptualization of being at risk is a relatively recent innovation that is bound up with the crisis thinking of the 1980s. The concept of *being at risk* encapsulates an outlook which is dramatically different from the classical notion of *taking a risk*. The formulation 'to take a risk' contains the assumption that individuals can both exercise choice and choose to explore and experiment. Taking a risk has as its premise active subjects whose actions have the potential to realize positive outcomes and to alter their circumstances. In contrast, the concept 'being at risk' reverses the previous relationship between human beings and experience. To be at risk assigns to the person a passive and dependent role. To be at risk is no longer about what you do – it is about who you are. It is an acknowledgement of powerlessness – at least in relation to that risk. Increasingly, someone defined as being at risk is seen to exist in a permanent condition of vulnerability (Furedi 2006: ch. 2).

It can be argued that this perspective encourages the securitization of social policy. The vulnerable need to be not only supported but also protected. Hence the police are assigned a significant role in the management of vulnerability. This point was stressed by Sir Ronnie Flanagan – head of Inspectorate of Constabulary – when he argued that the police had to develop their ability to protect vulnerable people (cited in the *Guardian* 2006). Vulnerability-led social policy not only relies on policing its targets; it also adopts a highly interventionist style of behaviour management. The government's recently launched Family Interventionist Programme has as its focus 'early intervention' to prevent bad behaviour 'spiralling into offending'. According to one of its proponents Graham Allen, Labour MP for Nottingham North, 'our target is to break the cycle, so that the kids who are born into some of the poorest and most vulnerable families today have a realistic chance of getting the skills and qualifications they need to find a job and become active members of society' (BBC 2008). Prevention, pre-emption and policing are key dimensions of vulnerability-led social policy.

Fostering Insecurity

The question at issue is not whether one chooses vulnerability or resilience as the norm or defining condition of individuals and their community. Rather, the problem is the representation of resilience as merely an antidote to a prior problem. Downsizing the status of resilience to a secondary role also indicates that far from being natural it is perceived as a reaction that needs to be stimulated from the outside. If resilience is depicted as a kind of cultural pain-relief to a community suffering from an illness, it will lack any organic relationship to society. This orientation inevitably turns resilience into a secondary and relatively minor dimension of a community's response. Yet as the experience of the 7 July bombings, for example, indicates, people have 'natural coping mechanisms' and resilience can thrive during and even in the aftermath of a terrorist incident (Drury and Cocking 2007: 27). Although sections of the media celebrated the resilience demonstrated by the people of London, policy-makers continue to act as if this response was exceptional.

The tendency for policy-makers and experts to both internalize and recycle the paradigm of vulnerability is also regrettable because it uncritically serves to reinforce the passive side of public life. Yet recent reviews of the experience of human response to terrorism and violence indicate that policy-makers often underestimate the resilience of their citizens. According to one analysis of the evidence from the 1995 sarin attack in Tokyo, 'from 9/11, from the 2001 anthrax attacks, and from the 7 July 2005 London bombings' it appears that 'panic does not typically break out following a CBR terrorist strike or a mass casualty attack'. The authors conclude that 'society is reasonably resilient' (Sheppard *et al.* 2006: 223). A similar conclusion is also drawn by a recently published survey of the available evidence. It stated that 'far from being the typical reaction to a disaster, panic is actually rare' (Drury and Cocking 2007: 9). Interviews carried out with survivors of terrorist incidents also confirm the absence of mass panic and the relative absence of selfish behaviour. Accounts provided to researchers by survivors and witnesses to the 7 July London bombings indicate that although people talked of 'panic' there was no mass panic. The researchers observed that 'far from the classic stereotype of mass panic in disasters, we found next to no evidence for this concept in people's reactions to the July 7th bombings, despite the word "panic" being used quite liberally in both press and eye-witness accounts' (Drury and Cocking 2007: 24). In line with experience in comparable situations the survivors reported that cooperation and helping were common and that selfish behaviour was rare.

Disasters are, of course, terrible tragedies that can have devastating consequences for individuals and community alike. But disasters also provide an opportunity for a community to come to know itself and discover not only its weaknesses but also its strengths. Experience indicates that this process is invariably realized through the emerging informal organization that comes into being in the aftermath of a disaster. As Kendra and Wachtendorf's study of resilience in the aftermath of 9/11 argues, 'creative thinking, flexibility and the ability to improvise in newly emergent situations is vital' (Kendra and Wachtendorf 2002: 52). These responses are often the product of informal solutions arrived at under the pressure of unexpected events. It is a process through which individuals, local institutions and communities learn to develop their resilience. Unfortunately, the tendency to professionalize disaster response may deprive a community of an opportunity to develop its resilience and inadvertently reinforce a sense of passivity and helplessness.

In the post-9/11 environment, an intellectual reorientation towards the conceptualization of potential sources of community resilience is crucial. As Pupavac notes, 'salutogenic studies, which explore people's resilience, are relatively rare in trauma literature and have been overlooked in disaster planning in recent decades' (Pupavac 2004: 55). This point is echoed by

Joseph, Williams and Yule, who state that 'at present disaster research is constrained by its focus on maladaptive responses' (Joseph *et al.* 1993: 228). The relative absence of interest in what some psychologists call community 'hardiness' is understandable in light of the powerful cultural forces that promote the emotional sensibility of vulnerability (Waysman *et al.* 2001). Yet community resilience has proved to be a vital resource when people are confronted with adversity. Politicians and experts should not simply pay lip service to it but devise policies that are resilience-led.

As noted previously, one of the principal problems with the current conceptualization of resilience is that it leaves the prior premise of a universal state of vulnerability untouched. Resilience is used in a way that presupposes the primacy of vulnerability. It is the exception, the modifying factor – rather than the defining state. However, the experience of resilience is not one that can be reduced to a factor isolated from the rest of social experience. It is inextricably intertwined with the everyday life of a community. Underpinned by a sense of individual coherence gained through being embedded in a wider system of social interaction, it is not an individual attribute but part of a wider legacy of community life. It can be encouraged, cultivated or disrupted, but certainly not taught or imparted by well-intentioned professionals.

A technocratic orientation towards the issue of resilience is unlikely to engage the creative and problem-solving capacities of communities who are faced with a violent and destructive threat to their life. Such policies are also likely to institutionalize a top–down professional approach that will leave little room for local initiative. A highly centralized professional response cannot deal with every contingency. In the end, encouraging people to take responsibility for their well-being is essential for an effective response to an emergency situation. In reality, resilience cannot be taught. It is not a state that exists prior to an event. The ability to bounce back from a disruption and cope with dramatically desperate events cannot be learned through training. Resilience emerges through circumstances that are unexpected and therefore new. It develops through improvisation and adaptation to 'rapidly changing and usually ambiguous conditions' (Dynes 2003: 9).

The tendency to treat resilience as a technical problem diverts attention from the fact that the response of a community to a threat and its level of morale are influenced by its shared experience and values and the meaning attached to them. Communities that are bound together by a robust system of meaning are able to act with a sense of purpose in defence of their community and way of life. Shared meaning provides people with clear guidelines about what is expected of them in their interaction with members of their community. Of course, political leaders implicitly understand that the future of society is linked to its capacity to develop a sense of direction that can inspire the public. This sentiment is regularly expressed through statements that acclaim the need for a 'narrative' or clarity about society's values. However, such narratives or values cannot be invented. What governments can do is to encourage a cultural climate where people are able to freely exchange their views and develop their opinions on the basis of their experience. That requires that citizens are treated as mature and not as vulnerable adults.

Notes

1. This point is stressed on the web page of UK Resilience: 'The Government's aim is to reduce the risk from emergencies so that people can go about their business freely and with confidence. This website exists to provide a resource for civil protection practitioners, supporting the work which goes on across the UK to improve emergency preparedness' (http://www.ukresilience.info/).
2. For an example of a call for restraint in policy-making, see the speech by Sir Ken MacDonald QC, cited in 'DPP warning over "war on terror"' *BBC News*, 23 January 2007 (http://news.bbc.co.uk/1/hi/uk/6292379.stm).

References

Barnett, M. (2004), Congress must recognize the need for psychological resilience in an age of terrorism, *Families, Systems and Health*, 22, 1.

BBC (2008), 'Early Intervention' City Starts, *BBC On-Line News*, 28 April.

Beck, U. (2003), The silence of words: on terror and war, *Security Dialogue*, 34, 3.

Better Regulation Task Force (2000), *Protecting Vulnerable People*, London: Cabinet Office.

Cabinet Office Civil Contingencies Secretariat (2003), *Dealing with Disaster* (rev. 3rd edn), London: Cabinet Office.

Cabinet Office (2003), *Draft Civil Contingencies Bill: Consultation Document*. Available at: www.ukresilience.info/ccbill/draftbill/consult/4 resilience.htm (accessed 4 May 2006).

Cabinet Office (2007), Summary management unit's aims and objectives. Available at: http://www.cabinetoffice.gov.uk/about_the_cabinet_office/units.aspx (accessed 5 November 2007).

Clarke L. (2006), *Worst Cases: Terror and Catastrophe in the Popular Imagination*, Chicago: University of Chicago Press.

Clarke, S. E. and Chenoweth, E. (2006), The politics of vulnerability: constructing local performance regimes for Homeland Security, *Review of Policy Research*, 23, 1.

Cornish, P. (2007), *The CBRN System: Assessing the Threat of Chemical, Biological, Radiological and Nuclear Weapons in the United Kingdom*, London: Chatham House.

Cutter, S. (2005), The geography of social vulnerability: race, class, and catastrophe. Discussion organized by SSRC on 'Understanding Katrina: Perspectives from the Social Sciences'. Available at: www.understandingkatrina.ssrc.org/Cutter/pf (accessed 24 January 2006).

Directgov (2007), Tackling drugs; our community, your say (25 July). Available at: http://www.direct.gov.uk/en/Nl1/Newsroom/DG_069416 (accessed 6 November 2007).

Drury, J. and Cocking, C. (2007), *The Mass Psychology of Disasters and Emergency Evacuations: A Research Report and Implications for Practice*, Falmer: Department of Psychology, University of Sussex.

Durodie, B. (2005), Cultural precursors and psychological consequences of contemporary Western responses to acts of terror. In S. Wessely and V. N. Krasnov (eds), *Psychological Responses to the New Terrorism: A NATO-Russia Dialogue*, Amsterdam: IOS Press.

Dynes, R. (2003), Finding order in disorder: continuities in the 9-11 response, *International Journal of Mass Emergencies and Disasters*, 21, 3.

Edwards, C. (2006), *The Case for a National Security Strategy*, Demos Report, London: Demos.

Every Child Matters (2006), Risk and Resilience Workshop. Available at: http://www.everychildmatters.gov.uk/resources-and-practice/IG00100/ (accessed 7 October 2007).

Fairclough, N. (2000), *New Labour, New Language?* London: Routledge.

Freedman, L. (2005), The politics of warning: terrorism and risk communication, *Intelligence and National Security*, 20, 3.

Furedi, F. (2006), *Culture of Fear Revisited*, London: Continuum.

Furedi, F. (2007), *Invitation to Terror: The Expanding Empire of the Unknown*, London: Continuum.

Guardian (2006), Police assessments show improvements needed, 25 October.

Homer-Dixon, T. (2002), The rise of complex terrorism, *Foreign Policy* (January).

Horne, J. F. and Orr, J. E. (1998), Assessing behaviours that create resilient organizations, *Employment Relations Today*, 24, 4: 29–39.

IPPR (2006), Research projects: risk and resilience. Available at: www.ippr.org/research/teams/project.asp?id=1964&pid=1964 (accessed 11 October 2007).

Jenkins, M. J. (2006), The new age of terrorism. In D. Kamien (ed.), *McGraw-Hill Homeland Security Handbook*, New York: McGraw-Hill.

Johnson, R. (2002), Defending ways of life: the (anti-), terrorist rhetorics of Bush and Blair, *Theory, Culture and Society*, 19, 4.

Joseph, S., Williams, R. and Yule, W. (1993), Changes in outlook following a disaster: the preliminary development of a measure to assess positive and negative responses, *Journal of Traumatic Stress*, 6, 2.

Kendra, J. and Wachtendorf, T. (2002), Elements of resilience in the World Trade Center attack, Preliminary report published by the Disaster Research Center, Newark, DE: University of Delaware.

Kunreuther, H. and Michel-Kerjan, E. (2004), *Dealing with Extreme Events: New Challenges for Terrorism Risk Coverage in the U.S.*, Center for Risk Management and Decision Processes, Philadelphia: Wharton University of Pennsylvania.

Linenthal, E. T. (2001), *The Unfinished Bombing: Oklahoma City in American Memory*, New York: Oxford University Press.

Lipschutz, R. (1999), Terror in the suites: narratives of fear and the political economy of danger, *Global Society*, 13, 4.

Lord Chancellor's Department (1997), *Who Decides? Making Decisions on Behalf of Mentally Incapacitated Adults*, London: HMSO.

Mann, B. (2007), Protecting UK's critical infrastructure (1 July). Available at: http://www.contingencytoday.com/online_article/Protecting-the-UK_s-Critical-National-Infrastructure/416.

Mitchell, J. K. (2004), The fox and the hedgehog: myopia about homeland security in U.S. policies on terrorism. In *Terrorism and Disaster: New Threats, New Ideas. Research in Social Problems and Public Policy*, 11 (available on-line).

Mueller, J. (2006), Is there still a terrorist threat? The myth of the omnipresent enemy, *Foreign Affairs*, 85 (September/October): 234–45.

New York Times (1998), Is Big Brother watching? Why would he bother? We're all vulnerable, 12 January.

O'Brien, G. and Read, P. (2005), Future UK emergency management: new wine, old skin? *Disaster Prevention and Management*, 14, 3: 353–61.

Observer (2003), Dangerous pursuit of beauty: the media's notion that thinness is next to godliness plays havoc with vulnerable young minds, 9 November.

Office of Homeland Security (2002), *National Strategy for Homeland Security*, Washington, DC: Office of Homeland Security.

Omand, D. (2005), Countering international terrorism: the use of strategy, *Survival*, 47, 4.

Pupavac, V. (2004), Psychosocial interventions and the demoralisation of humanitarianism, *Journal of Biosocial Science*, 36.

Runciman, D. (2006), *The Politics of Good Intention*, Princeton, NJ: Princeton University Press.

Sheppard, B., Rubin, J., Warman, J. and Wessely, S. (2006), Terrorism and dispelling the myth of a panic prone public, *Journal of Public Health Policy*, 27.

Slovic, P. (2002), Terrorism as hazard: a new species of trouble, *Risk Analysis*, 22, 3.

UK Resilience (2007), Welcome to UK Resilience. Available at: http://www.ukresilience.info/ (accessed 3 October 2007).

Waller, M. A. (2001), Resilience in ecosystem context: evolution of the concept, *American Journal of Orthopsychiatry*, 71, 3: 1–8.

Waysman, M., Schwarzwald, J. and Solomon, Z. (2001), Hardiness: an examination of its relationship with positive and negative long term changes following trauma, *Journal of Traumatic Stress*, 14, 3.

8

Child Protection Social Work: Risks of Fears and Fears of Risks – Impossible Tasks from Impossible Goals?

Brian Littlechild

Risk assessment and risk management have recently developed as major areas of attention within practice, policy and management of child protection work in the UK, with a growing literature base (Munro 2002; Calder 2003; Thom *et al.* 2007; Webb 2007). Concepts of risk as constructed by the media, government and the public are increasingly impacting upon professional practices (Denney 2005; Morgan 2007).

In recent years, developments in risk discourses within central government agency policy and guidelines have meant that the risk enterprise has gained momentum. However, in the area of risk in relation to social work and social care, little work has been carried out to produce a social model of risk (Titterton 2005). At the same time, the Royal College of Psychiatrists states that 'evaluation of risk is an inexact actuarial science operating in a political arena' (Morgan 2007: 5). This then raises questions about the validity, as well as reliability, of risk assessments in the social care field – and particularly within the child protection arena as generated by central government mandatory guidance – which are required to be acted upon by the local authority agencies which have primary responsibility for child protection in the UK (HM Government 2006).

The chapter goes on to examine the fear which affects frontline workers, managers and child protection agencies as a result of their perception of the operationalization of risk strategies. This is approached from two interlinked perspectives. First, in relation to unrealistic expectations of prediction of risk by use of current risk assessment tools, and the subsequent fear for agencies of being subjected to damaging publicity in the media for a child abuse death. Second, from the perspective of individual workers and their concerns at being judged by the media and by politicians as culpable for such children's deaths by not assessing risk well enough, in an area of work where they are already often subjected to threats and stress from parent service users (Ayre 2001; Littlechild 2005a). Such unrealistic expectations can produce fear in workers of getting things 'wrong' in child protection work (now officially known as 'safeguarding children' – HM Government 2006), arising from methods of risk assessment which are based upon positivistic approaches, and the unobtainable certainties within modernity which are sought in such approaches, which, it will be argued, can provide only indicative areas for potential risks. Essentially, central government appears to have taken a view that in order to reduce the risk of child abuse deaths, the production of mandatory guidance and checklists for professionals will ensure that agencies and professionals carry out risk assessments and plan their work in standardized ways, and therefore reduce the risk to children, and risk to the government of negative and critical publicity. However, such controlling policies from central government can lead to fear and anxiety in social work professionals of not assessing, and eliminating, risk, as the government and their employing agencies are expecting them to do. Regulatory guidance can be seen to place social workers 'between a rock and a hard place', with a fear of not meeting all of the many government requirements set out in the regulations, while at the same time often being personally threatened by families where abuse of children is taking place. This last point – violence and threats from parent service users where their children are being investigated for possible child abuse – leads into the second main theme of the chapter. Such experiences of workers are ignored within media accounts and official government risk assessment policies and guidelines, and yet are known to have been a major feature in a high number of child abuse deaths where children have been known to the protection agencies (Department of Health 1988; Humphreys 1999; Littlechild 2005a, 2005b; Stanley and Goddard 2002).

The tensions, dichotomies and omissions in relation to the assessment of risk in current 'official' policy discourses are discussed, and how these impact upon fears produced in child protection work. In essence, it is argued that it is necessary to examine workers' and agencies' fears of risk, in part by the use of qualitative research methods, to understand all the relevant areas of risk in child protection work, and in turn, the risks engendered within child protection work of those fears.

Child Protection Policies, Risk and Government Fears

The main aim of the child protection system in the UK is to protect children from harm and to enhance their well-being (HM Government 2006). The discourses and political realities which have determined how we view children, and therefore how risks to them are viewed, have changed dramatically in the last century and a half. From a time in which children were seen as young adults, with no special protection from the demands of the labour market, from sexual abuse, or from abuse within families or in substitute care, the rapidly developing discourse has moved on to how children are developed and protected in terms of work, in terms of compulsory education and, most significantly for our purposes here, in relation to ideas about protection in the twentieth century from what now has come to be seen as abuse (Platt 1969).

Policies relating to the perceived need to protect children on an individual basis became more evident after the Dennis O'Neill inquiry in 1948, following the gross neglect and death of this young boy following his evacuation as a result of the Second World War to an unregulated foster family, and the public outcry and government inquiry following these events. This public inquiry was the first to be set up by the government, and was a mechanism reintroduced in the 1960s, which continues through to the present (Corby *et al.* 1998).

The next phase of development in policy on abuse relating to physical harm and neglect came about from the work of the National Society for the Protection of Children (NSPCC) and its promotion in the 1960s of the work of two paediatricians from the United States, the Kempes. Following the groundbreaking work of the Kempes in persuading the legal and social welfare authorities in the USA that parents could physically harm their children, the NSPCC brought these two doctors to the UK to develop policies in a similar vein. Their approach derived from a medical model of diagnosis concerning diagnosis of deliberately broken limbs, and led to child protection registers being presented as the main policy directive in relation to child protection from government at that time. The categories of abuse were extended and developed as time progressed, to include emotional and sexual abuse. The most recent addition to this list of types of abuse has been recognition of situations within families where children are emotionally abused, due to their living in an environment of domestic violence (HM Government 2006; Humphreys and Stanley 2006; Children Act 2004). The central overarching legal concept in relation to the abuse and protection of individual children is that of significant harm or the likelihood of significant harm as set out in the Children Act 1989.

The importance of these developments for the purpose of the current discussion relates to the socially constructed nature of child abuse, as acknowledged by the government in the publication of its document, *Child Protection: Messages from Research* (Department of Health 1995), and therefore the difficulties in agreeing what constitutes abuse. This document recognized that child abuse is more like pornography than whooping cough, with the consequent difficulties of determining within a socially constructed perspective what it is and how to respond to it, rather than the medically oriented model of diagnosis, and treatment, framed within a positivistic review of knowledge and intervention. Such recognition, it could be argued, might have led to the media and politicians understanding that it is not always possible to accurately predict, diagnose and therefore treat child abuse in a way which can lead to risk elimination; however, this is not the case (Ayre 2001; Cooper *et al.* 2003; Bostock *et al.* 2005). These formulations affect risk assessments in child protection work carried out within an environment where agency managers and professionals perceive that if they do not eliminate risk, they will be open to severe criticism and personal abuse, both from within their agencies, and from the media.

The Background to the Risk Culture

The development of concepts of 'risk' and of the 'risk society' (Giddens 1990, 1991; Beck 1992) have led to suggestions that the lack of trust in institutions and professionals has meant an increasing tendency to regulate professionals and their decision-making in order to determine and minimize risk. Parton

(1997) argues that the problem with current risk assessment approaches is that they lead to an environment in which social workers and their employing agencies will tend to make defensible rather than 'right' decisions – or avoid taking 'risky' decisions at all. Such an approach can mean that social workers are not encouraged – or even allowed – to take risks, as a result of a negative view of risk-taking within an agency (Stalker 2003).

One of the problems for child protection social work in recent decades is that it has been positively vilified by the media and politicians (Corby *et al.* 1998; Ayre 2001). In addition, it can be argued that the Labour governments since 1997 have been fearful of the publicity arising from further child abuse deaths, and have taken the view that more regulations and policies over the local authorities responsible for child protection and over the social workers they employ would reduce the risks of such deaths. However, the corollary of this has been an increase in the fear within social work of being blamed for such deaths. McLaughlin notes how procedural attempts to reduce uncertainty by way of managerialist strategies can be criticized for leading to professionals' anxiety and lack of confidence in their abilities to assess and make decisions, as 'failure to follow the correct procedure can leave the worker vulnerable to disciplinary or judicial action if things go wrong' (McLaughlin 2007: 1264).

Aldgate *et al.* (2007) argue that this state of affairs arises from the new managerialism promoted by New Labour, which consists of a controlling approach of technocratic micro-practice with an overwhelming focus on outcomes. The lack of trust in social work and social workers has been clearly evidenced by the increasing tendency of government to issue reductivist checklists for social workers to follow, a trend followed by local authorities employing social workers, despite the possibility of misplaced trust in the efficacy of such checklists, which are often at best incomplete in relation to potential confounding factors, for example in relation to the risks arising from violence against staff (Littlechild 2005a).

Within the burgeoning number of policy directives and guidance documents from central government in the child protection area, intended to reduce the risk of child abuse deaths, the first attempt at a risk assessment tool came in 1988 in the document known as the 'Orange Book' (Department of Health 1988). Within this guidance, there was only one brief reference to the nature and effects of violence from parents/carers in child protection work, which was removed in its replacement, the *Framework for Assessment* (Department of Health 2000). Understanding and acknowledging within policies and risk assessments the effects of fear produced by violence from parents/carers is returned to as a key area in relation to risks for such children later in this chapter.

In relation to such managerialist approaches which promote such risk assessment paradigms, Parton and O'Byrne state:

> Social work . . . has become very defensive, overly proceduralised and narrowly concerned with assessing, managing, insuring against risk . . . [and] during the 1990s we saw the introduction of sophisticated attempts to make social workers accountable for, and subject their

practice to, ever more detailed reviews, inspections, audits and managerial oversight and prescription. (Parton and O'Byrne 2000: 1)

Such managerial prescription and control based on government concerns are evident in relation to another policy area relating to children and young people – the youth justice field. This was illustrated following the murder of 2-year-old James Bulger by two 10-year-old boys, Jon Venables and Robert Thompson, and their subsequent trial. A media and political outcry in relation to these two young people led to calls for dire punishments for them based upon their being labelled as evil, and for policy changes towards a more punitive system of dealing with young offenders, resulting from 'the process [of] a politics of fear, even of "child hatred" . . . concerned simply to demonize, promote hostility and pursue the politics of vengeance' (Muncie and Hughes 2002: 12). A number of the features of the trial were criticized by the European Court of Human Rights, including the actions of the then Home Secretary, Michael Howard, who announced that the two boys would be kept in custody for a minimum of 15 years, in response to the media outcry following the murder. In 1997, the Court of Appeal ruled that this decision was unlawful, and the Home Secretary lost the power to set minimum terms for life-sentence prisoners under the age of 18 years. The High Court and European Court of Human Rights have since ruled that politicians can no longer decide how long a life-sentence prisoner can remain behind bars.

While this punitive turn of events started under the Conservative government of John Major in the 1990s, it was the subsequent Labour governments which delivered punitive policies, leading to the abolition of doli incapax in the Crime and Disorder Act 1998, as a direct result of the Venables and Thompson trials (see also Denney, this issue). Doli incapax had at the trial required the prosecution in criminal proceedings to prove that a young person aged between 10 and 14 knew that what s/he was doing was criminally wrong. This did not fit with the New Labour idea of holding young people criminally responsible for their actions in ways not seen in official policies for nearly a century. Such ideas of central state control as responses to media outcries have been evident in both child protection and youth offending policies.

Hetherington *et al.* (1997) in their study of child protection systems in Europe concluded that the highly bureaucratic, centrally controlled and proceduralized systems in the UK could not have evolved in the same way in any other European country. In youth justice the government created the Youth Justice Board in the 1990s. The Board has control over the assessments and decisions to be made by youth justice professionals by way of the ASSET checklist. The process is the same – the government wishes to eliminate risk of a 'problem' occurring, and reacts by attempting to control agencies and the professionals involved. This is achieved through greater direction over, for example, the judges and professionals involved in youth justice, and the social workers involved in child protection. The process is built upon fear, desire to control, and regulation, with a key element of such regulation being central government's construction, and requirement for use, of assessment tools, as evidenced in the youth justice and child protection fields in recent years.

Risk Assessment Methodologies and Tools: Reliable and Valid?

Developments in rationality and scientific endeavour are the basis and justification for current discourses which underlie contemporary risk-assessment and risk-management strategies. Kronenfeld and Glik (1991) saw the perception of risk in the medical sociology field as reflecting the shift in people's thought processes away from an emphasis on fate or luck, to notions of control. Scientific rationalism has become indisputably the dominant paradigm for explaining and predicting events in the social world. The risk assessment enterprise is based on the premise that we can know the world, and that we can determine cause and effect from observation of events within a positivist paradigm. It is these notions of predictability and control which become so important in risk assessment and decision-making. No longer, then, do accidents, incidents or tragedies just happen; they are seen to be predictable, assessable and preventable (Littlechild 2004). One key area of risk assessment within this paradigm is the knowledge arising from previous events, often predicated upon actuarial assessments.

Actuarially Based Assessments of Risk

Actuarial methods are the basis upon which many risk assessment strategies are based. It is used in many areas of assessing risk in business; so, for example, insurance companies predict the risk to a particular individual or situation, based on information they have built up in relation to a certain activity. Thus, in relation to driving a car, for example, risks to different age groups, dependent upon where they live, previous offences and accidents, etc., are collected and analysed over time. However, actuarial approaches do not try to predict or manage risk to individual drivers; they balance the risk to their business having to settle claims from drivers by assessing the likelihood of the number of individuals from within certain groups making claims on their insurance. What they do not try to do is to predict which individual, over a period of time, will make that claim on their insurance. In health and social care professions, this is what it appears that agencies and professionals are expected to do – to predict which individual will act in which ways over a given period of time – a process termed by Fitzgibbon as the 'actuarial fallacy' (Fitzgibbon 2007a). Such methods in relation to the social world are, however, not able to take into account the many and complex areas which intertwine to determine how a particular person will respond on a particular day, to a particular set of circumstances (Titterton 2005). In addition, Higgins et al. (2005) note that actuarial methods are unlikely to be of use in a population with low base rates, e.g. of certain types of violence, as such methods lead to large numbers of false positives being generated. This is the case for the child abuse and child protection fields.

Fitzgibbon proposes that the use of statistics as the basis of actuarial risk assessments can be misleading; so, for example:

A risk assessment which always predicts a lower likelihood of harm could be interpreted as being 95% accurate even if 5% of subjects assessed go on to cause future harm. (Fitzgibbon 2007b: 137)

In addition, it is very difficult to measure retrospectively the effectiveness of risk assessment models and tools. One recent media-defined 'scandal' concerned prisoners released from prison who had subsequently carried out serious offences after being risk-assessed. It was claimed that the Probation Service had assessed a 91 per cent chance of reoffending by the prisoner (*Guardian* 2006). However, it is not possible to test empirically the validity of such assessments/predictions, as it can never be known if it was an accurate prediction or not. Positivistic models arising from the importation of models of knowledge and prediction from the natural sciences, then, cannot be easily transplanted into the human sciences in areas such as offending or child protection.

The Place of Non-positivistic Knowledge

Government policy and guidance do not acknowledge that risk assessment policies and tools derived from positivist technical–rational approaches fail to appreciate the limitations on how possible it is to be prescriptive in relation to risk assessment. Such processes, which provide guidance for professionals, require to be based on a systematic review of the evidence, including untidy and distinctly non-positivistic sets of knowledge concerning how people construct their knowledge of the area they are involved in, and their attributions of the world and the motives of others. In the particular case of the child protection social work field, this includes how social workers in reality make their assessment and decisions as a result partly of power dynamics within certain types of abusing families, and threats of intimidation and violence against them by parents in such families. These areas are ignored in the Department of Health Assessment Framework (Department of Health 2000), and its successor, the Common Assessment Framework. These assessment frameworks are required to be used by local authorities, in relation to child well-being and protection. If such experiences and attributions are not included in decision-making based upon risk assessments in social work, it then becomes impossible to include guidance on these areas which affect the safety of workers, and the well-being of children with whom they work (Littlechild 2004, 2005a).

Goddard *et al.* (1999) present a number of criticisms of risk assessment procedures which they see encroaching upon professional social work assessments in child protection work in Australia, New Zealand, Canada and the USA, among other countries. They argue that assessments that do not recognize uncertainty cannot accurately reflect the complex set of factors which might present risks to children, and are no longer acceptable. Parton (1998) similarly argues that social work must move beyond such restricted and restrictive risk assessments, and rediscover ambiguity and uncertainty, as he terms it – i.e. that in the complex set of factors which drive human cognition, motivation and behaviour, we are often not able to predict risks fully, even with a wide range of actuarial information concerning risk factors.

Given these uncertainties, it would not appear to be in the clients' or workers' interests to make use of mechanistic and potentially problematic solutions, yet for the employing, responsible agency, the attractions of having a mechanistic system that will 'hold up' in court if sued for their actions is attractive (Carson 1996). This in turn may possibly lead to individual workers being reluctant to assess a case as 'low-risk', as this may create high risk for themselves individually as professionals. This then could lead to coercive intervention which is not appropriate for the needs and rights of that child, or family. The fear created by a system which expects risk elimination through increasingly centralized guidance – essentially checklists – cannot help professionals or clients if it induces fear.

Policy Changes from Individual Child Abuse Death Inquiries

In contrast to actuarial approaches, the other major influence upon child protection risk assessment policies is the findings of child abuse death inquiry reports, whereby policies in relation to child protection were significantly affected by the results of such inquiries based on actions or omissions, as found in one single case (Corby *et al.* 1998). There are significant problematic effects of trying to base child protection work and the risks within it upon single incidents, as so often happens after tragedies have occurred. Such responses can mean that the risk factors identified in that particular case have a disproportionate effect upon policies and practice, focusing only on the issues raised in that inquiry, and excluding more important general risks for the population served (see e.g. Butler and Drakeford 2003). Examining 'mistakes' retrospectively when they have led to tragedy is not necessarily a good way to assess and deal with risks within a particular area (Cooper *et al.* 2003; Bostock *et al.* 2005).

The Effects of Current Expectations of Risk Assessment Work on Child Protection Professionals: A Culture of Fear

While there is a need to ensure that social workers and their agencies are acting appropriately and without negligence in their work, the idea that risk can be eliminated is unrealistic and problematic for services, children and frontline workers. The fear of risk as set out in previous sections has to be confronted by social workers and their agencies in order to improve their services. This can only occur within a culture which accepts that such agencies and workers cannot always get every decision 'right', while acknowledging that workers and agencies alike need to take into account appropriately lessons from research which can aid ways in which risk is assessed and worked with. This recognition can then lead to other, more constructive ways of conceptualizing how social workers and social work agencies deal with risk. This can be seen in some elements of the health service delivery, and more recently considered for social work and social care: learning from 'mistakes' or 'near misses', as set out in the Social Care Institute for Excellence (SCIE) position document, *Managing Risks and Minimizing Mistakes in Services to Children and Families* by Bostock *et al.* (2005; see www.scie.org.uk). In the airline industry, there has been a realization that lessons can be learned from near misses, which has led to new reporting procedures. This has not occurred in social work and social care. Bostock *et al.* (2005) argue that mistakes happen in all forms of human endeavour, and what we should be attempting to do is to learn from mistakes. If we blame staff for what happens, and make them fearful of reporting difficulties, the reality of the problems can neither be systematically examined, nor action taken to remedy them (Kemshall and Pritchard 1996). Workers can become fearful of their work, of their clients, and of reporting their concerns, in case they are seen as too demanding, as troublemakers, or nervous and/or ineffective workers (Rowett 1986; Norris 1990). Such a culture of blame is unhelpful for agencies, workers, and clients (see Bostock et al. 2005). In a report for the independent political think tank, Demos, Cooper et al. (2003) have argued that the current trend of regulating social workers more and more by way of the use of such mechanisms as the previously mentioned Assessment Framework, may create greater risks rather than reducing risks for children. They propose that politicians and managers have to allow professionals to have greater space within which to make judgements, and for them not to be blamed if a child's abuse is not due to gross neglect of their duties.

The Effects of Fear on Child Protection Risk Assessments

One key area in relation to fear in child protection work relates to the impact of violent parent service users. This appears to have been ignored in policy and procedures. In order to be able to have a more comprehensive and effective assessment of risk in child protection policies, procedures and risk assessment tools, government bodies need to ensure that research and developments in these areas include the reality of the experiences of the workers involved. This is particularly important as we know that social workers construct their own realities and attributions within their work, which lead to actions which are not always foreseen by policy-makers and higher-level managers. Professionals can become 'street-level bureaucrats', actively changing policy goals in relation to their own beliefs and experiences (Gelsthorpe and Padfield 2003; Evans and Harris 2004). A vital element of any evidence base is knowledge and consideration of how social workers perceive their world of work and their professional agency within it. Yet this has not been a feature of any statements or assessment of risk in relation to child protection work in any of the government publications or guidance since the Orange Book document (Department of Health 1988). This is despite the range and depth of evidence demonstrating the extent and the effects of such violence and aggression in social work and social care in general, and serious child abuse situations in particular.

Research by Pahl (1999) on stress in workers in social services departments discovered that violence and threats of violence to social workers were one of the major areas of stress and fear for social work and social care staff, and particularly child care and child protection staff (see also Smith and Nursten 1998). Concerns about how violence from service users can negatively affect child protection assessments and decision-making processes have been raised by, for example, Reder et al. (1993), Farmer and Owen (1998), O'Hagan and Dillenburger (1995), and Stanley and Goddard (2002). Analysis of a range of child abuse death inquiry reports in the United Kingdom has highlighted how assessment, intervention and decision-making in child protection can be influenced by workers' concerns about clients' aggression in a small but critical number of threatening and violent situations. These sets of features are often present in the most severe forms of abuse, including child deaths (Department of Health 1991; *Guardian* 2002). This significantly affects workers' well-being, capacity to carry out their work effectively, and their commitment to that work (Norris 1990; Brockmann 2002).

What these studies also demonstrated, along with the findings of Norris (1990), was that a high proportion of incidents of threats and intimidation is not reported by social workers within their agencies. This means that the extent of the problem, and the precise nature and effects of it, cannot be monitored, evaluated or dealt with. Workers, because of their fears and anxieties, can fail to recognize the threats against them, and might not believe that reporting them would mean that they were supported, or that the matter would be dealt with satisfactorily by their agency – leaving themselves and their child service users at risk (Littlechild 2005a, 2005b).

Conclusion: Risks of Risk Assessments

This chapter has examined how risk of harm in child protection work is currently constructed in government documents and child protection agencies. It has been argued that it is necessary to examine the risks of risk assessments, as the centrally developed risk assessment agenda and its associated tools have (probably) inadvertently induced fearful perceptions in social workers. This is due to their concerns about the unrealistic expectation that they can, by the use of such tools, eliminate risk. At the same time other risks, such as violence from service users, are ignored in risk assessment tools. Current formulations of positivistic risk assessment approaches are based upon fears of central government in wishing to try to eliminate risk in areas in which they are seen to have responsibility, such as child protection, by way of controlling guidance and regulation. This then leads to unrealistic expectations of centrally formulated risk assessment within the social work and social care field, while at the same time government has clear expectations that social workers, if only they apply them properly, would be able to avoid child abuse deaths. This chapter has set out the evidence as to why this cannot be the case in terms of actuarial and positivistic-based approaches, and issues arising within single child abuse situations. It has also been argued that there are areas of risks for children which are ignored within official policy and guidance, which have to be confronted in order to protect children in ways which currently formulated positivist approaches of risk assessment tools have not achieved.

When we come to consider ways in which we need to take into account knowledge to produce effective policies to reduce risk to children, government needs to include research into how professionals make their decisions and why – otherwise there will always be unintended consequences. This is necessary to understand the processes which professionals go through, and the pressures and influences on them, while also gaining their commitment to approaches which reflect the reality of the situations they are put into by government policies themselves. In the human sciences, it is dangerous to assume that professionals are not human beings who construct their own worlds, methods of working, views about their employing agencies, and attributions about service users and society. This then requires the incorporation of knowledge about how professionals can be engaged to produce the desired policy outcomes. In furtherance of this, the work of Ruch (2007) examines issues of managerialism, supervision and child protection cultures, and the problems associated with them. Ruch concluded that there is a need to produce a model for the development of policies, procedures and support mechanisms for staff that includes the views and experiences of both service users and professionals to aid the pursuance of policy goals. This is undoubtedly the case in relation to child protection as examined in this chapter. At the same time, the results of systematic analysis of risk factors, which take into account the reality of the untidy worlds of human beings which do not fit easily with positivistic paradigms, can provide guidance for professionals to consider when carrying out their assessments – and for agencies to support them in this. Canton (2005) notes that while it may be that risk assessment tools can help frontline workers take into account the different types of risk factors, it will always be a professional judgement which will have to be applied to these areas of risk, to the particular situation and to the family and child with whom they are working, an approach advocated by the Social Care Institute for Excellence (Bostock *et al.* 2005), and the Demos reports (Cooper *et al.* 2003), referred to earlier.

Anxiety related to mechanistic risk assessment tools has increased fear in social workers, while the tools themselves do not contain all the necessary elements which pose dangers to children. For enhanced, effective risk assessments, government policies and guidance need to take into account different methods of understanding how professionals approach their work, and are affected by risk factors currently ignored in policy and guidance. The fear of reporting and not receiving support in relation to intimidation, harassment and aggression from parents/carers of children where there are investigations concerning abuse is an important example of this. Government guidelines also need to allow professionals, where they can justify this, to move beyond restrictive checklists. Such a change in culture needs to take into account the effects of the work, and the power dynamics within it, upon the workers themselves. This requires qualitative research to add to the mix of areas to be taken into account in order to develop effective policy and practice. It is proposed here that there are alternative means by which government objectives in terms of reducing risk to children can take account of research and theory which are more likely to produce the desired outcomes than the current formulations. Government policies need to encourage local authorities to allow social workers to address their various fears openly with their managers in a culture of support, rather than a culture of blame in relation to decision-making.

References

Aldgate, J., Healy, L., Malcolm, B., Pine, B., Rose, W. and Seden, J. (eds) (2007), *Enhancing Social Work Management: Theory and Best Practice from the UK and USA*, London: Jessica Kingsley.

Ayre, P. (2001), Child protection and the media: lessons from the last three decades, *British Journal of Social Work*, 31, 6: 887–901.

Beck, U. (1992), *Risk Society: Towards a New Modernity*, London: Sage.

Bostock, L., Bairstow, S., Fish, S. and Macleod, F. (2005), *Managing Risks and Minimising Mistakes in Services to Children and Families*, SCIE Report 6, London: Social Care Institute for Excellence.

Brockmann, M. (2002), New perspectives on violence in social care, *Journal of Social Work*, 2, 1: 29–44.

Butler, I. and Drakeford, M. (2003), *Social Policy, Social Welfare and Scandal*, Basingstoke: Palgrave Macmillan.

Calder, M. C. (2003), *Risk and Child Protection*, CareKnowledge Briefing no. 9, London: OLM CareKnowledge.

Canton, R. (2005), Risk assessment and compliance in probation and mental health practice. In B. Littlechild and D. Fearns (eds), *Mental Disorder and Criminal Justice: Policy and Practice*, Lyme Regis: Russell House Publishing, pp. 137–58.

Carson, D. (1996), The legal aspects of risk. In H. Kemshall and J. Pritchard (eds), *Good Practice in Risk Assessment and Risk Management 1*, London: Jessica Kingsley.

Cooper, A., Hetherington, R. and Katz, I. (2003), *The Risk Factor: Making the Child Protection System Work for Children*, London: Demos.

Corby, B., Doig, A. and Roberts, V. (1998), Inquiries into child abuse, *Journal of Social Welfare and Family Law*, 20, 4: 377–95.

Denney, D. (2005), *Risk and Society*, London: Sage.

Department of Health (1988), *Protecting Children*, London: HMSO.

Department of Health (1991), *Child Abuse: A Study of Inquiry Reports*, London: HMSO.

Department of Health (1995), *Child Protection: Messages from Research*, London: HMSO.

Department of Health (2000), *Framework for Assessment of Children in Need and Their Families*, London: Stationery Office.

Evans, T. and Harris, J. (2004), Street level bureaucracy, social work and the (exaggerated) death of discretion, *British Journal of Social Work*, 34: 871–95.

Farmer, E. and Owen, M. (1998), Gender and the child protection process, *British Journal of Social Work*, 28: 545–64.

Fitzgibbon, D. W. M. (2007a), Risk analysis and the new practitioner: myth or reality, *Punishment and Society*, 9, 1: 87–97.

Fitzgibbon, D. W. (2007b), Institutional racism, pre-emptive criminalisation and risk analysis, *Howard Journal*, 46, 2: 128–44.

Gelsthorpe, L. and Padfield, N. (eds) (2003), *Exercising Discretion: Decision-making in Criminal Justice and Beyond*, Cullompton: Willan Publishing.

Giddens, A. (1990), *The Consequences of Modernity*, Stanford, CA: Stanford University Press.

Giddens, A. (1991), *Modernity and Self-identity in the Late Modern Age*, Cambridge: Polity Press.

Goddard, C. R., Saunders, B. J. and Stanley, J. R. (1999), Structured risk assessment procedures: instruments of abuse? *Child Abuse Review*, 8: 251–63.

Guardian (2002), Ainlee Walker Inquiry, 19 December: 4.

Guardian (2006), An emergency package to hold high risk offenders, 21 April: 6–7.

Hetherington, R., Cooper, A., Smith, P. and Wilford, G. (eds) (1997), *Protecting Children: Messages from Europe*, Lyme Regis: Russell House Publishing.

Higgins, N., Watts, D., Bindman, J., Slade, M. and Thornicroft, G. (2005), Assessing violence risk in general adult psychiatry, *Psychiatric Bulletin*, 29: 131–3.

HM Government (2006), *Working Together to Safeguard: A Guide to Inter-agency Working to Safeguard and Promote the Welfare of Children*, London: HM Government.

Humphreys, C. (1999), Avoidance and confrontation: social work practice in relation to domestic violence and child abuse, *Child and Family Social Work*, 4: 77–87.

Humphreys, C. and Stanley, N. (eds) (2006), *Domestic Violence and Child Protection: Directions for Good Practice*, London: Jessica Kingsley.

Kemshall, H. and Pritchard, J. (eds) (1996), *Good Practice in Risk Assessment and Risk Management 1*, London: Jessica Kingsley.

Kronenfeld, J. J. and Glik, D. C. (1991), Perceptions of risk: its applicability to medical sociological research, *Research in the Sociology of Health Care*, 9: 307–34.

Littlechild, B. (2004), Risk assessment and social work values: problems and possibilities. In P. Erath, B. Littlechild and R. Vornanen (eds), *Social Work in Europe: Descriptions, Analysis and Theories*, Institut für vergleichende Sozialarbeitswissenschaft und interkulturelle/internationale Sozialarbeit (ISIS) e. V. Eichstätt, pp. 42–53.

Littlechild, B. (2005a), The stresses arising from violence, threats and aggression against child protection social workers, *Journal of Social Work*, 5: 61–82.

Littlechild, B. (2005b), The nature and effects of violence against child-protection social workers: providing effective support, *British Journal of Social Work*, 35: 387–401.

McLaughlin, K. (2007), Regulation and risk in social work: the General Social Care Council and the Social Care Register in context, *British Journal of Social Work*, 37, 7: 1263–77.

Morgan, J. (2007), *'Giving up the Culture of Blame': Risk Assessment and Risk Management in Psychiatric Practice – Briefing Document to Royal College of Psychiatrists*, London: Royal College of Psychiatrists.

Muncie, J. and Hughes, G. (2002), Modes of youth governance: political rationalities, criminalization and resistance. In J. Muncie, G. Hughes and E. McLaughlin (eds), *Youth Justice: Critical Readings*, London: Sage.

Munro, E. (2002), *Effective Child Protection*, London: Sage.

Norris, D. (1990), *Violence against Social Workers*, London: Jessica Kingsley.

O'Hagan, K. and Dillenburger, K. (1995), *The Abuse of Women within Child Care Work*, Buckingham: Open University Press.

Pahl, J. (1999), Coping with physical violence and verbal abuse. In S. Balloch, J. McLean and M. Fisher, *Social Services: Working Under Pressure*, Bristol: Policy Press.

Parton, N. (1997), Child protection and family support: current debates and future prospects. In N. Parton (ed.), *Child Protection and Family Support: Tensions, Contradictions and Possibilities*, London: Routledge.

Parton, N. (1998), Risk, advanced liberalism and child welfare: the need to rediscover uncertainty and ambiguity, *British Journal of Social Work*, 28: 5–27.

Parton, N. and O'Byrne, P. (2000), *Constructive Social Work: Towards a New Practice*, Basingstoke: Macmillan.

Platt, A. (1969), *The Child Savers: The Invention of Delinquency*, Chicago: University of Chicago Press.

Reder, P., Duncan, S. and Gray, M. (1993), *Beyond Blame: Child Abuse Tragedies Revisited*, London: Routledge.

Rowett, C. (1986), *Violence in Social Work: Institute of Criminology Occasional Paper No. 17*, Cambridge: Cambridge University Press.

Ruch, G. (2007), Reflective practice in contemporary child-care social work: the role of containment, *British Journal of Social Work*, 37, 2: 659–80.

Smith, M. and Nursten, J. (1998), Social workers' experiences of distress: moving towards change? *British Journal of Social Work*, 28: 351–68.

Stalker, K. (2003), Managing risk and uncertainty in social work: a literature review, *Journal of Social Work*, 3, 2: 211–33.

Stanley, J. and Goddard, C. (1997), Failures in child protection: a case study, *Child Abuse Review*, 6, 1: 46–54.

Stanley, J. and Goddard, C. (2002), *In the Firing Line: Violence and Power in Child Protection Work*, Chichester: Wiley.

Thom, B., Sales, R. and Pearce, J. J. (eds) (2007), *Growing Up with Risk*, Bristol: Policy Press.

Titterton, M. (2005), *Risk and Risk Taking in Health and Social Welfare*, London: Jessica Kingsley.

Webb, S. A. (2007), *Social Work in a Risk Society: Social and Political Perspectives*, Basingstoke: Palgrave Macmillan.

9

Fear of Others: Social Exclusion and the European Crisis of Solidarity

Gerard Delanty

Introduction

It has been recognized for some time that a feature of the current age is widespread anxiety. For some this suggests an 'age of anxiety' that has now taken on a new dimension as a result of the penetration of risk and uncertainty into all spheres of life. Anxiety is an existential condition that is primarily psychological, but has a wider social and political application for contemporary society. It arises with increased levels of insecurity that can be related to risk and to the plethora of uncertainties that globalization has opened up. Whether there has been a measurable increase in risk and insecurity is a different matter, but it does appear to be incontrovertible that current times involve an increase in the experience of risk and the loss of secure reference points. As a sociologically relevant category, anxiety refers less to a generalized psychological condition than to a cultural mode of experience that has entered into social and political discourses around security, welfare, migration, environment and health. But what is objective and what is real are not two different things, for the discursive construction of reality takes on an objectivity of its own and becomes a reality when it enters into policy-making. September 11th has come to symbolize 'dangerous times' and a spirit of anxiety that goes beyond the reality of terrorist attacks (Appadurai 2006; Bauman 2006). This attitude, which defines the cultural spirit of the age, has had far-reaching social and political implications. Adversity has been inextricably linked with the symbolic construction of otherness and with the unknown and uncertain. Securitization has entered into the heart of the European project at a time when Europe's relation to the wider world has become more important (Huysmans 2005).

These issues are explored in this chapter with respect to increased levels of anxiety around migration in European countries. There has been a noticeable shift in popular views of the EU in recent years towards increased scepticism. Euroscepticism is not confined to a small minority of defenders of the nation state but has a wider resonance in the populations of many countries. It would not be inaccurate to say that the EU is suffering from a crisis in its legitimacy. However, while this is unlikely to extend beyond the present level of limiting further expansion, it has taken a widespread popular form and is a significant challenge for the EU in so far as it aims to develop a deeper and more expansive sense of political community. The fiftieth anniversary of the EU in 2007, in contrast to its inauguration in the Treaty of Rome, was marked by a certain sense of anxiety rather than of optimism for the future. While the violent nationalism that was a feature of Europe during the first half of the twentieth century may have disappeared from the face of Europe today, nationalism has returned in a different guise. It is less a project of states than a project of parties to the extreme right. But its significance goes beyond the specific question of nationalism since, as will be argued in this chapter, the rise of the extreme right and nationalism more generally is a product rather than a cause of a more pervasive social and cultural crisis of political community.

The argument is that there is an emerging crisis of solidarity with Europeanization and this is centrally about anxieties about peoplehood. With the emergence of a European political community that has diminished national sovereignty at a time when global forces are also undermining nation states, both Europe and migration become linked as sources of instability for many people. Anxieties about Europe and migration are linked with fears of a clash of civilizations and anxieties about crime and social securities.

The first section discusses the discourse of crisis that has surrounded the European project since about 2005 and which can be related to the enlargement of the EU and resulting uncertainties as to the nature of political community and peoplehood. This will lead into a critical analysis of the link between anxiety and fear of others. It is argued that xenophobia is connected with anxiety. The third section takes the theme of anxiety up with respect to changes in the nature of socio-economic relations. The chapter concludes with some reflections on the problem of social justice and recognition.

European Political Community and the Crisis of Solidarity

At the heart of the European project is an uncertainty about the very definition of peoplehood as that which constitutes the defining feature of political community. As the EU moves beyond purely market objectives, cultural and social questions have come increasingly to the fore. But these have not brought with them a more inclusive notion of political community, and the very notion of a European sense of peoplehood has been fraught with major controversies. Although a polity comparable to that of national societies does not exist as such, it is nonetheless possible to speak of an emerging political community and transnational polity. This too has brought to the fore questions of who are members of the polity and to what notion of peoplehood does it appeal. This situation has led to the emergence of different visions of Europe. As will be argued in what follows, an anti-institutional vision of Europe is gaining ground and is being nurtured by feelings of anxiety over peoplehood and resistance against migrants and minorities.

We can speak of three competing models of the European project. It would not be an exaggeration to speak of a clash of cultures, in the sense of a clash of different visions of what Europe is and where it is going. These are as follows: a vision of Europe as a transnational suprastate, a vision of Europe as a postnational political community of rights, and a vision of Europe based on core values of peoplehood as embodied in both national and European traditions. The latter two visions have emerged in opposition to the first. By far the dominant vision of Europe is that associated with what might be called the official EU ideology: a vision of Europe that is primarily based on the political level of the state. In this dominant discourse Europe is a matter of the transnationalization of the nation state by a post-sovereign suprastate whose main legitimization is that it is able to solve the problems that have beset the nation state in an age of globalization. The EU is thus able to integrate the economies of its member states while protecting them from the wider global context. This is primarily a functional, if not a technocratic, legitimization. So long as it delivers the goods and achieves a legitimacy through efficiency, it has the support of citizens. This concept of Europe has considerable appeal and can even command a degree of loyalty, although only minimal identity. But its support basis, which tends to be nationally variable, is relatively limited due to the predominance of domestic politics. When other issues come to the fore, it loses its capacity to be a source of legitimization.

Competing with this official vision of Europe as an emerging transnational state are two other competing visions. One of these is a largely leftist position that sees Europe in terms of a civic conception of the polity as a political community based on rights. As best illustrated in the writings of Jürgen Habermas, the European project exhibits some signs of a postnational democracy based on the rights of the individual and a republican constitutional order (Habermas 1998, 2001). Rather than see Europeanization in terms of a transnationalization of the nation state in the direction of a supranational state, an essentially civic conception of Europe is posited as the ideal. This vision of Europe is based on rights as opposed to efficiency. It is a vision of Europe that is clearly highly pertinent to the challenges facing European societies in integrating diverse groups of peoples. Given the scale of human mobility within the EU, a rights-based conception of the political has a huge relevance (Eriksen 2005). While not entirely in opposition to the technocratic model of Europe, it does point to a democratization of the EU in the direction of a greater role for civil society. As a strongly normative model, it is not a vision of Europe that has found strong support among electorates. It has not succeeded in articulating a model of identity, other than the relatively thin identity of what Habermas (1998) has called a 'constitutional patriotism', that is, an identity focused on the abstract principles of the constitution as opposed to the substantive values of a people.

In opposition to both of these visions of Europe is an alternative one that has some considerable support among electorates. This is a vision of Europe based less on rights than on the core values of peoplehood. Such values are generally seen as embodied in national traditions, but they can also be embodied in the very idea of a European political heritage. In this view, which is often expressed in anti-European sentiments, the European project has lost its ability to connect with the core values of peoplehood, which include rights, but also include a wider sphere of values such as those of solidarity and social justice. While often taking a nationalist and populist form, this defensive stance with regard to Europeanization can claim to represent an important tradition within the European political heritage. At the core of this is a social conception of society based on the values of solidarity and redistributive justice. This is generally associated with culturally specific conceptions of peoplehood, as defined in largely national categories.

These three competing visions of Europe, with their respective emphasis on efficiency, rights and values, are often overlapping. The rights-based model of Europe associated with Habermas makes certain assumptions about the nature of peoplehood, for instance, and generally assumes that a European version of a national community is possible. The official discourse of European identity associated with the EU often makes appeals to a vaguely defined notion of a European people based on a unity in diversity. But as visions of Europe they embody fairly distinct modes of legitimization and, even if taken for granted, understandings of political community and peoplehood.

Efficiency can no longer be the only justification for the EU, which must devise different kinds of legitimization, which also cannot derive from the principle of subsidiarity or purely regulatory policy-making. The expansion in the competences of the EU has unavoidably led to its politicization and to a questioning of its democratic basis. There is a widespread perceived lack of accountability, whether justified or not. In addition, there is a nascent fear of the social consequences of the liberalization of markets, a fear that is now increasingly associated with global markets and with migration. It is this that is more significant than the issue of the so-called democratic deficit. The social question is becoming more and more important and as it does there will be a deepening crisis of the European project. The three dominant visions of Europe are unable to address this challenge due to their limited horizons and the failure to see that the social question of solidarity and social justice cannot be solved without the creation of an entirely new vision of a European society. The model of Europe favoured by the EU is one of political coordination of functions and has relatively little to say on questions of identity and solidarity. It is often associated, whether rightly or wrongly, with a neo-liberal agenda. The rights model suffers from a more or less total neglect of issues of social justice, operating with a narrow rights-based view of the polity as a civic order. The social contextualization of political community is thus neglected. While more explicitly addressed to issues of social justice, the defence of peoplehood fails to offer a robust vision for the future since it is trapped within a limited national horizon and does not recognize the internal pluralization of national societies as an accomplished fact. However, the relative success of this values-based vision of Europe is undoubtedly due to its capacity to articulate widespread concerns about social issues, such as welfare and jobs.

The question of social values such as welfare and social security has become bound up with a debate about the nature of Europeanization at a time when the European project is entering a new phase. As the earlier modes of justification have ceased to command the necessary support and new ones have not yet emerged, a situation of uncertainty has arisen. What is significant is not this fact alone but that the present situation of uncertainty has developed alongside other experiences of uncertainty. This double bind will be discussed in more detail below. The point of the present discussion is that the way Europeanization has unfolded in recent years has provided preconditions for a culture of anxiety to emerge with Europe as a focus. European integration was once predominantly supported by both the left and the right in the early years. This has largely been reversed today, with the right mobilizing opposition against a social democratic left that has largely taken over much of the politics of the right.

Increasingly, with the shift towards centre-right politics and the defusing of the traditional left and right parties of the mainstream, new kinds of populist and nationalist parties are gaining ground. Nationalism has returned in a different guise; it is less a project of states than a project of parties associated with the extreme right. Euroscepticism is now being linked with right wing-influenced agendas concerning migration and a general hostility towards a broadening of political community. The extreme right in many cases has been able to take over the political positions not only of the right but also of the left. At least two related developments can be noted. There is increased opposition to Europeanization, on the one side, and, on the other, there is growing resistance to migration. Until the constitutional crisis relating to the draft constitutional treaty in May 2005, when Dutch and French voters overwhelmingly rejected the proposed treaty, these were not connected. It is evident that these are now linked. Clearly, the EU had put itself up for a severe test of popular endorsement, and not surprisingly it did not pass this test.

The present discussion has emphasized the situation in western Europe where the crisis of Europeanization is more acutely developed. Until recently the UK was generally regarded as the main Eurosceptic country, but this group now includes a wider range of countries. Interestingly, however, the UK has not witnessed the same degree of right-wing resurgence as has been the case in the smaller and traditionally more pro-Europe countries, such as Belgium, the Netherlands and Denmark. There are some exceptions, such as Finland and Ireland, which have not experienced the rise of the extreme right, but this now has a foothold in many of the small western European countries – Denmark, Belgium, Austria, the Netherlands, Sweden and Norway – whose social models have been challenged by the wider cultural transformation of Europe, on the one side, and on the other by the steady decline of social democracy. The question of a crisis of solidarity can be posed differently with respect to Central and Eastern Europe, countries that have only recently joined the EU and for whom Europeanization has often been connected with the recovery of national sovereignty. In many of these countries nationalist movements have gained increased ground and while there has been a general acknowledgement of multiculturalism the reality is that Central and Eastern Europe lags considerably behind western European countries on multicultural issues. Attitudes to the EU are largely instrumental and, in many cases, the vision of a postnational Europe has little substance other than a means of distantiation from Russia. Moreover, there are already signs of regional blocs emerging with different attitudes to Europe.

Finally, the controversy over Turkey's bid for EU membership is a further illustration of the growing anxiety and uncertainty that has arisen around the European project. The resistance to Turkey is clearly linked to fears of migration of large numbers of Turks. Already there are some 3.5 million Turks in EU countries, with the largest number in Germany. With a population of 70 million in Turkey, many people fear that the EU in its current form does not have the capacity to absorb such a large country, which shares borders with some of the least stable parts of the Middle East. Turkey's bid for EU membership has been linked with the spectre of an Islamification of Europe, despite the fact that it is one of the most secular countries in the world in terms of the separation of church and state.

Anxiety and Fear of Others

The question of Europe has become embroiled in a crisis over solidarity that is very centrally about peoplehood; it is about who belongs and who doesn't belong to the political community. This is a crisis that cannot be understood only in terms of attitudes about Europe, for it is a crisis that is nurtured by anxieties from many sources and has many reference points, ranging from crime to national security, jobs and welfare. The global wider discourse of the clash of civilizations, anti-European sentiments, right-wing and populist nationalism merge, leading to numerous discourses of anxiety, which have a spill-over effect on many other fields. The EU appears to be caught in a contradiction of removing frontiers between countries within the EU while attempting to establish frontiers with the non-EU (see Rumford, this volume). Although it is unlikely to succeed in reproducing national-style frontiers, the erosion of national frontiers within an EU that is also expanding in size has unleashed considerable opposition and anxieties concerning where the line between self and other should be drawn (see Delanty and O'Mahony 2002; Holmes 2006; Delanty et al. 2007).

What is anxiety? A distinction should be drawn between anxiety and fear, although they cannot be too sharply differentiated since anxiety could be seen as a form of fear. Fear concerns a threat that presents itself in terms that have a certain objectivity. Anxiety is a fear that is either objectless or where the object of the fear is less apparent or manifest. In other words, anxiety is a fear that cannot easily be given substance and produces in the subject a feeling of loss of autonomy. Freud provided a useful theory of anxiety that can be applied to the current situation. Renata Salecl has commented that for Freud in *Inhibitions, Symptons and Anxiety*, anxiety has to do with expectations of a danger that does not manifest itself (Wilkinson 1999; Salecl 2004: 19; Robin 2005). This suggests that anxiety arises in situations when the object is opaque or even invisible. In this respect anxiety is different from fear, which is based on an external threat to the self. Fear relates to a clear danger that is threatening, while anxiety relates to a situation of uncertainty. So anxiety arises when the self is threatened by dangers that do not take the form of an objective threat and where the relation between external object or reality and an internal self is not clear-cut. In anxiety the self lacks autonomy and mastery. An important dimension of anxiety is the lack of knowledge of

Gerard Delanty

the danger that is manifest. It may be the case that anxiety is induced by those situations that present themselves as new and thus as threatening.

It is clear that anxiety can arise in many situations, and preconditions need to be suppressed or normalized in order that the subject might cope with the external world and the unknown. Anxiety is constantly present in people's lives and a source not only of pathologies but of normal identity-building. Freud drew attention to the link between anxiety and fantasy. It was a central aspect of Freud's theory that anxiety is coped with by fantasy in order that the self might live with anxiety, which can otherwise easily destabilize the self. Fantasy provides a corrective in harmonizing the relationship between the self and the external world, allowing the subject to prevent the emergence of anxiety. Through fantasy, the source of the anxiety is transformed into an objectified problem that can be easily externalized and rationalized. A prevalent form that fantasy takes is a story that makes sense on the level of a narrative. While Freud's concerns were largely with the psychopathology of individuals, his work has a broader application to socio-cultural expressions of anxiety and fantasy.

The notion of anxiety as a feature of the age was famously invoked by W. H. Auden in his *Age of Anxiety* in 1948 and has been referred to by social scientists as a social phenomenon (Pahl 1995; Furedi 1997). Furedi relates it to panics around issues of safety while Pahl sees it as a condition that is exacerbated by the flexible work economy. C. Wright Mills (1959) believed that the experience of anxiety was a prevalent condition and one of the major tasks of the 'sociological imagination' to alleviate. The theme of anxiety has been central to the work of Ulrich Beck and Zygmunt Bauman, for whom anxiety is a constitutive feature of contemporary late modern society. Bauman (2006) has characterized this as a condition of 'liquid fear', which arises in a situation of social liquidity wherein the solid foundations of social institutions and substantial identities collapse into a plethora of individualized situations and precariousness. Wilkinson, in an examination of the notion that we are experiencing a heightened and novel state of anxiety, argues that public representations of anxiety do not necessarily correspond to the actual anxieties people experience as a form of personal distress (Wilkinson 1999). Empirical evidence appears to confirm rising levels of anxiety – stress, depression, suicide – associated with work and family life and with men more likely to suffer from anxiety-related problems and those in lower socio-economic groups more prone to anxiety than other groups. There is clearly a difference between anxiety as a psychological condition experienced by an individual and anxiety as a socio-cultural condition by which social problems are represented. The nature of collective and individual phenomena such as identity, trauma and anxiety are different and relate to each other in complex ways. People who suffer from anxiety due to work or family distress may not be responsive to wider societal crises such as global warming while those who may be anxious about the future may not suffer from anxiety as a form of psychological distress. Clearly society cannot be sick in the way an individual may be.

Notwithstanding Wilkinson's reservations on the socio-cultural application of the notion of anxiety and its wider generalizability as a collective phenomenon, the Freudian notion of anxiety has a relevance to the fears that have around European integration and globalization. There is arguably a connection between fear of the other as expressed in racist and xenophobic discourses and the notion of anxiety as a fear that does not have a clearly defined sense of an object. In other words, the symbolic logic at work in fears of others – or xenophobia – corresponds more closely to the symbolic structure of anxiety in that the objectivity of the fear is often objectless and has to be sustained by fantasy. But this symbolic logic has a more general application to the anxieties of the age. Many of the fears that have become central to people today are indeed invisible and intangible. The anxieties of the risk society – ecological catastrophe, biological terrorism, global warming, the rise of biotechnology and genetic engineering – as illustrated by Ulrich Beck provide many examples of a generalized condition of uncertainty that must be constantly rationalized by people in everyday life. This does not necessarily translate into mental distress in the psychological sense of the term. The risk society, as noted by the editor in his introduction to this volume, has now become a risk control society that has touched many areas of life. Potentially everything is subject to risk assessment and surveillance (Rose 1999). The anxieties nurtured by this situation concern issues that are not easily made tangible and are either invisible or highly abstract. Fear of crime and security emergencies in response to terror threats are similarly thriving on a culture of anxiety in which the objective threat must be imagined and given symbolic form. This is where fantasy comes in and offers a way to imagine in concrete and meaningful ways what is otherwise distant and abstract. In other words, the symbolic logic is one of a normalization of fears. It is in this sense, then, that the notion of an 'age of anxiety' is not an inaccurate characterization of current times. As Wilkinson argues, citing Kierkegaard, 'there is an important sense in which anxiety always announces itself to us as something new, since it appears to thrive upon our capacity to look towards the future and anticipate potentially threatening situations (Kierkegaard 1980; Wilkinson 1999: 452).

This account of anxiety as a symbolic process at work in contemporary society is particularly pertinent to an understanding of the new racism, or, as it is often referred to, everyday racism. A feature of racism in Europe today is a shift in the focus of hostility away from colour and race towards more social and cultural characteristics, for instance protecting jobs, concern about welfare benefits, cultural incompatibilities or differences. It is this shift away from the 'biological' racism of the industrial and colonial period that warrants the term 'new racism' (Macmaster 2001). In the new racism xenophobic attitudes, masculinities and 'ordinary' prejudices merge in subtle ways and become easily routinized. For this reason Essed (1991) uses the term 'everyday racism'. The normalization of racism can be found on many levels and takes different forms, in the media, in education, in policing, in work. This normalization might lead to the incorrect conclusion that racism has disappeared, when in fact it has simply taken more subtle forms (*Race and Class* 2001; Fekete 2001). It may also be pointed out that the normalization of racism in less overt forms in fact disguises an increase in racism.

This is evident in the way the extreme right in many countries has entered the mainstream by refining its electoral programmes, using less overt forms of racism and use. The move away from overt racism allows these parties to expand their electoral support as populist-nationalist parties (Rydgren 2003a, 2003b). In many cases the extreme right denies any connection with racism and justifies its policies in terms of the language of liberty, justice and rights. The recodification of the racialized subject as culturally incompatible facilitates the potential labelling of any group or individual as other. What in fact is occurring is a normalization of racism in political discourse in the public sphere as a process of 'othering' (Van Dijk 1985; Wodak and Van Dijk 2000). In the case of minorities and migration today the shift to cultural modes of racism as a form of othering is in part a response to the fact that much migration in Europe is internal and the 'others', while being racialized, are not identifiable as races as such. In this sense it is possible to speak of what Blok (1998), following Freud, terms a 'narcissism of minor differences'. Furthermore, the existence of anti-racism and various forms of anti-discrimination legislation in official policy disguises considerable racism in the everyday practices of institutions (Lentin 2004). The other becomes a source of anxiety because it can be anyone.

The episode in September 2005 when offensive cartoons depicting the Muslim prophet Muhammad appeared in Danish and Norwegian newspapers encapsulates this trend towards a normalization of racism. This was not an isolated episode, for the cartoons were reprinted in many European countries. The immediate consequences were not just confined to Europe but were global, with public burnings of the Danish flag in many Islamic countries throughout the world; in some cases the EU flag was burned. The defence of the cartoons was generally in the name of liberal values such as free speech.

The normalization of racism through the articulation of symbolic constructions of otherness is a result of the mobilization of society around cultural notions of peoplehood. Many countries generally associated with progressive multiculturalism are now questioning multiculturalism. In the UK this is reflected in the new concern with British values. The Dutch case is the most striking example of a broader move beyond multiculturalism. Following the murders of the politician, Pym Fortuyn, in 2002, and in 2004 of the film-maker Theo van Gogh, the Netherlands experienced a move to the right which culminated in the No vote to the constitutional treaty in 2005. This shift occurred not as a rejection of liberal values but as a defence of them against the perceived threat from multiculturalism and transnationalism.

Multiculturalism is being increasingly portrayed as undermining integration. Although not an outright attack on multiculturalism, Robert Putnam has recently argued that diversity does not always support integration. It would appear that multiculturalism is under attack and seen as a cause of social break-up; it is also held responsible for the decline of national models of social integration. The retreat from multiculturalism is occurring at a time when culture is increasingly becoming contested and open to multiple meanings, making any notion of peoplehood difficult. Peoplehood is not normally questioned and when it is in question it becomes uncertain. It is not the case that in the past people agreed with certain definitions of nation-hood or peoplehood, but rather they were less challenged in their collective identity. The anxieties that are manifesting themselves are not unconnected with fears that national identities may no longer be able to sustain themselves against stronger and more assertive migrant or ethnic identities. This is one of the anxieties that is taking shape around the so-called war on terror. The security of the state has lent itself to concerns about the viability of collective identities at a time when such identities have lost the power to offer secure reference points.

Insecurity, Social Fragmentation and the Erosion of Solidarity

The rise of the extreme right throughout Europe, with some exceptions, is a product of social fears being channelled into political support for right-wing parties, whose support derives from social anxieties and fears. It is a case of a generalized anxiety becoming expressed in fear of others. Immigrants have been the obvious targets for these parties who have frequently been able to combine fears of immigration with anxieties over jobs and welfare. The Europe-wide trend to third way and centre right-style politics has created a space for such parties to exploit social fears. Such anxieties, combined with the perceived loss of national sovereignty and changes in the nature of employment, are fertile ground for xenophobic currents. The European project of the transnationalization of the nation state is occurring at the same time as the state is retreating from the social commitments with which it had been associated. The proposed European constitution did little to address such concerns and seemingly was a continuation of the transnationalization of the nation state. Such developments lead to the affirmation of nation and statehood.

Racism and xenophobia are sustained by the decline of class- and nation-based solidarities rather than by a turn in the political culture to the right. Throughout Europe, there has been a progressive weakening of class and nation as foundations of solidarity. The resulting anxieties are easily translated into xenophobia as well as more direct expressions of racism. Central to this is the loss of traditional forms of status due to changes in the nature of work and family life. European integration began in the post-Second World War period on the basis of industrial society and the consolidating welfare states that were closely allied to industrial economies in a period of economic growth. The current phase of Europeanization is occurring in very different circumstances.

There has been a decisive shift from the industrial society of the early period of European integration to the current post-industrial information society in which a 'New Economy' based on knowledge, technical innovation and global markets has come into existence. This is a society that has witnessed the decline of class politics and changed relations between elites and masses whereby the elites can no longer rely on the traditional forms of loyalty and obedience. Consciousness of inequalities and social problems as class-based is less likely in the context of what Bauman (2000) terms societal liquidity; instead, problems become framed in different and often more culturally diffuse ways, of which the language of identity and 'ways of life' discourses are among the major vehicles for the expression of social discontent. The rebellious masses include the middle class, whose political dissatisfaction has increased due to the precariousness of their social situation and the perceived loss in status and reward. The New Economy has brought with it greater insecurities for the middle class, for whom professional occupations and educational attainment no longer guarantee the allocation of rewards and status (Sennett 1998, 2006). This is very well illustrated in the crisis over pensions, which encapsulates the experience of the future as one of uncertainty. It is arguably the case that the new wave of anxieties is due to changes in the circumstances more of the middle class than of the working class. While a large number of the population still enjoy secure employment, the number who have insecure employment has risen considerably, as has that of the marginalized.

Axel Honneth (2004) has commented on the paradoxes of self-realization in contemporary society. The individualism of self-realization has become intertwined with a consumption-driven tendency with the result of increasing rather than decreasing suffering. Self-realization as self-development is one thing, but another is the social discontent that arises when freedom becomes translated into, on the one side, a productive force to facilitate flexibility in the deregulated hyper-capitalist economy and, on the other, a force compelling people into putting an undue emphasis on immediate gratification. Boltanski and Chiapello (2007) have referred to this as the 'new spirit of capitalism', which in their analysis has moved from the older forms of economic and moral security to forms of organization that, while giving more autonomy to workers, generates greater insecurity. In an insightful analysis of what he calls the 'vertigo of late modernity', Jock Young (2007) has written about the rise of new middle-class anxieties in a situation in which work has become a source of disappointment. The vertigo of late modernity 'leads large sectors of people in the lower to middle part of the class structure to experience what Nietzsche called *ressentiment*, a feeling of anger, bitterness, powerlessness, which searches out culprits and mobilises difference' (Young 2007: 10). The social conditions that give rise to this are insecurities of status and of economic position. One of his central arguments is that of the precariousness of inclusion. Reward through merit is no longer a reliable guide to the future. Late modernity brings with it a sense of the randomness of reward and a chaos of identity (Young 2007: 34–5). Success has become a lottery, and while there are increased opportunities for self-realization through instantaneous consumption, nothing is certain. The possibility of downward mobility is ever-present. This is a situation in which class-based forms of awareness and solidarity are undermined by a pervasive fragmentation of collective experience. The line separating the included and the excluded is not one that can be easily drawn in a credit-driven society of consumption and the casualization of work. In his insightful analysis, Young argues against the polarity of an included middle class that is contented and secure and an excluded underclass that lacks an interest in the values of the middle class. Both, obviously in different ways, experience a sense of the incoherence and precariousness of fairness, on the one side, and on the other a pervasive insecurity that has consequences for their sense of status and recognition. 'Psychodynamically, *ressentiment*, whether of the moral indignation of the middle class or the feelings of humiliation of the poor, are assuaged by attempts to essentialise identity, to achieve ontological fixity and closure' (Young 2007: 206). What Young draws attention to is a major change in the nature of class in contemporary capitalism. The middle class has experienced a major crisis of upward mobility, with insecurity now a prospect facing much of the middle class. It has become revanchist, rejecting political programmes aimed at inclusion since such a politics does not benefit only it but also the working class. In short, the middle class supported inclusionary policies only so long as it was the chief beneficiary.

Young people in particular are more prone to insecurity. A recent study of young people presents wide-ranging empirical evidence of the impact of major societal changes as one of insecurity (Blossfield *et al.* 2005). This insecurity is yet more intensified for those at the margins of society and constitutes a social malaise. A striking example of this was the riots in France in November 2005, when ethnic minority groups, mostly of North African background, reacted to the death of two Muslim youths in a French suburb. This was the event that provoked violent clashes with the police and involved burnings of some 9,000 cars and several public buildings. Widespread anger and resentment against poverty and marginalization, and against the circumstances in deprived working-class suburbs, was the background to these events, which were quickly repeated in several other European countries. Although on a smaller scale than in France where a state of emergency was declared, in Germany, Spain, Belgium and the Netherlands there were also riots involving the burning of cars and buildings. It was not only resentment at high employment and social deprivation that played a role in the riots. The negative image of Islam in France and the popular view of the middle class that the French Muslim ghettos are hotbeds of Islamic militancy were important factors in politicizing the Muslim youths to rebel against their social and cultural marginalization. The riots can be seen as symptomatic of a social malaise in western European countries where a new kind of poverty and social marginalization is developing and in which migrants and ethnic communities are most likely to be based. It may be an exaggeration to say that the traditional class conflict has been replaced by a conflict of migrants versus citizens, but there is some truth to it as far as the most visible cleavages today are concerned. Quite a different case were the riots in the small northern English towns of Burnley, Oldham and Bradford in 2001 when white working-class groups engaged in acts of hostility against Asian minorities. This episode illustrates very well resentment against groups whose fortunes were perceived to be more favourable. The white working class had suffered a loss in socio-economic position resulting in a pervasive undermining of the bonds of solidarity and community spirit. Internally weakened social discontent was projected outwards against the large Asian community.

The social predicament discussed here is one of social fragmentation that is conducive to diverse expressions. Crime is one such product of discontent and is fuelled by economic insecurity and deprivation, as Young (2007) argues. Discontent can be mobilized in different ways to produce resentment

at the well-off or against migrants. Discontent is fuelled by relative deprivation, not absolute deprivation, and with the disappearance or narrowing of
cultural differences it is given an additional impetus. As migrants take on
board more of the values of the core society they lose their separateness and
easily become targets of hatred and resentment. Notions of the otherness of
migrants or ethnic communities are reinforced by the erosion of community
and solidarity within the core population.

It is conceivably the case, then, that the rise in nationalism and xenophobia
is connected with the transformation of work, family and status rather than
due to the appeal of the extreme right. Anxiety about the future is a key
dynamic in this. As argued earlier, anxiety is fuelled by the experience of
insecurity which is not simply an existential condition that can be explained
by psychopathologies but has its roots in socio-economic conditions and the
wider transformation of capitalism. The cultural crisis of Europeanization is
to a large degree a crisis in community and solidarities. The undermining of
class and nation as substantive sources of identity as a result of Europeanization and globalization has heralded widespread feelings of insecurity and
anxiety.

Conclusion: Social Justice and Recognition

The paradox in all of this is that while migrants are becoming more and
more plural and transnational and where cosmopolitan orientations are
much in evidence, national societies are now losing much of their pluralism. The
European project is on the defensive and multiculturalism is in question.
Many countries are undergoing a re-nationalization of collective identities.
Although such developments should not be exaggerated as amounting to
what Wacquant (2007) calls 'advanced marginality', it is possible to speak of
a crisis of solidarity at the core of European integration. The EU has not
succeeded in developing a collective European identity that is in any way an
alternative to national identity and the best that it can achieve is a nested
identity that is compatible with national identity and in many cases is
derivative of national identity. There is considerable resistance to a deepening
of Europeanization and a growing association of Europeanization with
globalization. It would appear to be the case that resistance to Europe and
fears about market forces have become embroiled in anxieties about identity
and security for the future. This is a situation in which multiculturalism has
become the first casualty.

The way out of the current crisis is unclear. It could be suggested that one
possibility should be the recovery of a sense of collective purpose that has
been lost. The European project has been mainly a project of the transnationalization of the European nation state, having gone far beyond its earlier
rationale of market integration. As Rumford (this volume) argues, on the one
side, the EU has been built on a commitment to mobility – of goods, capital,
labour and services – while on the other hand it has now become concerned
with imposing restrictions on mobility in the name of security. This, too, is a
further example of the crisis of European solidarity. However, the way
forward cannot simply be defined in terms of mobility, whether more or less

is what is desirable. It seems to be essential that the EU becomes associated with a social programme in which there is an affirmation of forms of recognition that go beyond formally legal categories. A commitment to social justice and solidarity is absent and it is this that is clearly a major source of social discontent. However, there is room for some hope. Solidarity has been given specific mention in the EU's Charter of Fundamental Rights, which was adopted in Nice in 2000 and incorporated into the Constitutional Treaty in 2004 (Ross 2007). The preamble states that the Union 'is founded on the indivisible, universal values of human dignity, freedom, equality and solidarity'.

While social policy will continue to be implemented by national societies as required by the principle of subsidiarity that is the defining tenet of the EU, this need not exclude the possibility of a new vision of Europe built around social justice and solidarity. The commitment to solidarity, despite its elusive nature, invoked in the Constitutional Treaty may be a basis to inspire social policy around a wider vision of a European model of society. It is essential that this is an inclusive notion and one that can address the rising tide of social discontent.

References

Appadurai, A. (2006), *Fear of Small Numbers*, Durham, NC: Duke University Press.
Bauman, Z. (2000), *Liquid Modernity*, Cambridge: Polity Press.
Bauman, Z. (2006), *Liquid Fear*, Cambridge: Polity Press.
Blok, A. (1998), The narcissism of minor differences, *European Journal of Social Theory*, 1, 1: 33–56.
Blossfield, H.-P., Klijzing, E., Mills, M. and Kurz, K. (eds) (2005), *Globalization, Uncertainty and Youth in Society*, London: Routledge.
Boltanski, L. and Chiapello, E. (2007), *The New Spirit of Capitalism*, London: Verso.
Delanty, G. and O'Mahony, P. (2002), *Nationalism and Social Theory*, London: Sage.
Delanty, G., Wodak, R. and Jones, P. (eds) (2007), *Migration, Belonging and Exclusion in Europe*, Liverpool: Liverpool University Press.
Eriksen, E. (ed.) (2005), *Making the Euro-Polity: Reflexive Integration in Europe*, London: Routledge.
Essed, P. (1991), *Understanding Everyday Racism*, Newbury Park, CA: Sage.
Fekete, L. (2001), The emergence of xeno-racism, *Race and Class*, 43, 2: 23–40.
Freud, S. (1979), *On Psychopathology: Inhibitions, Symptoms and Anxiety and Other Works*, London: Penguin Books.
Furedi, F. (1997), *Culture of Fear: Risk-taking and the Morality of Low Expectation*, London: Cassell.
Habermas, J. (1998), *The Inclusion of the Other: Studies in Political Theory*, Cambridge, MA: MIT Press.
Habermas, J. (2001), *The Postnational Constellation*, Cambridge: Polity Press.
Holmes, D. (2006), Nationalism in Europe. In G. Delanty and K. Kumar (eds), *Handbook of Nations and Nationalism*, London: Sage.
Honneth, A. (2004), Organized self-realization, *European Journal of Social Theory*, 7, 4: 463–78.
Huysmans, J. (2005), *The Politics of Insecurity: Fear, Migration and Asylum in the EU*, London: Routledge.
Kierkegaard, S. (1980), *The Concept of Anxiety: A Simple Psychologically Orienting Deliberation on the Dogmatic Issues of Hereditary Sin*, Princeton, NJ: Princeton University Press.

Lentin, A. (2004), *Race and Anti-Racism in Europe*, London: Pluto Press.

Macmaster, N. (2001), *Racism in Europe*, London: Palgrave.

Mills, C. W. (1959), *The Sociological Imagination*, New York: Oxford University Press.

Pahl, R. (1995), *After-Success: Fin-de-Siècle Anxiety and Identity*, Cambridge: Polity Press.

Race and Class (2001), Special Issue: *The Three Faces of British Racism*, 43, 2.

Robin, C. (2005), *Fear: History of an Idea*, Oxford: Oxford University Press.

Rose, N. (1999), *Powers of Freedom*, Cambridge: Cambridge University Press.

Ross, M. (2007), Promoting solidarity: from public services to a European model of competition? *Common Market Law Review*, 44: 1057–80.

Rydgren, J. (2003a), Mesolevel causes of racism and xenophobia, *European Journal of Social Theory*, 6.

Rydgren, J. (2003b), *The Populist Challenge: Political Protest and Ethno-Nationalist Mobilization in France*, Oxford: Berghahn Books.

Salecl, R. (2004), *On Anxiety*, London: Routledge.

Sennett, R. (1998), *The Corrosion of Character: The Personal Consequences of Work and the New Capitalism*, New York: Norton.

Sennett, R. (2006), *The Culture of the New Capitalism*, New Haven, CT: Yale University Press.

Van Dijk, T. (1985), *Prejudice in Discourse*, London: Sage.

Wacquant, L. (2007), Territorial stigmatization in the age of advanced marginality, *Thesis Eleven*, 91: 66–77.

Wilkinson, I. (1999), Where is the novelty in our current 'age of anxiety'? *European Journal of Social Theory*, 2, 4: 445–67.

Wodak, R. and Van Dijk, T. (2000), *Racism at the Top: Parliamentary Discourses on Ethnic Issues in Six European States*, Klagenfurt, Austria: Drava.

Young, J. (2007), *The Vertigo of Late Modernity*, London: Sage.

10

'We Don't Have to Take This': Zero Tolerance of Violence against Health Care Workers in a Time of Insecurity

Jonathan Gabe and Mary Ann Elston

It is regularly claimed that we live in insecure times (Vail 1999). Insecurity, fear and risk are said to have seeped into the fabric of people's lives and now dominate their thinking. Alongside concerns about natural hazards such as earthquakes and floods, people are said to be increasingly fearful of endogenous dangers such as environmental pollution, crime and occupational injuries. One work setting that is considered to be risky is health care, where violence from patients and others is said to be a cause for concern for health care workers. Support for this comes from the British Crime Survey, which regularly reports that doctors and nurses are among those most at risk of threats and assaults in the workplace (Budd 1999, 2001; Upson 2004). In this chapter we review the current UK government's policy of 'zero tolerance', which has been developed ostensibly to minimize the risk of such violence, and consider the reasons for its introduction and some of the potential consequences. The chapter starts with an account of the policy, the definition of violence that underpins it and how it has been measured, and assesses the evidence regarding prevalence. This is then interpreted in the context of wider policies of zero tolerance to crime, and debates about risk, anxiety and insecurity.

The NHS Zero Tolerance Zone Campaign and Beyond

The UK cross-government 'NHS Zero Tolerance Zone' (ZTZ) campaign was launched in 1999, ostensibly in response to professional and political concern about violence against health care workers from the public (GMSC 1994, 1995; DoH 1999a; NHS Executive 1999, 2000; RCN 1998). The campaign required National Health Service (NHS) organizations to develop preventive and 'zero-tolerant' risk management strategies and aimed to raise awareness among staff in general practice surgeries and hospitals about the need to report violent incidents to their employers or managers. It spelt out the action that might be taken against perpetrators and set targets for reducing incidents of violence and aggression by 20 per cent by 2001 and 30 per cent by 2003. The key message to NHS staff and to the public was that attempts to intimidate should no longer be accepted as an occupational hazard. A repeatedly used ZTZ slogan was: 'We don't have to take this' (DoH 1999a, 1999b). This slogan would seem to be in line with the broader policy objective of the current Labour government of countering disruptive challenges to the everyday lives of people by seeking to build resilience, as the latter was no longer deemed to be able to flourish by itself. According to Furedi (this volume) the promotion of resilience is motivated by the belief among policy-makers that society has become vulnerable to a growing range of threats to its security. In the face of such vulnerability the role of policy-makers is to develop policies to anticipate risk and help people to withstand shock so that they can 'bounce back'.

In the case of general practice, specific Department of Health initiatives made new provision for persistently violent patients to forfeit the right to be registered with a GP within their immediate locality and called for local development schemes to be established to deal with such patients where necessary (e.g. involving the employment of security guards at particular surgeries). In 2001, all GP practices were sent a poster to display in their waiting rooms, stating that 'Violent patients will be reported to the police and struck-off the GP's list' (NHS Executive 2001a).

Between 1997 and 2002, the Department of Health announced at least fourteen 'key initiatives aimed at reducing and ultimately preventing violence and aggression against NHS staff'. These included consecutive relaunches of the ZTZ campaign (NAO 2003a: 41).

In 2004 the NHS in England announced plans for what has been claimed to be the largest ever training programme in the UK, if not in Europe: a one-day 'conflict resolution course' to be made available to all frontline NHS staff – potentially 730,000 people (Oxtoby 2004). Two years later, in June 2006, the government indicated that it was supporting proposals from the NHS Counter Fraud and Security Management Service (CFSMS) to create a new offence of causing nuisance or disturbance on NHS premises or against NHS staff working in the community. NHS security officers were to be given authority to remove offenders physically without assistance from the police. They would be able to refer offenders to the magistrate's court for a fine of up to £1,000, whether or not the police brought charges under criminal justice law. In the words of the health minister, Caroline Flint, 'NHS staff deserve respect, not abuse. That is why we are sending a clear message to the small minority who are abusive, drunken or behave anti-socially on NHS premises, that this will not be tolerated' (DoH 2006). The headline in the press release announcing the policy made reference to 'bullies' being 'shown a red card', drawing an analogy with the way in which serious misbehaviour is dealt with on the football pitch, with offenders being sent off by the referee. The rhetoric was about being 'tough' on offenders and encouraging a 'culture of respect' which would be enforced where necessary. These sentiments are in line with New Labour's claim to be tough on crime, as well as its causes, and their general policy of promoting responsible citizens who must eschew anti-social behaviour (Clarke 2005). Also referred to was the claim that there had been a fifteen-fold increase in prosecutions by the CFSMS since it had taken charge of violence minimization in the NHS, and the hope that evidence of such action would make staff more confident to report incidents. In September 2007 it was announced by the Health Secretary Alan Johnson, at the Labour Party conference, that £97 million was being set aside to provide personal safety alarms to staff who wanted them to combat violence, and to pay for more private prosecutions by NHS staff who have been assaulted (Helm 2007). There is thus a clear continuity in the thinking between these latest initiatives and the initial ZTZ campaign, with a consistent emphasis on staff resilience, responsibilizing individual patients and threatening to forfeit their right to health care.

Behind the ZTZ campaign and recent training and safety and security initiatives is a recognition that work-related violence is a major financial as well as human risk facing the NHS. The direct cost of violence to the NHS was estimated by the National Audit Office (NAO) in 2003 to be at least £69 million per annum. (It is important to note that this estimate did not include the costs of staff replacement, treatment or compensation. In addition, this estimate took 'no account of the human costs, such as physical and/or psychological pain and increased stress levels, which are known to be substantial, nor the impact of violence and aggression on staff confidence and retention'.) It was also estimated by the NAO that violent incidents represented 40 per cent of all recorded health and safety incidents in the NHS (NAO 2003a: 4, 9).

In addition to issues of cost these policy developments also reflect pressing NHS concerns about recruitment and retention of staff, such as nurses and general practitioners. It is no surprise that the ZTZ initiative was based in the human resources section of the NHS Executive until 2003. Subsequently, as referred to above, responsibility for violence has passed to the newly established NHS Counter Fraud and Security Management Service, perhaps reflecting the development of risk thinking about violence in the NHS (Elston *et al.* 2006).

While it is clear that violence against NHS staff has been high on the policy agenda since the late 1990s, what needs to be established next is how violence has been defined in such policy documents and statements. We now turn to consider this issue.

Classifying Violence: Can Risk Be Calculated in a Rational Manner?

There has been much debate in policy and academic circles about how to define violence (e.g. Hearn and Parkin 2001). In line with the views of feminists that attention should be broadened from physical violence (specifically physical assaults involving injury) to take account of the impact of verbal abuse and aggressive acts regardless of whether physical injury has been caused (e.g. Kelly and Radford 1996), a more inclusive definition has been adopted by policy-makers. The ZTZ campaign has thus formally adopted the following inclusive definition of work-related violence, provided by the European Commission:

Box 1

What does workplace violence involve?

Physical violence

- assault causing death
- assault causing serious physical injury (requiring hospital treatment)
- minor injuries requiring first-aid
- physical attack not causing injury (kicking, biting, punching)
- use of weapons and/or missiles
- sexual assault

Non-physical violence

- verbal abuse, swearing or shouting, name-calling and insults
- racial or sexual harassment
- threats – with or without weapons
- physical posturing and/or threatening gestures
- abusive telephone calls or letters
- bullying
- deliberate silence

Source: NAO (2003a: 46).

[Work-related] violence means any incident where staff are abused, threatened or assaulted in circumstances related to their work, involving an explicit or implicit challenge to their safety, well-being or health. (Wynne *et al.* 1997)

NHS organizations and their staff are expected to follow this definition in recording incidents of violence. This helps to standardize its meaning and renders violence rationally calculable. The current official definition of violence in the NHS highlights the impact of violence on staff, including much more than physical assaults, as shown in box 1. The prevailing message of ZTZ to NHS staff is that they 'don't have to take' these behaviours, regardless of the state of physical or mental health of the perpetrators. For example, the ZTZ definition recognizes that receiving abusive or threatening phone calls from a patient's relative might have greater impact on a health care worker's 'well-being or health' than being scratched by a very elderly, confused patient. However, in either incident this behaviour ought to be reported to a manager or (in the case of general practice) employer.

It seems, however, that this inclusive definition of violence is not universally used by the NHS and other health care organizations or in current research. An example of this lack of consensus can be seen in the research on violence in acute in-patient mental health care commissioned by the UKCC. In this research, the term 'violence' is specifically associated with physical force, as distinct from 'abuse' or 'aggression' (Wright et al. 2002). Guidelines recently issued by NICE relating to the same clinical area also follow this definition (NICE 2005: 82).

Of course, drawing a terminological distinction between violence and verbal abuse, for example, does not imply that the latter should be looked upon as insignificant. In addition, using the term 'violence' inclusively does not disqualify drawing distinctions between sub-types of violence, as exemplified when the ZTZ campaign launched an initiative focused on harassment (NHS Executive 2002). Also, being able to make such distinctions in data may be very important, for example, when considering the meaning of different types of incident to 'victims'.

More importantly for the present argument, however, is the consequence of adopting a more inclusive definition. It almost goes without saying that the more inclusive the definition of 'violence' used, the greater the reported prevalence rate of unpalatable incidents. For example, in health care work, verbal abuse is more frequently experienced than physical assault. As an illustration of this point take, for example, a readers' survey in the *Nursing Times* in 2004 which reported that approximately nine out of ten nurse respondents had been verbally abused at work at some time in their career (Anonymous 2004; Norris 2004). If these respondents were representative of nursing as a whole, virtually all nurses should expect to have at least one episode of verbal abuse (i.e. of violence according to the ZTZ definition) in a nursing career. Thus, violence comes to be established as a very frequent, statistically normal experience for nurses. Similarly, a study of violence experienced by general practitioners (Elston et al. 2002) reported that 75 per cent had been verbally abused in the last two years, whereas 10 per cent reported being assaulted. If verbal abuse is taken as the indicator of violence, then prevalence is much greater than if assaults are taken as the measure.

Increasing the variety of behaviours that are counted as work-related violence not only turns 'violence' into a moderately normal experience for doctors and nurses. It also widens the number of persons who are defined as perpetrators of violence. As a result, what was a rare, deviant minority is transformed into potentially any patient or member of the public. Thus, adopting an inclusive definition of violence has involved employing a rather different understanding of violence from one that sees patients' violence as a consequence of their health problems.

Measuring Risk: What Is the Prevalence of Violence?

Faced with the variety of definitions described above, it is clear that statistical evidence on the prevalence of violence to UK health care staff needs to be approached with caution (see Wells and Bowers 2002; Committee of Public Accounts 2003; Lee and Stanko 2003). Two main types of data on work-related violence need to be distinguished: organizational records and victim surveys. In the case of organizational records, it is commonly acknowledged that many incidents of violence and aggression at work go unrecorded, even in those organizations where reporting procedures and definitions have been long established. It seems that doctors are particularly reluctant to report health and safety incidents (NAO 2003a: 18), although this also appears to be the case with nurses (O'Beirne and Gabe 2005). A study comparing videotape evidence with incident reports in a psychiatric in-patient setting identified 155 videotaped assaults (not all by patients on staff), in contrast to 12 officially recorded incidents over the study period (Crowner et al. 1994). There may be many reasons for such under-reporting. These include: staff dismissing incidents as trivial (including serious incidents); discounting them because of the patient's medical condition; being put off by apparently cumbersome reporting procedures; and believing that making a report would bring little benefit and possibly disadvantage (e.g. stigma in the face of perceived professional incompetence) (Cembrowicz and Shepherd 1992; Beale 1999).

It is evident that changes in reporting practices may result in artefactual changes in recorded rates of work-related violence. The NHS ZTZ programme appears to be a case in point. The aims of the programme included the improvement of management systems for reporting and recording violence within NHS organizations, the universal adoption of the inclusive ZTZ definition of violence, and an increased use of such systems by staff. Even partially meeting these aims might be expected to result in an increase in recorded incidents of violence. Consequently, it is not surprising that the official record of incidents of violence against NHS trust staff in England has increased from approximately 65,000 in 1998/9 (before the ZTZ campaign had properly begun) to close to 84,000 in 2001/2, and 95,000 in 2002/3. This represents an increase of 46 per cent over five years.

When the National Audit Office reviewed the ZTZ campaign in 2003 it attributed much of the increase in officially recorded incidents to 'better awareness of reporting with more widespread use of the common [ZTZ] definition which includes verbal abuse'. While acknowledging that 'increased hospital activity, higher patient expectations and frustrations due to increased waiting times' might be relevant, the NAO's conclusion with regard to violence in NHS trusts was that:

> Wide variations in reporting standards, different definitions and continued under-reporting, make it impossible to say conclusively how far the increase in reported violence reflects an actual increase in incidents or measures how trusts, individually or overall, are performing. There also remains a high and varied level of under-reporting of incidents (which we estimate is around 39 per cent). (NAO 2003a: 2)

The second type of data source is the 'victim' survey: this relies on retrospective data, usually collected by structured questionnaire, about the experience of violence of samples of health care workers. Usually, these data show higher prevalence rates (the likelihood of workers having been a victim over a specified time period) than organizational records for comparable work settings. However, comparing evidence from different surveys can be difficult because of variations in operationalizing and measuring violence, and sampling differences. There is also the problem of response bias with surveys on this topic. Those who have been the victims of work-related violence may be more likely to reply than those who have not, resulting in an overestimate of risk. And this may be the case even if the original sample was representative of the population being targeted. Surveys like that mentioned earlier in the *Nursing Times* should be treated with particular care on these grounds, and also because readers of the article who participated in the survey may not be representative of nursing in general, in terms of the work they do and the work-related violence they experience.

One well-respected source of survey data on work-related violence in the UK is the British Crime Survey (BCS), conducted regularly since 1991. Based on a large, nationally representative sample (approximately 36,000 respondents in 2002/3) (Budd 1999, 2001; Upson 2004) and with a response rate of over 70 per cent, the BCS is probably not subject to the response bias mentioned above. However, it uses a more restrictive definition of violence than, for example, that used in the ZTZ campaign, focusing on violence at work relating only to 'all assaults or threats which occurred while the victim was working and were perpetrated by members of the public', and not, for example, to verbal abuse (Budd 2001: 2). This definition reflects the survey's broader concern with criminal offences in general and not just violence at work.

Contrary to the commonly held view that work-related violence is increasing, evidence from the BCS is that for workers in general the overall risk of being assaulted has *fallen* by 54 per cent from 1995, when it peaked, to 2004/5, and is now below that reported in 1991 when the BCS began (Home Office 2005). However, this survey, like others comparing a range of occupations (e.g. International Labour Organization *et al.* 2002; Wells and Bowers 2002), does reveal that the chance of being a victim of assaults and threats at work is greater for health workers than for most occupations, the exception being those in protective service occupations, for example police officers, fire fighters and prison service guards who report significantly more assaults (Upson 2004). Among health workers the prevalence rate is highest for nurses. In the latter case it seems that those in the UK are particularly at risk, with one recent international survey reporting that in Europe the prevalence of violence against nurses is higher only in France (Estryn-Behar *et al.* 2008).

A further recent source of national data is the annual NHS National Staff Survey (NSS) conducted by the Healthcare Commission since 2003. The fifth NSS, conducted in 2007, covered staff employed by 391 NHS trusts in England providing acute/specialist, ambulance, mental health and primary care services. Overall, the 2007 NSS found that, among staff responding, 13 per cent reported experiencing physical violence and 26 per cent some form of bullying, non-physical abuse or harassment from patients or patients' relatives during the previous twelve months. Figures were generally similar to those reported in 2006 and 2005, suggesting that the rates of violence were stable, compared to rates from the BCS. Primary care staff appear to be much less likely to be physically assaulted than those providing mental health nursing or emergency care, but the differences are less for non-physical violence (Healthcare Commission 2008).

Work-related Violence in a 'Risk Culture'

Regardless of the actual prevalence of work-related violence, this is still an issue that many health care workers are concerned about. It is difficult to establish the extent to which such concern arises from: direct experience of violence; changing perceptions of verbal abuse and other forms of non-physical aggression; increased awareness of reports of violence; or regular exposure to initiatives designed to prevent and manage violence. However, this concern about violence is in tune with the risk culture, and with the uncertainty expressed by NHS health care workers in general about how to minimize such risk. According to Annandale (1996), a culture has developed in the NHS in which patients are increasingly seen as risk-generators. In this context it is best to adopt the 'precautionary principle' approach to risk management and assume it is better to be 'safe than sorry', even in the absence of clear-cut evidence of risk (Kemshall and Wood, this volume). With the reconstruction of patients as consumers with enhanced rights and expectations, as a result of a series of NHS reforms first introduced in the 1980s, new demands for accountability have arisen. These have in turn resulted in increased self-surveillance and defensive clinical practice on the part of health care staff. Annandale is concerned mainly with clinical risks, patient safety and malpractice allegations. However, her analysis is also relevant to work-related violence in a variety of ways. References to increasingly demanding consumers who are quick to emphasize their rights occur in many accounts of the allegedly growing problem of violence to NHS staff (e.g. NAO 2003b: 2; Hart 2004: 264; Oxtoby 2004: 23). Put another way, the generators of risk in the new risk culture are defined as coming from not just the small group of 'the seriously mad' or 'the very bad', but potentially from the majority, 'normal' public, particularly if an inclusive definition of violence is used.

This representation may have mixed consequences. On the one hand, doctors and nurses may come to see themselves as more vulnerable to violence, and feel under pressure to be more risk-aware. On the other hand, constructing aggressive and offensive behaviour from the public as 'out of order' and deserving of a robust reaction puts responsibility on the patient or employing organization. Like all employers, the NHS has a legal obligation to try and ensure the health and safety of its staff (NAO 2003b). In the next section we show how NHS policies for preventing and managing violence have been influenced by wider debates about zero tolerance in contemporary society.

Zero Tolerance as a Rhetorical Device

The NHS's zero tolerance campaign and more recent initiatives can also be understood in the context of debates around zero tolerance policing (ZTP). That term was first coined in the United States and was associated with New York's Mayor Giuliani and Police Commissioner Bratton's policy of 'hard policing' against both 'crime' and 'disorder' in the 1990s (Newburn 2002; Jones and Newburn 2004). It was seen as a necessary response to a crisis of urban governance and the need to respond quickly in neighbourhoods on the cusp of decline in order to halt a spiral of deterioration and criminality and address growing anxiety and fear among local residents. Underpinning the policy, therefore, was the acceptance of Wilson and Keeling's (1982) 'broken window' thesis that in order to have a major impact on 'serious crime' the police need to target and prioritize action against low-level disorder.

Although associated with conservative Republican politics, zero tolerance has been taken up and employed by the Labour government in the UK (Newburn 2002) (and by other governments around the world – Jones and Newburn 2006; Reiner 2007). In part this can be explained in terms of the power of the media in endorsing zero tolerance as a means of managing insecurity and reinvigorating faith in the ability of central and local state agencies to combat crime and promote an inclusive solidarity (Stenson 2000a). However, embarking on such a strategy can be double-edged as any subsequent failure to deliver a reduction in crime rates can open politicians up to public scrutiny and bring those agencies tasked with implementing the strategy into disrepute (see Kemshall and Wood, this volume).

Zero tolerance also chimes with New Labour's 'third way' strategy of being tough on crime and tough on the causes of crime (Downes and Morgan 2007), incorporating the New Right's emphasis on 'populist punitiveness' and the Old Left's concern with equality of opportunity. ZTZ was a way to justify increased spending on policing and on crime prevention and reduction strategies, while offering the prospect of enabling the police to regain control of neighbourhoods of the 'socially excluded', thereby creating the conditions for social and economic regeneration. Newburn (2002) argues that New Labour developed its policy of zero tolerance (and other crime control policies) in part as a way of appealing to middle-class voters, following lessons learnt from the electoral success of Bill Clinton and the Democrats in the USA after years in the political wilderness. The phrase 'zero tolerance' represents what Wacquant (1999) refers to as *mots d'ordres*, which have both powerful symbolic value and incite law and order. As Newburn suggests, it has a mesmeric quality that connects with a cultural predisposition to believe in an instant cure. According to Young (1999), two fallacies underpin this search for an easy miracle: first a cosmetic fallacy that social problems like violence are easy to deal with if the right treatment is found; and second, the fallacy that the 'social is simple', making interventions obvious and easy to identify. The adoption of zero tolerance can also be seen to reflect the influence of the punitive-penal policy complex – bureaucratic, political and moral entrepreneurial interests articulated through major neo-liberal think tanks which campaigned for zero tolerance crime control policies on both sides of the Atlantic in the 1990s (Newburn 2002; Jones and Newburn 2004). And finally, it can be seen as a rhetorical device to challenge complacency in the public services and to promote a culture and mindset conducive to continuous change and to meeting externally set targets (Stenson 2000b). As such, it fits well with the shift in policy around policing and criminal justice from (disciplinary) rehabilitation to containment involving risk assessment and risk management. It is against this background that New Labour's powerful attachment to the rhetoric of zero tolerance and its willingness to apply it to a range of policy areas, including violence against health care professionals, can be understood.

In the final two sections we elaborate further on how NHS policies for preventing and managing violence have been framed in terms of risk.

Regulating Risk through the ZTZ Campaign

It is apparent from the above discussion that the issue of violence in the NHS has been dominated by the vocabulary of risk assessment and risk management, and the regular mention of statistics. As we have demonstrated, research on work-related violence in health care has focused on trying to establish the calculable risk of violence to organizations or occupational groups, mainly for logistic reasons. Yet, as we have seen, the validity and reliability of most risk estimates are questionable. Efforts to encourage the use of a broad definition of violence and to improve the reporting of incidents of violence have resulted, in the short term at least, in a marked *increase* in recorded violence. By 2003, the NHS in England had failed by some margin to reach the national targets for incident reduction specified in the ZTZ campaign, even if some particular NHS trusts had done so (NAO 2003a). Furthermore, it was acknowledged that standardized reporting systems were still a long way from being implemented right across the NHS, and that under-reporting was still a serious problem for NHS risk management (NAO 2003a, 2003b).

As mentioned previously, organizational responsibility for violence within the NHS at central government level has shifted, arguably reflecting the development of risk thinking. In 2003, the newly established NHS Counter Fraud and Security Management Service (CFSMS) took over responsibility for violence from the human resources section of the NHS. According to the CFSMS chief executive, this signalled a shift in the campaign against violence from a 'moral crusade' to a professionalized, comprehensive security system for the NHS (Whitfield 2003), incorporating elements of the approach that CFSMS had employed to tackle fraud and corruption in the NHS (NHS Executive 2003).

This reorganization, like the NAO's involvement in evaluating the ZTZ campaign, assumes that parallels can be drawn between fraud, waste of public expenditure and violence as risks to the NHS. Such a view appears to resonate with some aspects of the governmentality approach to risk developed by Rose (1993) and Castel (1991). This posits that risk is best understood as a strategy of regulatory power by which populations are monitored and managed (Lupton 1999). Rose and Castel argue that risk thinking in contemporary Britain and other anglophone countries is characterized by an ideology of advanced liberalism which involves the dissolution of the autonomous acting subject to be replaced by conformity to bureaucratic processes based on abstract calculations.

When it comes to work-related violence, there is the opportunity for two sets of subjects to be dissolved. First, the idea that health care workers should behave autonomously and use their professional judgement to manage dangerous situations may be displaced by the requirement to follow routinized risk assessment protocols. Second, there is the potential for those perpetrating violence to be dissolved as autonomous individuals. In reality, the discourse on perpetrators in the NHS ZTZ campaign and more recent initiatives suggests that some perpetrators of violence against health care staff are in fact being 'responsibilized' rather than dissolved, in parallel with a general reorientation of penal policy in favour of holding offenders completely responsible for their actions and therefore liable to punishment. As we have suggested elsewhere (Elston *et al.* 2002), the favoured policy discourse that is emerging on violence in the NHS is primarily punitive. As the message on the posters relaunching the ZTZ campaign in 2001 stated: 'We don't have to take this – and we didn't': a message that was reinforced by pictures of newspaper cuttings about successful prosecutions for assaults on NHS staff (NHS Executive 2001a). In a similar vein, ZTZ leaflets and web pages provided clear guidance on involving the police and using the criminal justice system. The implication seemed to be that recourse to the police and the courts should be viewed as the normal organizational response, instead of leaving it mainly to the discretion of individual health care workers who have been the victims of violence. Decisions about further action, such as criminal prosecution, would then be a matter for the police and Crown Prosecution Service. A key initiative of the CFSMS at its inception was to develop 'a Memorandum of Understanding with the Association of Chief Police Officers that sets out what the NHS can expect from the police and what they can expect from the NHS around security, and in particular about dealing with violence and aggression towards staff' (NHS Executive 2003). More recently, we have seen that the government has given NHS security officers the authority to remove offenders physically without assistance from the police.

Consequently, much of the violence minimization campaign has presented perpetrators of violence against NHS staff as people against whom the NHS and its staff should be protected rather than as sick and distressed patients who cannot help their abusive behaviour and need professional care. By their behaviour these deviants are considered to have compromised their entitlement to care, regardless of whether criminal sanctions are instituted. Likewise, as noted previously, NHS trusts have been told to develop policies and procedures to withhold treatment from those deemed to be serial perpetrators of violence (NHS Executive 2001b) and for such individuals to forfeit their rights to be registered with general practitioners in their immediate locality (Elston *et al.* 2002). In other words, those who transgress in their interactions with health care professionals risk being excluded from the normal rights of citizenship, by having their access to NHS services restricted. Such exclusion is another theme of the Foucauldian analysis of governmentality and risk in advanced liberalism (Higgs 1998). It focuses on how individual recipients of welfare are measured and assessed against the norms and values of the model citizen and excluded and controlled if they do not conform.

For health care professionals, however, calls to limit access to treatment or to criminalize those who have been violent towards them seem to contrast sharply with a medicalized model which sees violence as caused by patients' underlying pathology, thereby absolving them of responsibility for their actions. The underlying tension between these two approaches may help explain why relatively few assailants of NHS staff have been prosecuted or had their normal citizenship rights to access curtailed (NAO 2003a), although prosecutions have apparently increased since the CFSMS took responsibility for violence minimization (DoH 2006).

Close scrutiny of the detailed ZTZ guidance on withholding treatment in fact reveals the difficulties involved in employing a blanket 'staff as victims to be defended' approach to risk reduction in a public health service. The guidance recognizes that patients who are mentally ill or under the influence of drugs or alcohol should be exempted from such sanctions (NHS Executive 2001b). However, how one determines which violent patients fall into the exempted category presumably depends primarily on clinical judgement. This argument parallels that developed by Rose (1998, 2000), who suggests that, under advanced liberalism, a distinction is increasingly drawn between those deviants who are judged to be 'low-risk' and those who are perceived to be 'high-risk'. While low-risk individuals may be channelled into 'circuits of reform' and offered quasi-contracts as part of a process of 'ethical recon-struction' under the surveillance of a professional, high-risk individuals are totally excluded from health and welfare services (or totally exempted from responsibility) and consigned to 'exclusionary gulags' (O'Malley 2006).

The violence minimization campaign's emphasis on encouraging NHS staff to attend training programmes such as one-day conflict resolution courses can also be seen from a governmentality perspective, as a form of 'new prudentialism', which increasingly places responsibility for risk protection in the hands of individuals (Lupton 1999). As Rose (1996) puts it, such prudentialism involves 'governance at the molecular level' of moral expectation. 'Good' citizens, as responsible and prudential, know what is expected of them and act accordingly (Kemshall 2006). From this standpoint, staff are being constructed through these courses as autonomous, self-regulating individuals who are expected to use the knowledge which has been acquired through the training provided to anticipate danger and avoid risk. In this sense, then, they are the primary site of risk management (Kemshall 2006). This in turn resonates with Annandale's (1996) argument mentioned earlier about the development of a risk culture in the NHS, especially the increased emphasis on self-surveillance in the face of risk from the majority 'normal' public, and not just from the minority of 'seriously mad' and 'very bad'.

In sum, official policies with respect to work-related violence in the NHS would seem to exhibit many of the characteristics of risk thinking identified by writers on governmentality in advanced liberalism. From this standpoint risk is best understood as a strategy of regulation, with decisions about individuals being based on protocols which can be employed to calculate risk. There is a potential tension between the model of the perpetrator implicit in much of the violence minimization campaign and the recognition that many perpetrators may not be wholly responsible for their actions at the time of an incident because of their medical condition.

Risk and Fear: Responding to the Perceived Risk of Violence

One of the possible unintended consequences of the adoption of an inclusive definition of risk, and the consequent apparent growth of violence against

NHS health care staff is an increase in fear and anxiety on the part of such staff. Various studies have pointed to the degree of fear of violence among such workers. Among doctors, GPs seem to be the most fearful, with between 35 and 66 per cent reporting being fairly or very worried in surveys (BMA 2003; Denney 2005). Analysis of the 2001/2 and 2002/3 waves of the British Crime Survey indicates that health and social welfare workers (which include nurses and paramedics) are the most fearful of all the occupations covered, with 36 per cent of those at potential risk being very or fairly worried about assaults and 42 per cent about threats. Health professionals (medical practitioners and pharmacists) are the third most worried with 27 per cent similarly concerned about assaults and 40 per cent about threats (Upson 2004).

While it seems clear that a significant number of health care workers are fearful of violence there is no empirical evidence of an increase in fear related to the DoH's violence minimization policy, although it is theoretically plausible that this might be so. Wilkinson (2001), for example, suggests that it is quite possible for knowledge of risk (in this case the risk of violence) to unsettle as much as reassure people. Both positions find support in the work of scholars engaged in debates around risk. Giddens (1991) and Beck (1992) take the former position and argue that the greater people's knowledge of risk, and hence 'risk consciousness', the more the likelihood that their anxieties will be aroused and their sense of insecurity increased. Giddens suggests that public debates about crime, alongside a plethora of other risks such as food scares, environmental pollution and health risks, create a 'generalized climate of risk', which for most people becomes a source of unspecific anxieties. People become saturated by an ever-increasing amount of information about societal risks as the result of the growth of a risk culture and this creates constant worry. Similarly, Beck contends that we now live in a 'risk society' and that the hazards we face are the product of modernity and not easily calculable. In this late modern world the claims of experts about hazards expressed in public debate contradict each other and result in 'manufactured uncertainty'. Responding to such uncertainty becomes all the more difficult as a result of ever-increasing individualization and the reduced influence of traditional structuring institutions such as the family and welfare state. Free from traditional constraints, people anxiously seek new certainties. Yet they are also expected to be self-reliant, and to both seek knowledge about risks and manage them rationally.

Both of these theorists argue that public knowledge of risk makes people more uncertain about their ability to live in safety. In contrast Douglas (1985, 1992; Douglas and Wildavsky 1982) provides an alternative interpretation of the culture of risk. She is concerned with the way in which people are able to use their knowledge of risk to cope with their anxiety and existential doubts. Rather than see risk consciousness as causing people to question and criticize accepted understandings of the social order, the culture of risk is said to shore up people's convictions about how people should live and what should be done to maintain their preferred way of life. Those who are perceived to threaten this way of life are blamed and treated as 'others', thereby reinforcing social solidarity around an agreed set of values about how people should behave. Instead of creating uncertainty and evoking anxiety, knowledge of risk, such as the risk of violence, functions to provide a clear focus for people's fear and how to respond to maintain a preferred way of life. On this view, the state's violence minimization policy is most likely to serve the function of a forensic device to identify the threat from risky others and reinforce social solidarity and a sense of moral order in the hospital or general practice surgery.

Conclusion

In this chapter violence against health care staff has been taken as an example of the way in which insecurity, risk and fear have come to dominate thinking about service delivery in the UK. It is clear from the evidence reviewed that violence has been identified as an issue for health professionals working in all settings in recent years, and that these staff are at relatively high risk of work-related violence. At the same time, it has been suggested that there is a need to keep a sense of proportion. The willingness of the British government to adopt an inclusive definition of violence has meant that so-called 'low-grade' violence such as verbal abuse is now accepted as violence. This, along with the efforts of nursing and other organizations to improve incident reporting, may have resulted, at least in the short term, in a marked increase in the amount of violence that is recorded.

It has been argued that the way work-related violence has been framed as a policy issue exemplifies the dominance of the discourse of risk management in contemporary health policy and the encouragement of conformity to bureaucratic processes based on abstract calculations. This is shown by the emphasis on statistics and quantitatively defined targets, and the expansion of the category of risk behaviour and of risk generators so that violence comes to be represented as a normal 'risk of the job' but one that 'we don't have to take', as in the ZTZ campaign. Those advocating this governmentality approach to risk (Castel 1991; Rose 1996, 1998) see the requirement that health care professionals follow routinized protocols for managing dangerous situations in place of professional judgements as leading to the dissolution of the autonomous acting subject. At the same time, encouraging NHS staff to attend conflict resolution training as part of the ZTZ campaign can be seen as a form of 'new prudentialism', with staff being expected to use the knowledge acquired in training and take responsibility for anticipating danger and avoiding risk (Rose 1996; Lupton 1999; Kemshall 2006). Advocates of governmentality also claim that the risk management approach may lead to the perpetrators of violence being dissolved as autonomous individuals. However, it has been shown that in the case of the ZTZ campaign and related NHS policy guidelines, some perpetrators of violence against health care staff have in fact been responsibilized rather than simply dissolved, paralleling a general shift in penal policy in favour of holding offenders fully responsible for their actions. This runs counter to health professionals' traditional medicalized model, which focuses on the needs of patients for professional clinical assistance even, or especially, when violent. Reconstructing perpetrators of violence against health care staff as deviants rather than sick has in turn resulted in these deviants facing the prospect of forfeiting their right to treatment, and thus the normal rights of citizenship. Such exclusion provides further support for the governmentality approach to risk in advanced capitalism (Higgs 1998), and reveals how the discourse of risk can serve to simultaneously responsibilize citizens and reinforce governance (Mythen 2008).

Framing work-related violence in terms of risk, as found in the ZTZ campaign and related government policies, also reinforces the belief in an illusory 'risk-free society' (Aharoni 1981). Against this, evidence of an apparent increase in violent crime may help to cultivate a culture of fear (Glassner 1999). We have seen that there are two contrasting interpretations in the sociological risk literature. On the one hand there are those like Giddens (1991) and Beck (1992) who argue that people's greater knowledge of risk and thus 'risk consciousness', following campaigns such ZTZ, are likely to increase anxiety and a sense of insecurity. In contrast, others such as Douglas (1985, 1992; Douglas and Wildavsky 1982) suggest that increased risk awareness may shore up people's convictions about how people should behave and what should be done to maintain the moral order. Both interpretations are plausible, but the empirical evidence of continuing fear of violence following the ZTZ campaign suggests that those who see campaigns that aim to heighten risk consciousness as feeding a culture of fear are more likely to be correct.

Finally, New Labour's policy of zero tolerance of violence against health care professionals needs to be understood as driven in part by concerns about the financial cost of violence and the problems of staff recruitment and retention in the face of such violence, and as being informed by wider debates about crime control and zero tolerance policing. As regards the latter, Newburn (2002) has argued, the phrase 'zero tolerance' connects with a cultural predisposition for an instant cure. According to Young (1999), this search for an easy miracle suggests that social problems like violence are easy to deal with if the right solution is found, and that having faith that such interventions as zero tolerance of violence against health care staff will work falsely assumes that the 'social is simple'. Those health care staff who face violence as an everyday reality, however, know how problematic such assumptions are. Rather than relying entirely on a 'top–down' violence minimization strategy based on enhanced internal reporting and auditing, exclusion and criminalization of transgressors and the evocation of 'we don't have to take it' to promote resilience, it may be more advantageous to engage health care staff to develop violence minimization policies in their own organizations. Such an approach would draw on these professionals' 'local knowledge' of patients and the communities they come from to develop strategies which might help them recognize potentially dangerous behaviour from patients and empower them to make safe challenges to such patients, taking into account their health as well as risk status.

Acknowledgement

This chapter draws on and develops an argument originally applied to violence against nurses in Elston, Gabe and O'Beirne (2006).

References

Aharoni, Y. (1981), *The No Risk Society*, New Jersey: Chatham House.
Annandale, E. (1996), Risk culture and nursing in the new NHS, *Sociological Review*, 44: 416–51.
Anonymous (2004), Verbal abuse of health care staff is a problem we must tackle together, *Nursing Times*, 100, 31 (3 August): 15.
Beale, P. (1999), Monitoring violent incidents. In P. Leather, C. Brady, C. Lawrence, P. Beale and T. Cox (eds), *Work-related Violence: Assessment and Intervention*, London: Routledge, pp. 69–86.
Beck, U. (1992), *Risk Society: Towards a New Modernity*, London: Sage.
British Medical Association (BMA) (2003), *Violence at Work: the Experience of UK Doctors*, Health Policy and Economic Research Unit, London: British Medical Association.
Budd, T. (1999), *Violence at Work: Findings from the British Crime Survey*, London: Home Office.
Budd, T. (2001), *Violence at Work: New Findings from the 2000 British Crime Survey*, London: Home Office and Health and Safety Executive.
Castel, R. (1991), From dangerousness to risk. In G. Burchell, C. Gordon and P. Miller (eds), *The Foucault Effect: Studies in Governmentality*, Hemel Hempstead: Harvester Wheatsheaf, pp. 281–98.
Cembrowicz, S. P. and Shepherd, J. P. (1992), Violence in the Accident and Emergency Department, *Medicine, Science and the Law*, 32: 118–22.
Clarke, J. (2005), New Labour's citizens: activated, empowered, responsibilized, abandoned? *Critical Social Policy*, 25: 447–63.
Committee of Public Accounts, House of Commons (2003), *Protecting NHS Hospital and Ambulance Staff from Violence and Aggression: 39th Report, Session 2002–3*, London: Stationery Office.
Crowner, M. L., Peric, G., Stepcic, F. and Van Oss, E. (1994), A comparison of videocameras and official incident reports in detecting inpatient assaults, *Hospital and Community Psychiatry*, 45: 1144–45.
Denney, D. (2005), Hostages to fortune: the impact of violence on health and social care staff, *Social Work and Social Sciences Review*, 12, 1: 16–28.
Department of Health (DoH) (1999a), *Health Service Circular 99/226. Campaign to stop violence against staff working in the NHS: NHS Zero Tolerance Zone*, London: Department of Health.
Department of Health (DoH) (1999b), *We Don't Have to Take This: Resource Pack*, Leeds: NHS Executive.
Department of Health (DoH) (2006), Bullies who threaten NHS staff are shown the red card as new figures reveal 1 in 22 NHS workers suffer violence. Department of Health News Release. Available at: http://www.dh.gov.uk/en/Publicationsandstatistics/Pressreleases/DH_4135962 (accessed 13 May 2008).
Douglas, M. (1985), *Risk Acceptability According to the Social Sciences*, London: Routledge and Kegan Paul.
Douglas, M. (1992), *Risk and Blame: Essays in Cultural Theory*, London: Routledge.
Douglas, M. and Wildavsky, A. (1982), *Risk and Culture: An Essay in the Selection and Interpretation of Technological and Environmental Dangers*, Berkeley: University of California Press.
Downes, D. and Morgan, R. (2007), No turning back: the politics of law and order into the millennium. In M. Maguire, R. Morgan and R. Reiner (eds), *The Oxford Handbook of Criminology*, 4th edn, Oxford: Oxford University Press.
Elston, M. A., Gabe, J., Denney, D., Lee, R. and O'Beirne, M. (2002), Violence against doctors: a medical(ised), problem? The case of National Health Service general practitioners, *Sociology of Health and Illness*, 24, 5: 575–98.

Elston, M., Gabe, J. and O'Beirne, M. (2006), A 'risk of the job'? Violence against nurses from patients and the public as an emerging policy issue. In P. Godin (ed.), *Risk and Nursing Practice*, Basingstoke: Palgrave Macmillan.

Estryn-Behar, M., van der Heijden, B., Camerino, D., Fry, C., Le Nezet, O., Conway, P. M. and Hasselhorn, H.-M. (2008), Violence risks in nursing: results from the European 'NEXT' Study, *Occupational Medicine*, 58: 107–14.

General Medical Services Committee (GMSC) (1994), *Women in General Practice*, London: GMSC/British Medical Association.

General Medical Services Committee (GMSC) (1995), *Combating Violence in General Practice: Guidance for GPs*, London: GMSC/British Medical Association.

Giddens, A. (1991), *Modernity and Self-Identity: Self and Society in the Late Modern Age*, Cambridge: Polity Press.

Glassner, B. (1999), *The Culture of Fear: Why Americans Are Afraid of the Wrong Things*, New York: Basic Books.

Hart, C. (2004), *Nurses and Politics: The Impact of Power and Practic*, Basingstoke: Macmillan.

Healthcare Commission (2008), *2007 NHS Staff Survey*, London: Commission for Healthcare Audit and Inspection.

Hearn, J. and Parkin, W. (2001), *Gender, Sexuality and Violence in Organizations: The Unspoken Forces of Organization Violations*, London and Thousand Oaks, CA: Sage.

Helm, T. (2007), Johnson spells out plan for 'personal' health service, *Daily Telegraph*, 26 September: 13.

Higgs, P. (1998), Risk, governmentality and the reconceptualisation of citizenship. In G. Scambler and P. Higgs (eds), *Modernity, Medicine and Health: Medical Sociology towards 2000*, London: Routledge, pp. 176–97.

Home Office (2005), *Violence at Work: Findings from the 2003/04 and 2004/5 British Crime Survey*, Supplementary Tables to Online Report 04/04. Available at: http://www.homeoffice.gov.uk/rds/notes/october_summaries.html (accessed 21 January 2008).

International Labour Organization, International Council of Nurses, World Health Organization, and Public Services International (2002), *Framework Guidelines for Addressing Workplace Guidelines in the Health Sector*, Geneva.

Jones, T. and Newburn, T. (2004), The convergence of US and UK crime control policy: exploring substance and process. In T. Newburn and R. Sparks (eds), *Criminal Justice and Political Cultures*, Cullompton: Willan Publishing.

Jones, T. and Newburn, T. (2006), Three strikes and you're out: exploring symbol and substance in American and British crime control politics, *British Journal of Criminology*, 46: 781–802.

Kelly, L. and Radford, J. (1996), 'Nothing really happened': the invalidation of women's experience of sexual violence. In M. Hester, L. Kelly and J. Radford (eds), *Women, Violence and Male Power*, Buckingham: Open University Press, pp. 19–33.

Kemshall, H. (2006), Sexuality and risk. In G. Mythen and S. Walklate (eds), *Beyond the Risk Society*, Maidenhead: Open University Press.

Lee, R. M. and Stanko, E. A. (eds) (2003), *Researching Violence: Essays on Methodology and Measurement*, London: Routledge.

Lupton, D. (1999), *Risk*, London: Routledge.

Mythen, G. (2008), Sociology and the art of risk, *Sociological Compass*, 2: 299–316.

National Audit Office (NAO) (2003a), *A Safer Place to Work: Protecting NHS Hospital and Ambulance Staff from Violence and Aggression. Report by the Comptroller and Auditor General*, London: Stationery Office.

National Audit Office (NAO) (2003b), *A Safer Place to Work: Improving the Management of Health and Safety Risks to Staff in NHS Trusts. Report by the Comptroller and Auditor General*, London: Stationery Office.

National Institute for Clinical Excellence (NICE) (2005), *Violence: the Short-term Management of Disturbed/Violent Behaviour in Psychiatric In-patient Settings and Emergency Departments*, London: National Institute for Clinical Excellence. Available at: http://www.nice.org.uk (accessed 26 February 2005).

Newburn, T. (2002), Atlantic crossings: 'policy transfer' and crime control in the USA and Britain, *Punishment and Society*, 4, 2: 165–94.

NHS Executive (1999), *NHS Zero Tolerance Zone: Managers' Guide – Stopping Violence against Staff Working in the NHS: We Don't Have to Take This*, Resource Pack, Leeds: NHS Executive.

NHS Executive (2000), *NHS Zero Tolerance Zone: Primary Care*. Available at: http://www.nhs.uk/zerotolerance/general/criminal.htm (accessed 23 September 2000).

NHS Executive (2001a), *NHS Zero Tolerance Zone Campaign: Phase III*, Leeds: NHS Executive.

NHS Executive (2001b), *Zero Tolerance Zone Phase IV: Withholding Treatment from Violent and Abusive Patients in NHS Trusts*, HSC 2001/18, Leeds: NHS Executive.

NHS Executive (2002), *Dealing with Harassment by NHS Service Users: A Guide for Managers and Staff*, Leeds: NHS Executive.

NHS Executive (2003), *NHS Zero Tolerance Zone: Campaign Update 31–7–03*, Leeds: NHS Executive.

Noble, P. and Rodger, S. (1989), Violence by psychiatric in-patients, *British Journal of Psychiatry*, 155: 384–90.

Norris, R. (2004), The shocking truth about verbal abuse, *Nursing Times*, 100, 31: 12–13 (3 August).

O'Beirne, M. and Gabe, J. (2005), Reducing violence against NHS staff: findings from an evaluation of the Safer Surrey Hospital Initiative, *Crime Prevention and Community Safety: An International Journal*, 7, 2: 29–39.

O'Malley, P. (2006), Criminology and risk. In G. Mythen and S. Walklate (eds), *Beyond the Risk Society*, Maidenhead: Open University Press.

Oxtoby, K. (2004), Silence the abuse, *Nursing Times*, 100, 31: 22–5 (31 August).

Reiner, R. (2007), Political economy, crime and criminal justice. In M. Maguire, R. Morgan and R. Reiner (eds), *The Oxford Handbook of Criminology*, 4th edn, Oxford: Oxford University Press.

Rose, N. (1993), Government, authority and expertise in advanced liberalism, *Economy and Society*, 22, 3: 283–99.

Rose, N. (1996), Governing 'advanced' liberal democracies. In A. Barry, T. Osborne and N. Rose (eds), *Foucault and Political Reason: Liberalism, Neo-Liberalism and Rationalities of Government*, London: UCL Press.

Rose, N. (1998), Governing risky individuals: the role of psychiatry in new regimes of control, *Psychiatry, Psychology and Law*, 5, 2: 177–95.

Rose, N. (2000), Government and control, *British Journal of Criminology*, 40: 321–39.

Royal College of Nursing (RCN) (1998), *Dealing with Violence towards Nursing Staff*, London: RCN.

Stenson, K. (2000a), Reconstructing the government of crime. In G. Wickham (ed.), *Socio-legal Politics: Post-Foucauldian Possibilities*, Aldershot: Dartmouth.

Stenson, K. (2000b), Some day our prince will come: zero-tolerance policing and liberal government. In T. Hope and R. Sparks (eds), *Crime, Risk and Insecurity*, London: Routledge.

Upson, A. (2004), *Violence at Work: Findings from the 2002/2003 British Crime Survey: Home Office Online Report 04/04*, London: Home Office.

Vail, J. (1999), Insecure times: conceptualising insecurity and security. In J. Vail, J. Wheelock and M. Hill (eds), *Insecure Times: Living with Insecurity in Contemporary Society*, London: Routledge.

Wacquant, L. (1999), How penal commonsense comes to Europeans: notes on the translantic diffusion of the neoliberal doxa, *European Societies*, 1, 3: 319–52.

Wells, J. and Bowers, L. (2002), How prevalent is violence towards nurses working in general hospitals in the UK? *Journal of Advanced Nursing*, 39, 3: 230–40.

Whitfield, L. (2003), Catch them if he can: the interview – Jim Gee, *Health Service Journal*, 113, 5877: 30–1 (16 October).

Wilkinson, I. (2001), *Anxiety in a Risk Society*, London: Routledge.

Wilson, J. Q. and Keeling, G. (1982), Broken windows, *Atlantic Monthly*, March: 29–38.

Wright, S., Gray, R., Parkes, J. and Gournay, K. (2002), *The Recognition, Prevention and Therapeutic Management of Violence in Acute In-Patient Psychiatry: A Literature Review and Evidence-Based Recommendations for Good Practice*. Prepared for the United Kingdom Central Council for Nursing, Midwifery and Health Visiting, London: UKCC and Institute of Psychiatry.

Wynne, R., Clarkin, N., Cox, T. and Griffiths, A. (1997), *Guidance on the Prevention of Violence at Work*, Luxembourg: European Commission.

Young, J. (1999), *The Exclusive Society*, London: Sage.

11
Risk and Welfare

Bent Greve

Since Beck published his book on the risk society in 1992, the concept of risk has been prominent in many analyses of societal development and everyday life. The consequences of risk for the need for a welfare state and the impact on development outside traditional areas of the welfare state have also been raised. Risk was, in many ways, one of the core reasons for the development of the welfare state after the industrial revolution, i.e. to cover risk of unemployment, risk of work accidents, sickness and income during old age. Risk has always been a fact of life for humankind, and neither the individual nor the market has always been able to cope with it. This has implied a need for a collective effort to ensure help when needed (i.e. the tribe, the municipality, the state). Economic security has historically been high on the agenda for welfare state development, although issues such as belonging, participation and well-being have also been part of the gradual development of welfare states. The erosion of nation states and the 'familiar territory', as Rumford argues, has also made risk, fear and insecurity part of everyday life in modern times.

Given the long history of risk, it is not surprising that a concept of *new* risk has entered the analysis (cf., for example, Taylor-Gooby 2004). Whereas risk associated with the emergence of the welfare state is still in play, at least to some extent, the new risk is often seen as that arising from the transition towards a post-industrial state, including the impact of the break-up of families and anxiety from external threats such as terrorism. Changes in lifestyles and the establishment of life-course social policy have therefore also been part of a new area of activity for welfare states. The gender dimension has been more important in these new areas of risk than in the old type, given that traditionally there was a mainly male-dominated work–life system with a male-breadwinner model. Despite discussion of marketization and privatization, the role of the state has been further expanded, for example with regard to care for children and leave arrangements. Care for children has made it possible to have a dual-breadwinner model; however, bringing up children as a single parent has also been possible, albeit with a new type of risk – that of living in poverty. Children are constantly at risk, and this has created a need for the welfare state to offer various types of surveillance and policy measures to prevent their neglect and abuse, as Littlechild points out.

In relation to personal security, the demand by the state for personal responsibility has had as a result a growth in private business. The possible interaction between state and market is thus often more profound than it seems at first sight. The state has a role with regard to preventative measures to reduce risk and increase safety (Greve 2007b).

The state's role as provider of security in its, by now, many facets has thus not been reduced, as the move to more private delivery in many welfare states might lead one to believe. This is due to the fact that people wish to have security with regard to income, work, family, community and health (Layard 2005). Quality of life seems in all EU countries to be related to 'having an income, enjoying a satisfactory family life and having good health' (European Foundation 2007: 4). Use of the labour market to provide many types of welfare benefits (Greve 2007a) is a way of making a distinction between those who have access to a large variety of benefits, and those left dependent on social welfare. The gap in living standards between these groups may perhaps be even greater than it used to be.

At the same time welfare societies, by enacting legal regulations in relation to crime, terror, etc., have made people more aware of risk, and perhaps even more fearful than they would have been without these interventions. The market thus still does not provide everything the individual needs, not with regard to old risks, and even less, perhaps, in relation to many of the new risks. The willingness to pay for new risks, despite there being no clear relation between payment and an increased level of physical security, is one of modern society's peculiarities. A reason for people being willing to pay more for security than can be justified from a rational viewpoint might be that 'we hate loss more than we value gain' (Layard 2005: 135). When we hate loss more than gain we are also seemingly willing to pay for precaution, which cannot be argued from an economic or a social perspective, but only from the perspective of fear and anxiety.

A consequence of the increase in risk can be social division manifesting in more spatial divisions, as shown in the chapter by Rowland Atkinson. Risk becomes self-reinforcing as this spatial division implies a tendency for the rich to live together with other rich people, and the poor with other poor people. Gated communities and separation also in other areas of life in society (e.g. education, health, and sport) imply a risk of a less cohesive society and thereby the creation of a vicious cycle.

Society's increased exposure to new varieties of fears, and also perceived threats, has changed our understanding of what welfare can be considered to be. If welfare is understood not only as a guarantee of daily bread and a decent standard of living, but also, as in the more classical social indicator discussion, of security and a sense of belonging, then welfare debates about changes in social policy have to be broader than who gets what at what time during the life cycle. This is to a large extent what the chapters in this volume show. One example is the chapter by Gabe and Elston, who look at risk for health care workers, arguing that the gradually more inclusive definition of violence has also increased the reported incidence of violence, which in turn implies that more people are perceived as being a risk to society.

The welfare state as a piggy-bank, as Barr has labelled it, will therefore, by the classical approach to welfare, not be able to deliver what the electorate wants. Even a high level of income and consumption will not make voters happy if they feel that their daily life, including their working life and security, is under pressure.

The perception of security is highly individual, and this can explain why in most western countries, despite the lack of firm evidence, punishment and 'being tough on crime' have great popular electoral support. It might therefore seem that using more of society's scarce resources to combat crime and terrorism cannot be explained by rational economic calculations, but rather as a response to feelings of anxiety.

Global terrorism and crime cannot necessarily be counteracted through traditional policies alone, and as Sen reminds us (2007: 79):

> The confusion generated by an implicit belief in the solitarist understanding of identity poses serious barriers to overcoming global terrorism and creating a world without ideologically organized large-scale violence.

In most OECD countries more people are now in prison than in 1992. On average, the growth has been from 102 per 100,000 inhabitants in 1992 to 132 per 100,000 in 2004, with the United States having the highest rate (OECD 2007). Despite this, there is no clear evidence that risk has been reduced or that increased happiness can be detected. As Denney points out, this might be related to the fact that people considered as being a risk to the public sometimes have less justice than before 9/11.

Life courses now differ from the way they used to be. The male-breadwinner model is less prevalent than before, marriage break-up more frequent, and this implies that women especially have a higher economic risk than they used to. Longer time spans in education and as pensioners have also changed the need for various types of redistribution of income over the life cycle.

How the boundaries of the local, the nation state and the EU have an impact on individual citizens is not clear. Fear and anxieties about the EU and migration, as Delanty discusses, have had implications for support and understanding of the European project. This further emphasizes the need for a greater European focus on social justice and solidarity. Still, the implication of this is in contradiction to the European focus, that social policy is seen mainly as a prerogative of nation states. If more welfare policies are transferred to the supranational level, this can increase fear among individuals that the support they need might evaporate, i.e. it might be more difficult to persuade decision-makers at a greater distance to take initiatives where the benefits are not clear to the decision-makers.

Risk cannot be, even with everyone's best effort, completely removed. This implies that if policy-makers make such a promise, even for high-risk offenders, then the result can be a mistrust of policy-makers, as even the best programme will fail to ensure that risk will disappear. This is discussed in the chapter, with a focus on MAPPA, by Kemshall and Wood. There might be a very high level of administrative cost with only a limited impact on the number of offenders.

Nevertheless, it is important to try to assess risk as a way of both reducing fear and using the available resources as well as possible. The interaction between risk assessment and social work is therefore important. This includes a requirement not to overemphasize the possible options and outcomes of doing risk assessment. There is also a problem of how to balance the fear of reporting abuse, which might be damaging to the family, against not reporting, which can lead to child abuse which could have been prevented. This balance between intervention and non-intervention, and the need for integrating various viewpoints in the analysis, is clearly framed in the chapter by Littlechild (see my earlier comment).

Fear, anxiety and welfare policies are therefore today framed differently from the way they were in the wake of the development of the welfare state, when risk of losing one's job, having an accident at work and not being able to support the family were core concerns. Whether the welfare state is also able to cope with the new types of risk in a rational way is more open to question. Policy-makers seem more interested in trying to analyse rationally the costs and benefits of different policies to cope with risk. This implies a 'risk' that societies will spend more on surveillance, prisons, sanctions and preventive measures than on ensuring the core of the welfare state's *raison d'être* – securing a decent living standard for all.

References

Barr, N. (2001), *The Welfare State as Piggy Bank: Information, Risk, Uncertainty, and the Role of the State*, Oxford: Oxford University Press.

European Foundation for the Improvement of Living and Working Conditions (2007), *First European Quality of Life Survey: Key Findings from a Policy Perspective*, Dublin: European Foundation for the Improvement of Living and Working Conditions.

Greve, B. (2007a), *Occupational Welfare: Winners and Losers*, Cheltenham: Edward Elgar.

Greve, B. (2007b), Prevention and integration: an overview, *European Journal of Social Security*, 9, 1: 3–10.

Layard, R. (2005), *Happiness: Lessons from a New Science*, London: Penguin.

OECD (2007), *Society at a Glance: OECD Social Indicators 2006*, Paris: OECD.

Sen, A. (2007), *Identity and Violence: The Illusion of Destiny*, London: Penguin.

Taylor-Gooby, P. (ed.) (2004), *New Risks, New Welfare*, Oxford: Oxford University Press.

Index

Index

Index

Index

Iraq war 7, 9–10
Islam *see* Muslims

Jenkins, M.J. 93
job satisfaction, and financial planning 22, 23
job security, and financial planning 24, 25, 30, 31
Johnson, Alan 133
Joseph, S. 99
justice
 and New Labour policies 15
 redistributive justice 119
 social justice 3, 119, 128–9

Keeling, G. 139
Kendra, J. 88, 98
Khan, M. 31
Kierkegaard, S. 123
Kitzinger, J. 53
Kronenfeld, J.J. 108

Labour Party *see* New Labour policies
Lash, S. 21, 30
Lawrence, Frances 15
Lawrence, Philip 15
Lawrence, Stephen 14
learning disabilities, people with, and financial
 planning 25–6, 31
Lees, L. 45
legislation
 Anti Social Behaviour Act (2003) 12
 Anti Social Behaviour Orders 12
 Anti-Terrorism Crime and Security Act
  (2001) 8
 Care Standard Act (2000) 96
 Children Act (1989) 105
 Civil Contingencies Bill 87
 Civil Partnership Act 14
 Crime and Disorder Act (1998) 12
 Criminal Justice Act (1991) 55
 Criminal Justice Act (2003) 54, 55, 58
 Criminal Justice and Court Services Act
  (2000) 13, 55, 58
 Disability Discrimination Act (2005) 14
 Human Rights Act (2000) 8, 14, 15
 NHS and Community Care Act (1990) 10
 Prevention of Terror Act (2005) 9
 Race Relations Amendment Act (2000) 14
 Terrorism Act (2006) 9
Leisurewatch 65
Lelkes, O. 31
lesbians, and financial planning 21, 22–3, 29, 31
Liberty 77
Lieb, R. 60
Linethal, E.T. 95
Lipschutz, R. 95
liquid fear 71, 122
London
 7 July bombings 4, 7, 9, 98
 remodelling of urban spaces 39
low-income workers, and financial planning 20,
 22
Lupton, D. 21
Lyon, E. 53

McGrew, A. 73
McLaughlin, K. 106

McNulty, Tony 79
Major, John 10, 107
male-breadwinner model 150, 152
*Managing Risks and Minimizing Mistakes in Services to
 Children and Families* (SCIE) 110
Mandela, Nelson 9
Mann, Bruce 87–8
manufactured uncertainty 143
MAPPA (Multi-Agency Public Protection
 Arrangements) 13, 55, 56–7, 58–61, 61–2, 65–
 6, 152
market failure, and urban policy 41, 48
Marvin, S. 47
Massey, D. 38
media
 and child protection work 103, 104, 106
 and public protection 54
 on vulnerability 96
 and youth justice 107
Menezes, Jean Charles de 13
mental illness 15
 and the NHS Zero Tolerance Zone
  campaign 142
middle class, and insecurity in modern
 society 126–7
migration in European countries, anxiety
 around 116–17, 125–8
Mills, C. Wright 122
Mirza, M. 31
mistakes, learning from, in child protection
 work 110–11
modernity
 reflexive modernity and human rights 13–15
 and risk society 4–6
 vertigo of late modernity 126
Monckton, John 60
Morgan Report (1991) 12
Muhammad, prophet 124
multi-agency working
 and housing policy 44
 and public protection 63
multiculturalism 124–5
 and the European Union 120
Muslims
 and community safety 12, 13, 29
 and discourses of fear 11
 in Europe 121, 127
 and financial planning 23, 24, 25, 28, 31
 and the normalization of racism 124

NAO (National Audit Office), and the NHS Zero
 Tolerance Zone campaign 133, 136, 138
nationalism 83
 and European integration 117, 118, 120, 128
National Society for the Protection of Children
 (NSPCC) 105
Nazism, and global borderlands 81, 82
Negri, A. 73
neighbourhoods
 social composition of 40–1
 zero tolerance policing 138–9
 see also communities
neo-liberalism, and European integration 119
Netherlands
 and the European Union 120
 and multiculturalism 124

157

Index